BATTLESHIP

BATTLESHIP

PHILIP KAPLAN

AURUM PRESS

For Claire and Joe

First published in Great Britain 2004 by
Aurum Press Ltd
25 Bedford Avenue
London WC1B 3AT

ISBN 1 85410 902 2

1 3 5 6 4 2
2004 2006 2008 2009 2007 2005
Printed and bound in Singapore by Imago

overleaf: The USS *Missouri*, BB-63, being towed to her berth at Ford Island, Pearl Harbor, Hawaii, where she can be visited by the public. right: The battleship USS *California*, BB-44, after the 7 December 1941 Japanese attack on United States Navy ships and facilities at Pearl Harbor.

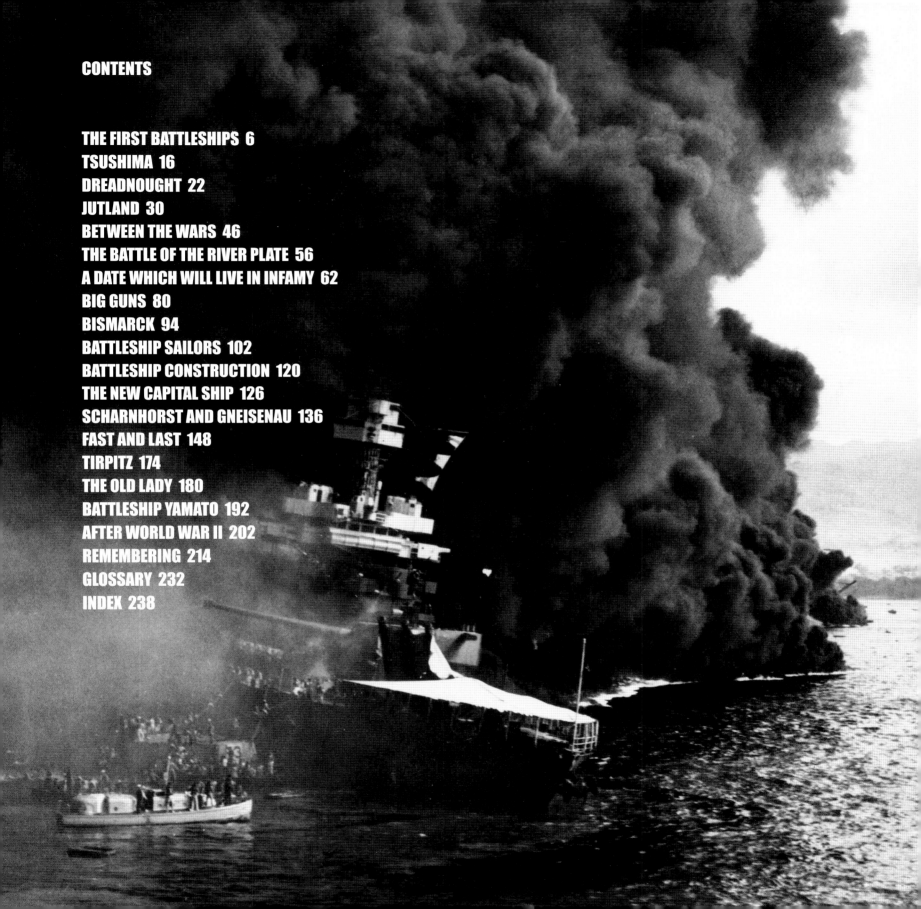

CONTENTS

THE FIRST BATTLESHIPS

Sailor, harrowing the seas,
Your eyebrows caked with
salt / No harbour siren's
kiss / Shall ever melt.
– from *Song*
by Gordon Symes

Borne each by other in a
distant line, / The sea-built
forts in dreadful order
move; / So vast the noise,
as if not fleets did join,
But lands unfixed, and
floating nations strove.

Now passed, on either side
they nimbly tack; / Both
strive to intercept and
guide the wind; / And, in its
eye, more closely they
come back, / To finish all
the deaths they left behind.
– from *Annus Mirabilis*
by John Dryden

right: The *Duke of
Wellington* in 1855,
flagship of the British
Royal Navy Baltic Fleet.

BATTLES HAVE BEEN fought at sea for thousands of years, but naval warfare entered a new era in the late fifteenth century, when cannon became the principal armament of warships. From this period until the second half of the nineteenth century, when steam supplanted sail in the world's navies, naval tactics were dominated by the 'line of battle'. This formation, consisting of a line of ships sailing, parallel with or at an angle to a similar line of opposing ships, enabled the rows of guns along the ship's side to bring maximum fire power to bear on the enemy. A ship that was big and powerful enough to take its place in the line of battle was called a 'ship of the line' or a 'battleship'.

Ships of the line might vary quite significantly in size and armament—in Nelson's navy they might carry anything between 74 and 120 guns— but they were all significantly superior to frigates, sloops, brigs and the other lesser naval craft; they were all what navies later came to call 'capital ships'.

Preserved in the historic Naval Dockyard at Portsmouth, England, are three examples of 'capital ships', one from the beginning of the age of 'classical' naval warfare, one from its zenith and the third from the point when steam began to eclipse sail. The Tudor *Mary Rose*, the oldest of these, was commissioned in 1509 by King Henry VIII, as the first real warship of the young Royal Navy. Named after the king's favourite sister, *Mary Rose* was launched at Portsmouth in 1511 and became the flagship of the Royal Navy. She was 127 feet long at her waterline, with a beam of 38 feet and a draught of 15 feet. Her ultimate displacement, after being refitted, was 727 tons.

Mary Rose was constructed of oak and elm and armed with muzzle-loading guns made of cast bronze and breech-loading guns of wrought-iron. In order to ensure that her guns were made to the highest standard of the day, the king imported the finest gun-founders from France. Her armament also included a large number of skilled bowmen whose task was to kill the crewmen of enemy vessels. She was normally manned by a crew of between 300 and 400.

Unlike most fighting ships of the time, the *Mary Rose* was designed specifically as a warship. Mindful of her role as a defence against England's potential enemies, which included France and Scotland, the king himself specified how she was to be equipped; the result was an innovative vessel which can legitimately be described as the prototypical battleship. Rather than having her guns mounted mainly on the 'castles' at either end of the hull like her predecessors, her designers pioneered the use of big guns in a row down each side of the hull near the waterline, enabling her to fire broadside barrages at enemy vessels. In another break from tradition, her planking was positioned edge-to-edge in a Carvel-type construction, rather than being overlapped. This technique made for a much more watertight hull.

In 1512 the *Mary Rose* took part in her first battle. In September of the previous year the Pope and the King of Aragon had entered into an alliance against Louis XII of France. In January 1512, the English Parliament voted to ally the country with Spain and preparations were made for *Mary Rose* to sail as flagship of Admiral Sir Edward Howard. On 10 August that year she led 25 other warships in an attack on the French fleet at Brest which Admiral Howard estimated at 222 ships. He immediately attacked the French flagship, the 790-ton *Grande Louise*. At the end of the two-day raid, Howard returned to Portsmouth in triumph, having captured 32 French vessels and 800 seamen.

Mary Rose campaigned effectively for the king through the subsequent years during which Henry devoted much money and effort to fortifying his coastal approaches against attack by the French. At Portsmouth an enormous chain boom extending to the Gosport shore, to seal off the

I am a great inventor, did
you but know it.
I have new weapons and
explosives and devices to
substitute / for your
obsolete tactics and tools.
Mine are the battle-ships
of righteousness and
integrity— The armour-
plates of quiet conscience
and self-respect— The
impregnable conning-
tower of divine
manhood— / The Long
Toms of persuasion—
The machine guns of
influence and example—
The dum-dum bullets of
pity and remorse— / The
impervious cordon of
sympathy— / The
concentration camps of
brotherhood— / The
submarine craft of
forgiveness— / The torpedo-
boat-destroyer of love—
And behind them all the
dynamite of truth! / I do
not patent my inventions.
Take them. They are free
to all the world.
– from *War and Hell*
by Ernest Crosby

harbour entrance was installed. In a two-month campaign against France in 1544, English forces captured the port of Boulogne, tightening their control over the Channel. By spring of 1545, however, Henry faced the prospect of a major French attack on Portsmouth, his principal naval base on the south coast, which was intended to destroy Henry's warships and other vessels in their anchorage, and to sever English supply lines to Boulogne. On 18 July, the French fleet anchored in St Helen's Roads near the Isle of Wight. As commander-in-chief of his forces, the king waited at Portsmouth for the threatened French landings. His fortifications there included the Square and Round Towers which oversaw the deepwater channel, and the gun batteries of Southsea Castle. Treacherous shallows near the harbour posed an additional hazard to the enemy ships.

The French had assembled a fleet of 225 ships with 30,000 men, while Henry faced them with just 100 ships and 12,000 men. He met with his naval commanders and then went ashore to watch his fleet sail out to meet the enemy. His ships turned south out of Portsmouth harbour, between Spit Sand and Horse Sands; but although there were some clashes between the two sides that day, little resulted from the early exchanges of cannon fire before night fell.

The following day the sea was calm and the French galleys advanced on the English warships, attempting to draw them out into open battle. Then suddenly the *Mary Rose* heeled over and sank. A French account claims that she was hit by French cannon. English accounts differ considerably, though they suggest that, while hoisting sail and preparing to get under way, *Mary Rose* suddenly heeled as she came about. Her gunports were open, with her cannon run out ready for action and as she heeled, seawater rushed over the gunport sills, destabilizing the vessel and causing her to capsize and quickly sink.

The *Mary Rose* was the main casualty of what

turned out to be little more than an inconclusive skirmish.

Attempts to raise her failed, and it was only in 1982 that she was lifted from the seabed and taken to the dockyard where she had been built.

In the two centuries that followed the sinking of the *Mary Rose,* Britain, along with France, the Netherlands, Portugal and Spain developed a large colonial empire, and a powerful naval fleet to oppose any threat to their freedom of the seas. Britain had the advantage numerically, but France and other nations were more advanced in the design and construction of warships that were larger, faster and more stable. However, the superior quality of the British crews and officers who excelled in their training, gunnery skills and discipline resulted in the dominance of the British fleet until the American War of Independence. In that conflict the French sided with the Americans against Britain and Spain allied herself with France, posing a combined invasion threat which the British had to take most seriously. Within a decade of the end of the American war, that threat became more substantial as Napoleon Bonaparte began his adventures across Europe. In 1783, the British were defeated by the Americans and the Royal Navy was no longer the feared force it had been for nearly three hundred years.

The most famous warship in British history is HMS *Victory*, the flagship of the Royal Navy fleet at Trafalgar. Crewed by 850 men, *Victory* was 226 long with a beam of 52 feet and a draught of 21 feet. She was built of oak, elm, fir and pine and her hull was sheathed in copper. Her armament was 102 cast-iron cannon ranging from 12 to 32-pounders, along with two 68-pounders. She spent the first years of the nineteenth century sailing at the head of the British fleet in the Mediterranean and Atlantic oceans for several years, trying to draw the French fleet into battle. Then, in October 1805, Admiral Villeneuve, in command of the

HMS WARRIOR
946

Launched on 29 December 1860, HMS *Warrior* might well have been called Peacemaker, for in her entire career at sea she never fired a shot in anger. Her mere presence in several encounters brought a calming effect to what otherwise would have been hostilities.

Her crew consisted of 42 officers, three warrant officers, 455 seamen and boys, 33 royal Marine officers, six Royal Marine non-commissioned officers, 118 Royal Marine artillerymen, two chief engineers, ten engineers and 66 stokers and trimmers. She served in the British fleet for many years before being relegated to the Reserve Fleet. In 1883 she was withdrawn from service and her masts and guns were stripped from her. In 1924, *Warrior* was put up for sale and the buyer then used her as a floating oil jetty at Pembroke Dock in Wales.

Now beautifully restored and preserved, *Warrior* may be visited and toured at the historic Naval Dockyard at Portsmouth, England.

"A black viscious ugly customer as ever I saw, whale-like in size, and with as terrible a row of incisor teeth as ever closed on a French frigate."
— Charles Dickens on HMS *Warrior*

far left: The *Alfred*, the first American battleship. left: HMS *Warrior* in 1874.

French fleet, took his warships out of port at Toulon to join with the Spanish fleet at Cadiz. Napoleon had abandoned whatever plans he may have had for invading England and his combined naval force was proceeding to Naples where they were to operate in support of troops against Italy.

Heading into what would be one of the last great open-sea battles of the age of sail, in the early hours of 20 October Nelson's force awaited that of Villeneuve and the Spanish commander, Rear Admiral Magon, in the Straits of Gibraltar off Cape Trafalgar.

Contrary to strict Admiralty policy, Nelson elected to attack the French and Spanish warships using a new tactic he had devised. He would lead his ships in two separate parallel battle lines at a nearly 90° angle to the enemy line, causing their ships to scatter and providing his captains with the opportunity to engage their opponents in ship-to-ship actions. In fact, this approach put *Victory* and his other ships in greater danger than the conventional tactic would have done, but Nelson took the risk, in the belief that the French and Spanish gunners were poorly trained and unskilled and the British gunners at least three times faster at their work than was the enemy.

At 11 a.m., on 21 October, the crew of *Victory* made her guns ready for action. With little wind, the ships of Nelson's force were making just one and a half knots as they approached the French and Spanish vessels. It was nearly 11.30 a.m. when Nelson sent his "England expects" flag signal to his fleet, followed immediately by the signal "Engage the enemy more closely". At about this time, some of the enemy ships began firing at Nelson's warships, checking their ranges, which were already very short. As the distance continued to close, *Victory* was taking hits and losing crewmen. She manoeuvred to slide between the French flagship *Bucentaure* and another enemy vessel, the *Redoutable*. While passing *Bucentaure* at a distance of less than 40 feet, the gunners of *Victory*

The oldest commissioned warship in the world, HMS *Victory*, is still manned by Officers and Ratings of the Royal Navy.

She now lies in Number Two Dry Dock at Portsmouth Naval Base, attracting more than 350,000 visitors annually. At the close of her active career, in November 1812, *Victory* was moored in Portsmouth harbour near Gosport. In 1921, the British government decided that the ship should be restored and preserved in commemoration of Admiral Lord Nelson, the Battle of Trafalgar, and Royal Navy supremacy in the days of sail.

left: A painting of HMS *Victory*, artist unknown.
below: A rare British stone cannon ball.

below: The *Merrimac*, one of the first ironclad gunboats built in America. right: The *Monitor*, after her fight with the *Merrimac* at Hampton Roads, Virginia in March 1862. Dents made by the heavy steel-pointed shot from the guns of *Merrimac* are visible near the porthole.

launched a broadside blast at the French flagship, hitting it with a force sufficient to cause nearly 400 casualties. The broadside exchanges continued and, by 4 p.m., the battle had ended in triumph for the British, and in tragedy as well. In the midst of the cannon fire, Admiral Nelson was mortally wounded by a French sniper.

One of the most important naval battles of all time, the British victory at Trafalgar re-established the Royal Navy as the dominant naval force in the world. Napoleon would not be invading England, and the world had witnessed what a well-led, well-trained and disciplined fleet could achieve, even when faced with an enemy whose vessels were faster and better armed. As Ian Johnston and Rob McAuley stated in their book *The Battleships*: "If ever there was an example of a 'battleship' that became a symbol of national pride, it is surely HMS *Victory*—still in commission in the Royal Navy, beautifully preserved and restored, she is the ultimate example of the power and majesty of a line-of-battle ship of 100 guns—an eighteenth-century ancestor of the great battleships that were to follow."

After Trafalgar, the British fleet sailed wherever it chose to go, virtually unchallenged.

Both the British and French navies were mightily impressed by the effectiveness of the new shells fired from 68-pounder guns on the Russian line-of-battle ships during their bombardment of Turkish warships at Sinope in the Crimean War of 1853. These shells, replacing cannon balls, exploded on impact with their Turkish targets, setting them on fire. The French and British answer to this new threat was a type of floating gun platform covered in four-inch armour plate. These gun-battery platforms were powered by steam engines giving them a speed of four knots and were manoeuvred into firing position by tugs. This combination of radical advances in armour and armament technologies would lead to the development of the twentieth-century battleship.

British domination of the seas extended into the later nineteenth century, when steam power and the industrial revolution made possible the first generation of metal-hulled vessels. The

development of shells or projectiles capable of breaching the hulls of vulnerable wooden warships had led to ironclads. Warships could be built to previously impossible sizes, but iron hulls brought with them the need to devise new and different armament, along with shells or projectiles capable of breaching these strong new hulls.

The navies of the world were no longer dependent upon the wind and its direction. Steam power, and the new screw propeller enabled an entirely new form of vessel to come into being, and in 1860, an important new battleship was completed, the first of four vessels of the *Gloire* class of French battleships. Though still rigged for sail, her design

In the sixteenth century, before the advent of commercial fertilizer, great quantities of manure were transported by ship. It was stored in dry bundles, weighing far less in that form than when wet, and in dry form it was not subject to fermentation.

When at sea, however, the manure occasionally became damp, causing the process of fermentation to begin. Methane gas is a by-product of this process, and the danger of its presence was soon discovered, probably by a seaman who brought a lighted lantern with him when he visited the cargo hold. Several ships were destroyed by mysterious explosions before the cause was discovered.

Once the cause of these explosions was understood, shippers began stamping the bundles: 'Ship High In Transit', directing cargo handlers to stow the bundles high enough in the ship to prevent water or damp from reaching the cargo.

featured engines developing 2,500 horsepower which drove a propeller shaft giving *Gloire* a top speed of thirteen knots. She had a crew of about 570 men. Her displacement was 5,630 tons. Her length was 255 feet at the waterline; her beam was 56 feet and her draught was 28 feet. She was armed with 36 6.4-inch muzzle-loading guns down both sides of her decks. She was protected by a 4.7-inch wrought iron armour belt which extended down both sides of her hull to a depth of five feet.

The French intended to build up to thirty *Gloire* class battleships; they actually completed ten. Limited iron-making capacity in France meant that only *Couronne*, of the first four ships in the class, would have an iron hull.

With the completion of *Gloire*, building activity on an ironclad warship for Britain was greatly increased. Two such vessels, *Warrior* and *Black Prince*, were under construction. They were modern, pioneering vessels whose technology would greatly influence future battleships and whose appearance, in 1861 and 1862 respectively, ended the brief lead which France had gained in warship design with *Gloire*.

A purpose-built battleship, the 9,137-ton *Warrior* significantly raised the standard for warships. Much faster, better armed and armoured than *Gloire*, the iron-hulled *Warrior* was an innovative fighting vessel that incorporated advances such as forced ventilation on the gundeck to get rid of smoke, a laundry with hand-operated washing machines, and a blast furnace in the boiler room to produce molten iron used in hollow shot. *Warrior* was 420 feet long with a beam of 58 feet and a draught of 26 feet. She had a 4.5-inch armour belt and her armament consisted of ten 110-pounders, 26 68-pounders and four 70-pounders. She carried a crew of 700 men. Like the *Victory*, *Warrior* has been lovingly restored and may be visited at the Naval Dockyard in Portsmouth.

In America, the Civil War of 1861-65 spurred the design and construction of what had been a European concept, the turret-gunned warship. To meet the challenge of the new CSS *Virginia* (formerly the steam frigate *Merrimac*), a low-set, floating battery armed with eight nine-inch guns set in armoured gun ports and two seven-inch rifled shell-guns, the US Navy commissioned the *Monitor*. Designed by inventor John Ericsson, *Monitor* was essentially a steam-powered raft which featured a rotating turret twenty feet in diameter housing two eleven-inch smooth-bore guns.

After encountering and sinking two US Navy frigates at Hampton Roads, near the entrance to Chesapeake Bay on 8 March 1862, *Virginia* was engaged the next day by *Monitor* in a three-hour battle. It ended inconclusively when both vessels withdrew, each unable to penetrate the armour of their adversary. This clash of new and unconventional warship types established that their heavy armour seemed invulnerable to attack, and that a layout of fixed guns along the length of a battleship was no match for a vessel with turret-mounted guns able to fire in any direction. It was clear, too, that the development of more powerful guns and shells would be crucial to overcoming the advances in armour plating that had been demonstrated by *Virginia* and *Monitor*. But, while these powerful new warships foreshadowed future developments, they had been designed solely for fighting in calm coastal water. Something quite different would be required for the new form of combat to come on the open seas.

By the last years of the nineteenth century, dramatic increases in production allowed steel to replace iron in the construction of warships. By then, steam had almost entirely replaced sails as the power source for such vessels. It was a time in which great maritime nations like Britain, Germany, Japan, Russia and the United States set out to build powerful and impressive new navies centred around giant, blue-water battleships.

$50,000 REWARD.—WHO DESTROYED THE MAINE?—$50,000 REWARD.

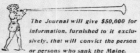

EDITION FOR GREATER NEW YORK.

The Journal will give $50,000 for information, furnished to it exclusively, that will convict the person or persons who sank the Maine.

NEW YORK JOURNAL
AND ADVERTISER

The Journal will give $50,000 for information, furnished to it exclusivly, that will convict the person or persons who sank the Maine.

NO. 5,572.   Copyright, 1898, by W. R. Hearst—NEW YORK, THURSDAY, FEBRUARY 17, 1898.—16 PAGES.   PRICE ONE CENT In Greater New York ; Elsewhere, and Jersey City, TWO CENTS

DESTRUCTION OF THE WAR SHIP MAINE WAS THE WORK OF AN ENEMY.

$50,000!
$50,000 REWARD!
For the Detection of the Perpetrator of the Maine Outrage!

The New York Journal hereby offers a reward of $50,000 CASH for information, FURNISHED TO IT EXCLUSIVELY, which shall lead to the detection and conviction of the person, persons or government criminally responsible for the explosions which resulted in the destruction, at Havana, of the United States war ship Maine and the loss of 258 lives of American sailors.

The $50,000 CASH offered for the above information is on deposit with Wells, Fargo & Co.

No one is barred, be he the humble but misguided seaman eking out a few miserable dollars by acting as a spy, or the attache of a government secret service, plotting, by any devilish means, to revenge fancied insults or cripple menacing countries.

This offer has been cabled to Europe and will be made public in every capital of the Continent and in London this morning.

The Journal believes that any man who can be bought to commit murder can also be bought to betray his comrades, **FOR THE PERPETRATOR OF THIS OUTRAGE HAD ACCOMPLICES.**

W. R. HEARST.

Assistant Secretary Roosevelt Convinced the Explosion of the War Ship Was Not an Accident.

The Journal Offers $50,000 Reward for the Conviction of the Criminals Who Sent 258 American Sailors to Their Death. Naval Officers Unanimous That the Ship Was Destroyed on Purpose.

$50,000!
$50,000 REWARD!
For the Detection of the Perpetrator of the Maine Outrage!

The New York Journal hereby offers a reward of $50,000 CASH for information, FURNISHED TO IT EXCLUSIVELY, which shall lead to the detection and conviction of the person, persons or government criminally responsible for the explosions which resulted in the destruction, at Havana, of the United States war ship Maine and the loss of 258 lives of American sailors.

The $50,000 CASH offered for the above information is on deposit with Wells, Fargo & Co.

No one is barred, be he the humble, but misguided, seaman, eking out a few miserable dollars by acting as a spy, or the attache of a government secret service, plotting, by any devilish means, to revenge fancied insults or cripple menacing countries.

This offer has been cabled to Europe and in London this morning.

The Journal believes that any man who can be bought to commit murder can also be bought to betray his comrades, **FOR THE PERPETRATOR OF THIS OUTRAGE HAD ACCOMPLICES.**

W. R. HEARST.

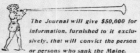

NAVAL OFFICERS THINK THE MAINE WAS DESTROYED BY A SPANISH MINE.

George Eugene Bryson, the Journal's special correspondent at Havana, cables that it is the secret opinion of many Spaniards in the Cuban capital that the Maine was destroyed and 258 of her men killed by means of a submarine mine, or fixed torpedo. This is the opinion of several American naval authorities. The Spaniards, it is believed, arranged to have the Maine anchored over one of the harbor mines. Wires connected the mine with a powder magazine, and it is thought the explosion was caused by sending an electric current through the wire. If this can be proven, the brutal nature of the Spaniards will be shown by the fact that they waited to spring the mine until after all the men had retired for the night. The Maltese cross in the picture shows where the mine may have been fired.

Hidden Mine or a Sunken Torpedo Believed to Have Been the Weapon Used Against the American Man-of-War---Officers and Men Tell Thrilling Stories of Being Blown Into the Air Amid a Mass of Shattered Steel and Exploding Shells---Survivors Brought to Key West Scout the Idea of Accident---Spanish Officials Protest Too Much---Our Cabinet Orders a Searching Inquiry---Journal Sends Divers to Havana to Report Upon the Condition of the Wreck.
Was the Vessel Anchored Over a Mine?

BY CAPTAIN E. L. ZALINSKI, U. S. A.

(Captain Zalinski is the inventor of the famous dynamite gun, which would be the principal factor in our coast defence in case of war.)

Assistant Secretary of the Navy Theodore Roosevelt says he is convinced that the destruction of the Maine in Havana Harbor was not an accident. The Journal offers a reward of $50,000 for exclusive evidence that will convict the person, persons or Government criminally responsible for the destruction of the American battle ship and the death of 258 of its crew.

The suspicion that the Maine was deliberately blown up grows stronger every hour. Not a single fact to the contrary has been produced.

Captain Sigsbee, of the Maine, and Consul-General Lee both urge that public opinion be suspended until they have completed their investigation. They are taking the course of tactful men who are convinced that there has been treachery.

Washington reports very late that Captain Sigsbee had feared some such event as a hidden mine. The English cipher code was used all day yesterday by the naval officers in cabling instead of the usual American code.

TSUSHIMA

WHEN NAVAL FORCES of Russia and Japan met in battle at 2 p.m. on 27 May 1905 off the island of Tsushima near the Straits of Korea, it was the first large engagement between big-gun warships. It was really a test of the warships and tactics of Britain versus those of France. Many of the Japanese ships involved were British-built, with mostly British weapons and equipment. The Russian vessels were largely based on French designs and engineering and the participating Russian shipyards were principally financed with French investment. The Japanese fleet at Tsushima included six battleships and nine armoured cruisers. Of these, all of the battleships and five of the cruisers were British-made.

In 1902 Britain and Japan had signed a formal alliance recognizing their common interest in preventing further expansionism by Russia. It was a mutual assistance pact whereby both nations would co-operate to help maintain the principle of free trade in Chinese waters, and a counter to the Russian threat to Korea, Manchuria and other countries in the region.

The war began when the Japanese navy conducted a surprise attack on the Russian Pacific Fleet at Port Arthur on mainland China on the night of 8/9 February 1904. Both Russia and Japan wanted control of the Far East seas, but the Russians had not imagined that the Japanese would go so far as war. In the raid, Japanese Imperial Navy Admiral Heihachiro Togo ordered five destroyers into the narrow harbour in a torpedo attack on the Russian fleet. Two of the seven Russian battleships sheltering in Port Arthur, *Tsarevitch* and *Retvizan*, as well as the cruiser *Pallada*, were hit, hampering the Russian fleet's capability long enough for Japanese forces to land in Korea virtually unopposed. These troops then advanced across the Yalu River to threaten the Russians at Port Arthur. The next day Togo, in his flagship the battleship *Mikasa*, led a force of sixteen warships in a bombardment of the vessels at Port Arthur. The

There is a tide in the affairs of men, / Which, taken at the flood, leads on to fortune . . .
– from *Julius Caesar*, Act IV, Scene III
by William Shakespeare

left and overleaf: Japanese battleships which participated in the Battle of Tsushima on the afternoon of 27 May 1905.

"Men appear to prefer ruining one another's fortunes and cutting each other's thoats about a few paltry villages, to extending the grand means of human happiness."
— Voltaire

Russian ships were blockaded in the port and some of the warships tried unsuccessfully to break the siege in an action on 25 February. Two Japanese battleships, *Yashima* and *Hatsue*, ran into Russian mines, exploded and sank.

As a young man, the Russian Tsar had been attacked by a lunatic while touring in Japan and ever since then had nursed a profound hatred of the Japanese. In April 1904, he resolved to use his Baltic Fleet to teach the Japanese a lesson they

would never forget, and to restore Russian prestige at the same time. But by late August the situation for the Russians had deteriorated dramatically. With their Pacific fleet bottled up, they were vulnerable to sea attack from the east; an intolerable situation. They determined to use any means necessary to eliminate this threat from Japan, including the rash measure of deploying their Baltic Fleet to the Far East.

Preparing to move the fleet halfway around the world was a logistical nightmare for Russian naval

"Diplomats are just as essential to starting a war as Soldiers are for finishing it. You take Diplomacy out of war and the thing would fall flat in a week."
— Will Rogers

" 'The Battleship Potemkin' has been famous for so long that it is almost impossible to come to it with a fresh eye. It is one of the fundamental landmarks of cinema. Its famous massacre on the Odessa Steps has been quoted so many times in other films (notably in 'The Untouchables') that it's likely many viewers will have seen the parody before they see the original. The film once had such power that it was banned in many nations, including its native Soviet Union. Governments actually believed it could incite audiences to action. If today it seems more like a technically brilliant but simplistic "cartoon" (Pauline Kael's description in a favorable review), that may be because it has worn out its element of surprise—that, like the 23rd Psalm or Beethoven's Fifth, it has become so familiar we cannot perceive it for what it is.

"The movie was ordered up by the Russian revolutionary leadership for the 20th anniversary of the Potemkin uprising, which Lenin had hailed as the first proof that troops could be counted on to join the proletariat in overthrowing the old order.

"As sketched by Eisenstein's film, the crew members of the battleship, cruising the Black Sea after returning from the war with Japan, are mutinous because of poor rations. There is a famous closeup of their breakfast meat, crawling with maggots. After officers throw a tarpaulin over the rebellious ones and order them to be shot, a firebrand named Vakulinchuk cries out, 'Brothers! Who are you

commander Admiral Zinovy Rozhestvensky. Rozhestvensky had been Russian Naval Attaché in London between 1892 and 1894 and was under no illusions about the capabilities of the British warship industry, especially in comparison to that of Russia. Russia had no bases or port facilities of her own to serve the Admiral's ships along his route, compelling him to transport all the coal and provisions which his vessels required, as well as medical and repair capabilities and everything else that his men and ships would need for the voyage and the epic battle to follow.

Rozhestvensky steamed out of Kronstadt in late September. While moving through the North Sea on the night of 22 October, the Russian vessels somehow became involved in a confusing and tragic action in which they fired on four British fishing trawlers, setting them on fire. Britain readied for war with Russia and sent out cruisers to stalk the Baltic warships as they passed down the Channel and on towards Spain. But tempers cooled as the Russian ships proceeded further south.

Admiral Rozhestvensky split the Baltic Fleet in two as it approached Tangier at the end of December. He sent the smaller vessels through the Suez Canal and took the big ships around the Cape of Good Hope. The difficulties he faced were considerably increased when, on 1 January 1905, a signal arrived informing him that the Japanese had taken Port Arthur. At the end of his extremely demanding journey he would no longer have the use of either the battleships of Russia's Pacific Fleet, or the Port Arthur facility. He would have to take his fleet on to the only other port open to him, Vladivostok, via the straits between Japan and Korea. The admiral informed the Tsar by telegram that the best he could do at that point was to break through to Vladivostok. The Tsar replied angrily that the admiral's mission was "to master the Sea of Japan". The pragmatic admiral felt little optimism about the fate his squadron would face

when it encountered the Japanese Fleet in its home waters.

On 27 May, the Russian Baltic Fleet reached a position near the island of Tsushima. Awaiting it was Admiral Togo and his fleet, with four battleships, including Togo's flagship *Mikasa*, *Fuji*, *Asahi* and *Shikishima* in the vanguard. They were accompanied by 20 cruisers of which ten were heavy, 21 destroyers and several smaller vessels. The 15,000-ton battleships were armed with four twelve-inch guns and fourteen six-inch guns each and could make 18 knots. The Russian fleet had the advantage in numbers with eleven battleships, four of them new. They displaced 13,500 tons each and carried four twelve-inch guns and twelve six-inch guns. Their maximum speed was 17.5 knots. As he led his fleet into battle, Togo signalled them: "The fate of our Empire rests on this action. Let every man do his utmost."

The seas were high as the opposing fleets closed the distance between them in the early afternoon of the 27th. In the difficult conditions, the Russian admiral brought his fleet in at nine knots, while Admiral Togo elected to charge at top speed. At the precise moment, Togo's ships turned to cross the 'T' of the Russian vessels, positioning the Japanese warships so that all of their big guns could be brought to bear on the Russians, who, for their part could only reply with their forward weapons.

Shortly after firing commenced, it was clear that the Japanese crews were serving their guns, sighting and firing with greater efficiency than their opponents. Massive fires soon raged in the Russian ships *Alexander III*, *Osliabya* and *Suvarov*, the flagship of Admiral Rozhdestvensky. The forward turret of *Osliabya* was destroyed and in half an hour further damage caused her to capsize and sink. A shell smashed into the bridge of *Suvarov*, seriously wounding Rozhestvensky, who was evacuated to a destroyer soon afterwards when it was apparent that *Suvarov* could not be saved. By late afternoon, heavy smoke and mist were obscuring the battle area, reducing Togo's ability to target the Russian ships accurately. The conditions enabled the Russians to quickly regroup and withdraw towards Vladivostok. But the ships of the Japanese pursued the Russians and continued to pound them. Their heaviest fire was directed at the battleships *Borodino* and *Alexander III*, both of which were sent to the bottom of the straits by early evening. Now Togo launched his destroyers in a torpedo attack which soon resulted in the sinking of the battleship *Sissoi Veliki* and the cruisers *Vladimir Monomakh* and *Admiral Makarov*. The one-sided battle continued into the following day, with the Japanese destroying most of what remained of the Russian fleet. When it was over, just three Russian vessels, a cruiser and two destroyers, all badly damaged, managed to limp into port at Vladivostok. The final score amounted to eleven Russian warships sunk, four captured and three interned in the Philippines. Japanese ship losses amounted to three torpedo boats. The Russians lost 5,045 sailors killed, with 6,106 taken prisoner. Japan lost 110 killed and suffered 590 wounded. The Russian fleet had been annihilated and Russia was no longer a world-class sea power. The Odessa mutiny of June 1905, during which the crew of the battleship *Potemkin* shot their officers and took control of the ship, served to underline the weakness of the Russian political and naval establishment.

The Battle of Tsushima is seen by most historians as one of the most important and decisive engagements in naval history. It demonstrated the ship-killing power of the big gun at sea and confirmed the dangers posed by torpedoes. It produced in the Japanese a sense of pride in their achievement and a confidence that they were a significant naval power and would continue to be one in the future.

The rest of the world was in awe of what the Japanese had achieved at Tsushima. Europe was shocked and surprised at the outcome, and alarmed at the prospect of a new and possibly more aggressive posture on the part of Japan throughout Asia as her influence there expanded. With her defeat of the Russian fleet, Japan came to believe in the importance of shedding her dependence on foreign sources for her warships and weaponry. She began intense efforts to develop steel mills and shipyards, mainly for battleship construction at Kure, Sasebo and other ports. While her navy enjoyed its new command of the Far Eastern seas, Japan's armies in Manchuria were dominating that war front. With her ultimate victory she retained Port Arthur, the South Manchurian railway and an overarching position in Korea.

Observers at Tsushima attributed the Japanese victory to the better handling of their ships and to their highly disciplined adherence to sound naval doctrine and procedure. It is also fair to say that the quality of leadership in the Russian navy had declined greatly after the death of its key commander, Admiral Makarov, in the explosion of the battleship *Petro Pavlovsk* when it struck a Japanese mine near Port Arthur in April.

Perhaps most significantly, Tsushima served to point the way forward for naval tactics in the twentieth century. It demonstrated that fewer rounds, very well aimed and fired at a decisive range from the heavy guns of battleships, would yield far more effective results than many rounds delivered relatively quickly from lighter guns. The victorious Admiral Togo had proved a clever, formidable warrior, capitalizing on superior speed in his attacks at Tsushima, instilling in his crews efficiency, skill, determination, discipline and patience, all of which paid off handsomely in his overwhelming defeat of the Russian adversary. His prudent yet opportunistic management of his ships, and his facility in effectively employing both big gun and torpedo attacks, impressed the changing world.

shooting at?' The firing squad lowers its guns, and when an officer unwisely tries to enforce his command, full-blown mutiny takes over the ship."
— Roger Ebert, film critic

IT WAS THE RAPID DEVELOPMENT of steam turbine engines for sea-going vessels, particularly the designs of Charles Parsons, that had impressed the Royal Navy's Committee on Designs in their planning sessions for *Dreadnought*. In that period a number of ships of various types and sizes were being fitted with turbines and undergoing sea trials. Cunard was preparing to fit them into its new passenger liners, *Mauretania* and *Lusitania*. Turbine power was clearly the wave of the future in warship design.

In the first years of the twentieth century naval planners realized that the torpedo could no longer be dismissed as a mere novelty but had to be respected as a genuine threat. Torpedoes were becoming reliable, accurate weapons of substantial range. The obvious counter was to deploy larger-calibre naval guns which could strike the enemy from beyond torpedo range. The lessons of the Battle of Tsushima served to reinforce this new philosophy. In May 1905, the same month as Tsushima, the British First Sea Lord, Vice-Admiral Sir John 'Jackie' Fisher, put Britain in the forefront of a battleship revolution when he authorized construction of the first of an entirely new class of capital ships, the first 'all big-gun' battleship, HMS *Dreadnought*.

Fisher was no expert in the fields of warship design or naval gunnery, but he was determined that the Royal Navy would be modernized and prepared to meet the growing challenge posed by the German Fleet. His own challenge was to provide the navy with a new warship of great capability, but at relatively low cost. The British treasury would not stand for what might be perceived as an extravagance that would anger the taxpayers. *Dreadnought* would be expensive, so Fisher called for a substantial reduction in the British warship inventory and the scrapping of hundreds of ships which he claimed were 'too weak to fight and too slow to run away'. He also included cruisers in his list of eliminations, as he believed that the Royal Navy's future lay with a

DREADNOUGHT

HMS *Dreadnought* was the first all big-gun battleship and the first turbine-driven battleship.

below: HMS *Dreadnought* during her anchor trials—a postcard identifying her as the largest and most powerful warship in the world. left: *Dreadnought* in drydock

right: HMS *Dreadnought* steaming in 1906.

proliferation of submarines, destroyers and fast battleships. His cuts brought impressive economies along with a leaner and meaner fleet.

The most important single feature of *Dreadnought*, as compared with her predecessors, was the use of steam turbine power. This, and her further assets of heavy, long-range gun armament and improved armour, perfectly suited Fisher's main interest—to show the world, and especially Germany, France, Russia and the United States, that Britain still ruled the waves and would continue to do so.

Fisher believed in the value of a deterrent. Never one to shy from publicity, he decided to produce *Dreadnought* in a single year and to use the project as a means of impressing the world with Britain's naval invincibility, shipbuilding strength and industrial capacity. He was set on Britain being first to launch, conduct trials and operate the new class of battleship and was utterly ruthless in his pursuit of that aim.

His zeal for the project was most evident when a major delay was encountered in production of the gun turrets for the new vessel. To circumvent the problem, Fisher ordered a number of shortcuts; in particular, he had turrets, mountings and armour plates, which had been intended for two other battleships, *Lord Nelson* and *Agamemnon*, diverted for installation in *Dreadnought*. The 1,100 workers of the Portsmouth Shipyard laid down *Dreadnought* in October 1905 and by February 1906 the new ship had been launched. On 3 October, in a record-breaking building time, she was readied for preliminary trials. From the laying of her keel to completion, *Dreadnought*'s construction took just 366 days. In fact, her final fitting-out took an additional two months, but her coming-out party made all other capital ships in the world obsolete. Henceforth, battleships fell into two groups: pre-Dreadnoughts and Dreadnoughts—the word is still used as a generic for even the last generation of battleships.

Dreadnought was larger than any previous battleship. She looked, and was, formidable and revolutionary. With long, clean lines, and huge turrets spaced along her deck, she was a superb gun platform. Her performance during sea trials was gratifying; her gunnery judged excellent with two aimed rounds a minute fired per piece. Her structure was fully up to the stress of firing eight-gun broadsides. Powered by steam-driven quadruple-screw turbines, she was capable of 21.6 knots and had a range of 6,620 nautical miles at an average speed of ten knots. She was manned by a crew of 695 which, depending on operational requirements, would sometimes grow to as many as 775. She was 527 feet long with a beam of 82 feet and had an eight-inch to eleven-inch armour belt and eleven-inch armour on her five turrets, which mounted two twelve-inch guns each. Additional armament included 27 twelve-pounder guns and five eighteen-inch torpedo tubes. Fully loaded, *Dreadnought* displaced 21,850 tons, similar to that of the current Royal Navy aircraft carrier, HMS *Illustrious*.

Like many other prototypes, *Dreadnought* was not without faults, including a main belt armour that was too low and inadequate anti-torpedo boat guns. But such flaws were not to be repeated in the subsequent British dreadnoughts.

Britain was not alone in having concluded that the priorities for the next generation of battleships would be high speed and a unified primary armament of heavy guns with great size, range and accuracy. The planners and naval architects of the United States, Japan and Italy were all busily developing their own versions of the new vessel while *Dreadnought* was being constructed. The U.S. was actually well ahead of Britain in such development, with their *South Carolina* class battleship at the time of *Dreadnought*'s keel-laying. But *Dreadnought* was the first such ship afloat and with her arrival all other existing battleships became second rate.

Depictions of HMS *Dreadnought*, right and centre right, and other *Dreadnought*-era warships. far right: USS *South Carolina* in 1909, below: USS *Idaho*, BB-24, under repair, below right: the German battleship *Thuringen* in 1910. below far right: German battlecruiser *Von Der Tann* in 1910.

DREADNOUGHT.

H.M.S. "Dreadnought."

In addition to *Dreadnought*, Fisher intended the development of a new armoured cruiser, the battlecruiser. He had wanted to use 9.2-inch guns in this class of ships, but in the end was persuaded that it should be armed with 12-inch guns. The design was highly controversial in that, to achieve the required speed of 25 knots, a hull larger than that of *Dreadnought* was needed, and this, combined with the weight of the big guns, made it necessary to save weight elsewhere by using the ordinary light armour

HMS *Dreadnought* was completed in 1906 and was unlike any other battleship in existence. With steam turbine engines, previously used only in small naval vessels and a few liners, the impressive new British warship was armed with ten twelve-inch guns, equating to the firepower of more than two conventional battleships of her day, making her capable of sinking virtually any other battleship in the world.

"Battle, n. A method of untying with the teeth a political knot that would not yield to the tongue." – Ambrose Bierce, *The Devil's Dictionary*

right: The USS *Louisiana*, BB-19, an American contemporary of HMS *Dreadnought*, in April 1908 near Coronado, California.

of conventional armoured cruisers. HMS *Invincible* was the first ship of the new 'battlecruiser' class. She was followed in construction by sister-ships *Inflexible* and *Indomitable*. The keels for all three vessels were laid down during 1906 and all were completed in 1908. Like *Dreadnought*, the *Invincible* class battlecruisers were turbine-powered and were indeed capable of the 25 knot requirement. They carried four turrets, each mounting two 12-inch guns, but had only 4- to 6-inch main belt armour, and 7-inch armour on the barbettes, giving them only minimal protection.

Invincible was 567 feet long and displaced 17,370 tons. She had a top speed of 25.5 knots, a crew of 780 men and secondary armament of sixteen 4-inch guns and five 18-inch torpedo tubes.

Just as Admiral Fisher's efforts were producing results, fears began to surface in Britain about Germany's rapidly expanding warship inventory. To this point the British had been quietly confident of their ability to outbuild and outgun the other significant fleets of the world, and in doing so, retain supremacy of the seas. Then, in 1908, the Liberal British government decided to cut substantially the annual budget allocation for battleships. This action immediately sparked heated debate between the political parties about Britain's defence requirements and strategic priorities—and the associated costs. Economic reform was in the air and two British battleships under construction were cancelled. Concern at the Admiralty heightened when it was learned that the Germans were in fact accelerating their battleship construction effort, while the British were cutting back theirs. It appeared that the German battleship inventory could reach near parity with the British within three years. The argument continued in Parliament until the summer of 1909. The opposing factions in the Commons finally agreed on authorization for the building of four new dreadnoughts that year and

four more in 1910, providing that German battleship construction continued at the current pace. Additionally, both Australia and New Zealand expressed concerns at the looming threat to British Commonwealth naval supremacy and offered to pay for the construction of two new warships—battlecruisers—to be named *Australia* and *New Zealand*. The arms race between Britain and Germany in the run-up to the First World War resulted in construction by Britain of 32 battleships and 10 battlecruisers. In that period Germany built 19 battleships and 6 battlecruisers. Many other nations caught battleship fever, spending vast sums to purchase their share of the perceived power and prestige associated with a fleet of these impressive new vessels. The naval inventories of France, Russia, the United States, Italy, Japan, Austria-Hungary, Brazil, Argentina and Chile all began to swell with the new warships. It was the battleship boom of all time.

With all her promise, the record of *Dreadnought* in World War I was not particularly impressive. In her entire combat career, she was credited with the destruction of just one enemy vessel, a German submarine, which she rammed and sank. Britain's dreadnought fleet proved to be a rather high-maintenance affair which, after only two months of wartime operation, required significant refitting in its various home ports, denying the Royal Navy the service of two or three of the vessels at any given time in the war. When hostilities ended, the British public was profoundly opposed to everything related to that conflict, not least the costly weaponry, and a massive programme of warship scrapping began. *Dreadnought* herself went to the breaker's yard in 1923.

Dreadnought's significance lay not in her war record, but in her profound influence on the navies of the world, which led to a sea change in their capital ship philosophies and planning.

JUTLAND

"AND—about this Jutland fight?" I hinted, not for the first time. "Oh, that was just a fight. There was more of it than any other fight, I suppose, but I expect all modern naval actions must be pretty much the same." "But what does one *do*—how does one feel?" I insisted, though I knew it was hopeless. "One does one's job. Things are happening all the time. A man may be right under your nose one minute—serving a gun or something— and the next minute he isn't there." "And one notices that at the time?" "Yes. But there's no time to keep *on* noticing it. You've got to carry on somehow or other, or your show stops. I tell you what one *does* notice, though. If one goes below for anything, or has to pass through a flat somewhere, and one sees the old wardroom clock ticking, or a photograph pinned up, or anything of that sort, one notices *that*. Oh, yes, and there was another thing—the way a ship seemed to blow up if you were far off her. You'd see a glare, then a blaze, and then the smoke—miles high, lifting quite slowly. Then you'd get the row and the jar of it— just like bumping over submarines. Then, a long while after p'raps, you run through a regular rain of bits of burnt paper coming down on the decks— like showers of volcanic ash, you know."
— from *Sea Warfare*
by Rudyard Kipling, on the Battle of Jutland

On 31 May 1916, Vizeadmiral Reinhard Scheer, the German High Seas Fleet commander, ordered the deployment of Admiral Franz von Hipper's battlecruiser group from their North Sea ports. Scheer planned to entrap the British Grand Fleet, or as much of it as he could lure out of harbour. He sent the ships towards Norway in a bid to draw the British battlecruisers into intercepting his force. He then set out after his 5 battlecruisers, with a force of 22 battleships, 11 cruisers, 6 pre-dreadnoughts and 61 torpedo boats. His plan called for U-boats to mine the routes the British vessels would take out of their bases at Cromarty, Rosyth and Scapa Flow. The subs were then to be

below: HMS *Malaya*, sister ship of *Valiant*, *Barham* and *Warspite*.

"Hit your enemy in the belly, and kick him when he is down, and boil his prisoners in oil—if you take any—and torture his women and children. Then people will keep clear of you."
– Admiral of the Fleet Lord Fisher addressing the Hague Peace Conference of 1899

stationed near the British bases in an attempt to torpedo the enemy dreadnoughts as they emerged. The U-boat captains were further assigned to report back to Scheer on all British warship movements in the area. Additional reconnaissance was to be carried out by Zeppelin airships, to keep Scheer informed of the size and position of the enemy force he would be facing.

The British had begun intercepting and reading German naval messages in 1914 after the onset of the First World War. On 16 May 1916, suspicion was aroused at the Admiralty in London when it was learned that several U-boats had left their usual stations along the Atlantic trade routes. The Admiralty discovered on 29 May that the German High Seas Fleet had been ordered to readiness for activity at sea on 31 May and 1 June.

As though in concert with Scheer's plan, British battlecruisers commanded by Admiral Sir David Beatty promptly departed Rosyth to scout the area near Skagerrak strait. They were then to steam to within seventy miles of the Grand Fleet, which was heading south from Scapa Flow under the command of Admiral Jellicoe. Jellicoe had been ordered to take the fleet to an area roughly 100 miles east of Aberdeen. In the coming engagement with the enemy he was to report every movement to the operations room of the Admiralty, which would essentially run the battle from London. In the late evening of 30 May he led the fleet, in his flagship *Iron Duke,* from Scapa and positioned it on station at 2 p.m. the following day.

From the moment Beatty's battlecruisers left Rosyth, Scheer's scheme began to unravel. His U-boats did not manage to attack the enemy vessels as they cruised by, and with deteriorating weather in the area, the German airships were unable to operate. They flew later in the day, but, with minimal visibility, were of little use to Scheer who, at that point, lacked any up-to-date information about his opponents. He was unaware

that the entire British fleet was bearing down on him as his High Seas Fleet took up their position. In another curious turn of events, the Admiralty apparently misinterpreted an intercepted German message and signalled Jellicoe at midday that Admiral Scheer's flagship, *Friedrich der Grosse*, had not left its Jade River moorings near Wilhelmshaven. The commanders of both the British and German fleets were thus unaware that they were converging on one another.

As it happened, Admiral Jellicoe's Grand Fleet had been directed to operate in the precise area where Admiral Hipper's battlecruisers were headed. The long-anticipated clash of the two great fleets was now inevitable. Fate seems to have intervened once again when, in the early afternoon, cruisers of both sides departed from their formations to investigate a distant sighting which turned out to be a Danish steamer. The opposing cruisers spotted one another while about fourteen miles apart and immediately set out to close that distance. At this point, both the German and British commanders believed that they were successfully luring their opposite number into a trap. The British cruisers *Galatea* and *Phaeton* approached and fired upon the German cruiser *Elbing*, which returned fire. *Galatea* sighted Hipper's battlecruisers and immediately signalled their approach to Admiral Beatty who promptly changed course, heading south-east.

The quality of reconnaissance for both sides continued to deteriorate. A British seaplane, launched from the *Engadine*, was scouting in the area, trying to locate the main force of the enemy fleet. The crew only managed to spot the German cruisers. But in the next hour smoke columns from the British fleet were sighted by sailors on the German battlecruisers at the same moment that Beatty was receiving word about sightings of the German vessels from his ships. Beatty was eager for the confrontation and led a force of six battlecruisers into action against an enemy group of five such ships. He did not realize, however, that the main body of Admiral Scheer's High Seas Fleet was now bearing down on his force, as he and Hipper concentrated on outmanoeuvring one another over the next half hour. Beatty had changed course in an attempt to place his ships between Hipper's vessels and the German bases, while Hipper now swung his forces south-east, hoping to draw Beatty towards the German main force less than fifty miles away. The action was imminent and still neither Scheer nor Hipper knew that Jellicoe's main force was rapidly closing on them.

In the afternoon haze at 3.46 p.m., the seas and the weather were calm as the battle began in earnest. If either side had an initial advantage, it was the Germans, who had the sun behind them, illuminating the enemy vessels and making their own ships more difficult to see. Almost as soon as the firing began, roiling black clouds of coal smoke combined with the haze to further obscure the combatants.

Hipper's flagship *Lutzow* was at the head of the German battlecruisers, leading *Derfflinger*, *Seydlitz*, *Moltke* and *Von der Tann*. Beatty's flagship, *Lion*, was at the head of the British line of battlecruisers, and was followed by *Princess Royal*, *Queen Mary*, *Tiger*, *New Zealand* and *Indefatigable*. *Lion* was hit immediately by shells from *Lutzow*, which hit a turret and killed the entire turret crew. *Lion*'s magazines flooded and fires raged round the ship. By 4 p.m. the British battlecruisers had suffered several direct hits, while their German counterparts received just four. The most serious loss occurred when the *Von der Tann* hit HMS *Indefatigable* with three eleven-inch shells on her aft starboard quarter. Lurching out of line, the British vessel began to burn furiously as another shell from *Von der Tann* smashed into her forward twelve-inch gun turret, soon followed by yet another. Within seconds the stricken *Indefatigable* exploded in a massive

orange fireball and sank rapidly by the stern, rolling over as she went, taking more than 1,000 men down with her at 4.03 p.m. Only two of her crew survived.

By 4.25 p.m., *Derfflinger* had the range of *Queen Mary* and scored hits on her, causing an immense explosion which forced HMS *Tiger*, the next ship in the line, to urgently change course and dodge the wreck of *Queen Mary*. *Seydlitz* now joined the attack on *Queen Mary*, sending shells into her A and B magazines, which blew up with sufficient ferocity to tear the ship in two.

Petty Officer E. Francis, Ret., a survivor of HMS *Queen Mary,* described how he urged his shipmates to abandon ship: " 'Come on, you chaps, who's coming for a swim?' Someone answered, 'She will float for a long time yet,' but something, I don't pretend to understand what it was, seemed to be urging me to get away, so I clambered up over the slimy bilge keel and fell off into the water, followed, I should think, by about five other men.

"I struck away from the ship as hard as I could, and must have covered nearly fifty yards, when there was a big smash, and stopping and looking round the air seemed to be full of fragments and flying pieces. A large piece seemed to be right above my head, and acting on an impulse I dipped under to avoid being struck, and stayed under as long as I could, and then, came to the top again, and coming behind me I heard a rush of water, which looked very much like a surf breaking on a beach, and I realised it was the suction or backwash from the ship which had just gone. I hardly had time to fill my lungs with air when it was on me; I felt it was no use struggling against it, so I let myself go for a moment or two, then struck out, but I felt it was a losing game, and remarked to myself mentally, 'What's the use of you struggling, you're done,' and actually eased my efforts to reach the top, when a small voice seemed to say 'Dig out.'

"I started afresh, and something bumped against me. I grasped it and afterwards found it was a large

"The *Queen Mary* was next ahead of us, and I remember watching her for a little, and saw one salvo straddle her. Three shells out of four hit, and the impression one got of seeing the splinters fly and the dull red burst was as if no damage had been done, but that the armour was keeping the shell out. The next salvo that I saw straddled her, and two more shells hit her. As they hit, I saw a dull red glow amidships, and then the ship seemed to open out like a puff ball, or one of those toadstool things when one squeezes it. Then there was another dull red glow somewhere forward, and the whole ship seemed to collapse inwards. The funnels and masts fell into the middle, and the hull was blown outwards. The roofs of the turrets were blown 100 feet high, then everything was smoke, and a bit of the stern was the only part of the ship left above the water. The *Tiger* put her helm hard-a-starboard, and we just cleared the remains of the *Queen Mary*'s stern by a few feet."
– an officer in HMS *Tiger*

hammock; it undoubtedly pulled me to the top, more dead than alive, and I rested on it, but I felt I was getting very weak, and roused myself sufficiently to look around for something more substantial to support me. Floating right in front of me was a piece of timber (I believe the centre baulk of our pattern 4 target). I managed to push myself on the hammock close to the timber, and grasped a piece of rope hanging over the side. My next difficulty was to get on top, and with a small amount of exertion I kept on. I managed to reeve my arms through a strop, and then I must have become unconscious."

In only a few minutes *Queen Mary* went down with the loss of 1,285 men. There were nine survivors. Admiral Beatty now had just four battlecruisers remaining. The Germans still had five.

To the rescue now steamed four British *Queen Elizabeth* class battleships of the 5th Battle Squadron, *Warspite*, *Barham*, *Valiant* and *Malaya,* with fifteen-inch guns which were able to commence firing while still at a range of 19,000 yards. *Valiant* squared off against *Moltke* as *Barham* took on *Von der Tann*. At such a great range, the German ships could not respond and could only attempt to evade the British shells by changing course and zig-zagging. At this point Beatty needed time, pending the engagement of the entire Grand Fleet, and ordered a torpedo attack by his destroyers, causing Hipper to alter course. A 21-inch British torpedo rent a great hole in the side of *Seydlitz*, which reduced her speed but did not force her to leave her position among the German battlecruisers.

At last lookouts aboard one of Beatty's light cruisers spotted battleships of the High Seas Fleet twelve miles distant and signalled the admiral who brought his ships about in a feint as if to avoid engagement with the big German vessels. Actually, he was trying to coax them into proximity with the Grand Fleet. But sloppy communications left some of Beatty's ships in the dark about his intention

and they soon found themselves within the range of the German fleet.

The four *Queen Elizabeth* class battleships slowly manoeuvred round to improve their positions relative to that of the enemy and, as they did, both *Barham* and *Malaya* were hit and incurred casualties. The four British vessels were firing too and soon were laying shells down on the *Markgraf*, *Grosser Kurfurst* and the German battleships.

Describing his experiences in HMS *Malaya*, one of her sailors recalled: "I was Midshipman of the afternoon watch on May 31st, when a signal was received which seemed to excite the small crowd on Monkeys' Island, the crew name for the Upper Bridge, from which the Captain, or the Officer of the Watch, controls the ship, and being, like all snotties, very curious, I eventually mustered up enough courage to ask the Officer of the Watch what it was about, only to be snubbed for my pains. A few minutes later, however, the Captain sent me down to the Engineer Commander with a copy of a signal (which naturally, I suppose, I read). It was from the *Galatea*, reporting two enemy ships in sight. I duly returned to the bridge, after telling the Engineer Commander that the Captain wanted steam for full speed as soon as possible.

"I think we only realised that we were at last in for a proper action when we heard the battlecruisers firing ahead. We then began to get quite jubilant; so much so, that when a German shell landed abreast us on the port side about 500 yards short there was a positive cheer from the *Malaya*. Then we heard the other ships of our own squadron open fire, one after the other, ahead of us, each salvo helped on its way by a cheer. In our torpedo control tower we were so interested in what was going on, that when *Malaya* herself opened fire, the blast from 'X' turret's guns, which were only a few feet away from us, sat us down with a 'whump,' and the range-taker came down from his seat with a crash.

"From this time onwards my thoughts were really more like a nightmare than thoughts of a wide-awake human being. I don't think I felt fright, simply because what was going on around me was so unfamiliar that my brain was incapable of grasping it. Even now I can only think of the beginning of the action as through a dim haze. I remember seeing the enemy line on the horizon with red specks coming out of them, which I tried to realise were the cause of projectiles landing around us, continually covering us with spray, but the fact refused to sink into my brain. We were all the time rather excited, and our enthusiasm knew no bounds when we passed a sunken ship with survivors swimming around her. We never dreamt that it was one of our own battlecruisers; but it was the *Indefatigable*, and over a thousand dead men lay in her wreck. The same thing occurred when we passed the wreckage and survivors of the *Queen Mary*. Even when a man on some wreckage waved to us, we thought it must be a German wanting to be picked up. It is rather dreadful to think of now, especially as some men were not too keen on rescuing Germans after the *Lusitania* and similar atrocities, but I have often thought since how well it showed the confidence that we had in our own fleet that no one for a moment imagined that one of our own ships would be sunk so soon.

"All this time I was gradually getting my thoughts out of their 'dreamy' state, and was slowly beginning to realise that all these projectiles falling a few yards short and over were big ones, and that they were meant for us; and my thoughts, following their natural course, led me on to think of my life-saving waistcoat, which, like a fool, I had left in my sea-chest down below. There was no chance of getting it now.

"All this time we were being thrown about by the blast of 'X' turret, and we spent quite a portion of our time in ungraceful and rather painful positions on the deck, bumping against the range-finder, plotter and other things with sharp corners.

"Shortly after 7.30 pm we lost touch altogether with the enemy, and a lull in the action occurred.

35

After having a look at the damage done to 'X' turret,
I went forward, and was surprised to see a large
shell hole in the upper deck near No. 3 six-inch gun
starboard. The lower boom stanchion was buckled
out of all recognition, and the bread store was a
twisted heap of wreckage. I went down to the
battery, where everything was dark chaos. Most of
the wounded had been taken away, but several of
the killed were still there. The most ghastly part of
the whole affair was the smell of burnt human flesh,
which remained in the ship for weeks, making
everybody have a sickly nauseous feeling the whole
time. When the battery was finally lighted by an
emergency circuit, it was a scene which cannot
easily be forgotten—everything burnt black and bare
from the fire; the galley, canteen and drying room
bulkheads blown and twisted into the most
grotesque shapes, and the whole deck covered by
about 6 inches of water and dreadful debris; and
permeating everywhere the awful stench of cordite

fumes and of war. It is hardly surprising that the nerves of many of us were shaken, especially as the men below decks and in other stations away from the actual damage had never dreamt that we had suffered such damage or casualties.

"By the time it was dark we were all at our stations again. Some of the torpedo control tower's crew were lying on the deck, whilst the remainder kept a lookout."

As the ships of the British Grand Fleet steamed south to join Beatty's battlecruiser force which was still heading north, Admiral Jellicoe ordered three of his *Invincible* class battlecruisers, under the command of Rear Admiral Sir Horace Hood, to go to the aid of Beatty. After the various course reversals of both sides, the situation was now that Hipper's force was leading the entire German High Seas Fleet, pursuing Beatty's battlecruisers northwards, and steaming into the arms of the Grand Fleet; all seemed set for the confrontation

that the British had been seeking since the start of the war.

At 5.26 p.m. the light was changing as Beatty halted the northerly run of his ships to turn and re-engage Hipper. Now the advantage of illumination began to be with the British, who capitalized on it, badly damaging *Lutzow. Derfflinger* was starting to take on water due to severe bow damage and *Seydlitz* was afire. All the big guns of *Von der Tann* had been put out of action and Admiral Hipper was forced to bring his destroyers up in a desperate attack on the British line. It was then that Hood's three battlecruisers arrived to scatter the German destroyers.

Once again, a situation arose in which optimal intelligence based on thorough, up-to-the-minute reconnaissance was required by both sides. Information of this quality, however, was simply not available. Admiral Jellicoe, probably the best naval tactician in the world at the time of Jutland, had just seven miles visibility from the bridge of

Iron Duke and knew very little about the present position, speed and bearing of the enemy fleet. He did know that he had only a few moments to deploy the vessels of the Grand Fleet in such a way as to allow all their big guns to bear on the enemy as soon as they came within range. He quickly ordered the fleet to form a nine-mile-long single column. The move positioned his newest and most capable battleships to initiate the action, and was, according to most naval historians, probably the most effective deployment anyone could have achieved in the circumstances. As he completed the manoeuvre, Jellicoe's fleet was joined by the British battlecruisers.

In the relatively shallow water of the Jutland Bank off the coast of Denmark, sailors of the Grand Fleet witnessed a grotesque spectacle in the aftermath of an attack by *König* and *Derfflinger* on HMS *Invincible*. In the waning sunlight, *Invincible*, the flagship of Admiral Hood, was struck by a massive salvo that destroyed her mid-ships turrets, sending

fire into the magazines below, setting off an enormous explosion, that broke her hull into two. Both halves of the 570-foot-long battlecruiser then sank vertically, leaving the bow and stern standing out of the water like gravestones. Of her crew, 1,026 men died. Just six were saved.

The two great battle fleets now engaged in a series of gun actions. Jellicoe and the Grand Fleet crossed the 'T' of Scheer's High Seas Fleet and the German ships began to receive the full firepower of the British battleship line. It was Scheer who was trapped. His only option was a 180° "battle turnaway". All the German battleships accomplished the manoeuvre and, in the gathering mist of early evening, aided by a smokescreen laid by his destroyers, Scheer's force retreated.

At 6.56 p.m., Jellicoe had brought the Grand Fleet round to the south to cut off Scheer's escape route and, at 7.08, Scheer's 'T' was crossed again, exposing his ships to an even more devastating assault from the British battleships. What followed has been referred to as the 'death ride' of the German battlecruisers. Scheer ordered them to: "Charge the enemy. Ram. Ships denoted are to attack without regard to consequences." Leading the ride was *Derfflinger*, which quickly lost her fire control and two turrets in the ensuing action. *Lutzow* was hit and burned furiously. *Seydlitz* took five hits. In this phase of the battle, only two Grand Fleet ships suffered significant damage. *Colossus* was struck by two shells and *Marlborough* received a torpedo, but both ships were able to carry on. Firing continued until 8.35, but by then the main fleet action of Jutland was finished. Through the night, German battleships continued to fire on British cruisers and destroyers near the rear of the Grand Fleet. Jellicoe, however, was loath to risk substantial night action, fearing the likelihood of mistakes in ship identification as well as collision. Scheer, for his part, could not afford such reservations and took the risk in order

below left: A postcard depicting the super dreadnought HMS *Colossus* in 1911. below: 2nd Class battleship HMS *Revenge*.

H.M.S. QUEEN MARY

to shepherd his fleet back to the safety of Wilhelmshaven. Only his pre-dreadnought *Pommern*, which blew up when struck by a British torpedo, and *Lützow*, which had to be sunk by German destroyers when she could no longer maintain steam, were lost in the effort. On their return to Wilhelmshaven, *Seydlitz* and *Derfflinger* had both lost half their main armament. Hipper led them back in *Moltke*.

The eminent British historian Sir John Keegan has written of the battle: "By comparison with the losses suffered in contemporary battles on land—Verdun and the Somme, both fought in 1916—Jutland was not costly. The total number of sailors killed was 8,500, about 6,000 British, 2,500 German. It is the manner of dying that appals. Burns, rarely suffered in trench warfare, were a major cause of death, usually the result of boilers bursting or cordite catching fire. The doctors were bewildered by the symptoms. Often the victims seemed scarcely hurt at first but then displayed strange signs of deterioration and died within the day. Shell splinter wounds varied in nature from multiple pepperpotting to decapitation. What sailors feared most was drowning inside the ship. Shut in small compartments behind watertight doors, they could be overcome by a high-pressure gush through a shell hole. The quickest end was by the detonation of a main magazine, which destroyed the ship, the cause of the loss of *Indefatigable*, *Invincible* and *Queen Mary*."

Jutland was basically a draw. The German forces had sunk three British capital ships and three armoured cruisers. The British had sunk one capital ship and one elderly battleship. On the day after the battle, the British had possession of the battlefield and their Grand Fleet returned to its ports largely intact. It was refuelled, rearmed and essentially ready to put to sea again a day later.

In terms of the total numbers of men and ships lost, the German claim to victory was justified. The

left: Aboard the British battlecruiser HMS *Queen Mary*. below: The loss of the *Queen Mary* at Jutland.

far left top: German Admiral Reinhard Scheer, Commander-in-Chief of the High Seas Fleet in the Battle of Jutland. far left bottom: Admiral Franz von Hipper, commander of the German battlecruisers at Jutland. centre: World War I U.S. Navy reservists recruiting in New York during 1917, and left above: San Francisco Yeomanettes attached to the U.S. Naval Reserve in 1918. left: Symbolic of the Royal Navy's might at the turn of the century, HMS *Prince of Wales*.

British lost fourteen ships, the Germans eleven. Personnel losses amounted to 6,097 British and 2,551 German. Strategically, Britain's Grand Fleet still ruled the North Sea and the British still maintained their blockade of Germany. Technologically, the Germans had the edge with their big gun shells, which were filled with desensitized TNT (trinitrotoluene), a considerable improvement over the Lyddite-filled shells of the British. Certainly, both sides suffered from grossly inadequate communications.

The vast investment in ships and men which both sides had made during the prewar naval race had not brought to either the dividends which it had hoped for. The Royal Navy had failed to achieve the decisive victory which it sought, and would never get another chance to defeat the Germans in a fleet action. The grandly named High Seas Fleet, on the other hand, was now reduced to the role of a coastal defence force and acting as an adjunct to the less visually impressive but far more effective U-boat fleet.

With the Armistice of 1918, Germany lost her status as a great naval power. Under the terms of the peace Treaty of Versailles, her fleet was interned. In November 1918, the High Seas Fleet sailed from Wilhelmshaven to the Firth of Forth in Scotland, and later to its final destination, Scapa Flow. For months the Allies continued to discuss the ultimate fate of the German ships which lay at anchor in Scapa. The ships were in the care of German skeleton crews, overseen by British armed guards. With the Armistice due to expire on 21 June 1919, when the Treaty of Versailles came into effect, the German commander of the interned fleet, Vizeadmiral Ludwig von Reuter, took matters into his own hands. At mid-morning on the 21st Reuter ordered his crews to scuttle the ships.

In the next two decades most of the former German warships were raised from the waters of Scapa Flow and towed to Rosyth and elsewhere in Britain where they were eventually broken up for scrap. The battleships *Kronprinz*, *Markgraf* and *König* remain at the bottom in Scapa to this day.

right: A battleship of the Jutland period, the USS *New York*, BB-34, in May 1915.

above: *The Fleet's In!*, a
1934 painting by Paul
Cadmus for the Works
Projects Administration
depression recovery
programme of the U.S.

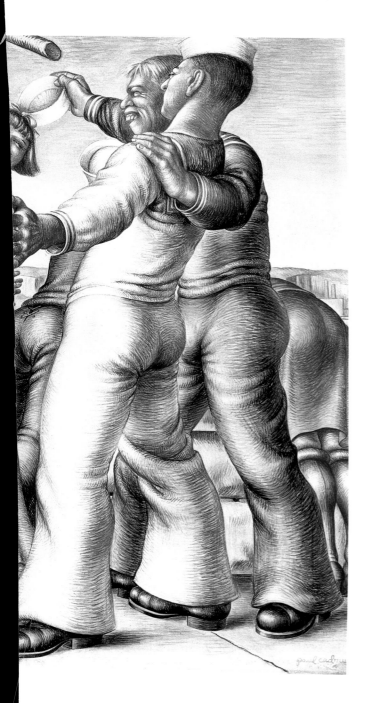

ANXIOUS TO take advantage of a peace dividend at the
end of World War I, Britain quickly scrapped nearly
400 of her warships, among them 40 capital ships. An
expansionist Japan, meanwhile, was expanding her
warship fleet at a rapid pace, with considerable
British support. In response to the Japanese naval
construction programme, the Americans began
building four *Maryland* class battleships; 32,500-ton
vessels armed with eight sixteen-inch guns, to
counter the new, similarly-armed *Nagato* class
battleships of Japan. By 1921, the United States had
a total of twelve battleships under construction. The
British fell behind the battleship curve and did not
join this arms race until 1925 when they authorized
construction of four new 46,000-ton battlecruisers.
They were unable to finance a further four capital
ships—48,500-ton battleships to be armed with
eighteen-inch guns.

In 1921 the administration of the new U.S.
president, Warren G. Harding, sponsored a major
conference on arms limitation held at
Washington. The conference led to a treaty in
1922 by which the five main naval powers, the
United States, Britain, France, Italy and Japan
agreed to limit capital ship tonnages as follows:
Britain and the United States were each confined
to a total of 525,000 tons, Japan was entitled to
315,000 tons, while France and Italy could each
have 175,000 tons. Individual capital ships would
be limited to a maximum of 35,000 tons with
armament no larger than sixteen-inch guns.
Britain and the United States would be limited to
a total aircraft carrier tonnage of 135,000, with
new carriers limited to an individual tonnage of
27,000. All lesser warships would be limited to
10,000 tons each with guns no larger than eight-
inch calibre.

SS *Michigan*, teaming after r I.

The Treaty of Versailles, signed on 28 June 1919, had decreed that Germany's future armoured warships could not exceed a displacement of 10,000 tons, with cruisers limited to 6,000 tons, and destroyers to 800 tons. Submarines and military aircraft were entirely prohibited.

Germany sought ways around the Versailles terms which it saw as excessively restrictive. It initiated clandestine projects such as a design bureau in the Netherlands that employed former wartime U-boat designers. The bureau was actually working for the German Admiralty, designing and supervising the construction of submarines for Turkey, Spain and Finland. These designs would later be utilized in the production of German U-boats for use in World War II. In another move to circumvent the Versailles rules, the Germans developed the design for an 'armoured ship', the *Panzerschiff*, or pocket battleship. It would, in fact, exceed the 10,000-ton limitation by 23 per cent and be armed with six eleven-inch guns and eight 5.9-inch guns. Its diesel engines gave it a speed of 26 knots, faster than most battleships of the time. By 1934, the Germans had completed three of the pocket battleships.

In a climate of austerity in the United States, the administration of President Herbert Hoover cut the pace of warship construction, planning and funding. By 1930, the U.S. was at the rear of the inventory and building race with only eleven such vessels completed or under construction. Leading the category was Japan with 125. Then came France with 119, followed by Italy with 82 and Britain with 74. In the background, Germany continued to rearm in secret.

Franklin D. Roosevelt was elected president of the United States in 1932 and, in the midst of the Great Depression era, presided over new funding for warship construction as part of the National Industrial Recovery Act approved by the Congress.

In January 1933, Adolf Hitler became Chancellor

of Germany and, by 1934, had joined Japan in with-drawing from the League of Nations. Japan and Germany were flouting the dictates of Versailles and the later Washington and London naval conferences. Hitler took the further illegal step of reintroducing conscription in Germany. France and Italy, both concerned about German pocket battleship development, began construction in the early 1930s of the *Dunkerque* and *Vittorio Veneto* class battleships, respectively—and the Germans started work on *Scharnhorst* and *Gneisenau* in 1935. In an effort to catch up with the other nations and counter the Japanese warship building programme, Roosevelt spearheaded the 1934 Vinson-Trammell Act which authorized work on approximately 100 new warships.

By the mid-thirties, Britain's warship fleet was largely in poor shape, run-down and mostly obsolete. Forming the core of the fleet were the remaining *Queen Elizabeth* and *Revenge* or R class battleships and the *Hood*. Planned in response to the four German Mackensen class battlecruisers of 1914, the 46,000-ton *Hood* was completed in 1920, the only one of her class of four battlecruisers to reach completion. The 34,000-ton *Nelson* and *Rodney* joined the fleet in 1927 as the first battleships to be designed to the newly imposed 35,000-ton limit. Meanwhile, flagrantly disregarding the treaty terms that bound her, Germany was building U-boats and rapidly rearming. In addition to submarines, her shipyards were hard at work on the design and construction of six new capital ships, at least one carrier, eighteen cruisers and dozens of destroyers.

At another conference of the big five naval powers, held in London in 1935, Japan insisted that she would not be bound by the Washington Treaty limitations. The head of the Imperial Japanese Navy, Admiral Isoroku Yamamoto, proposed the total abolition of the battleship. "These ships are like elaborate religious scrolls which old people hang up in their homes. They are purely a matter of faith, not reality. The battleship is as useful in modern warfare as a samurai sword." The other conferees rejected his proposal and the Japanese withdrew from the talks. The naval treaties that had helped keep the peace were unravelling.

A so-called London Protocol of the time found Britain and Germany agreeing that submarines were bound by international law not to attack merchant ships without warning. Britain's 1930s policy of non-alienation served to embolden Hitler, and Italy's Benito Mussolini, in their territorial adventurism. The United States felt embittered that the European nations appeared to be throwing away the hard-won peace after World War I, and the American people turned more and more isolationist as the decade wore on. In 1936, Germany began work on the battleships *Bismarck* and *Tirpitz*, both of which would greatly exceed their officially allowed displacement and, in this uneasy world climate, Japan was busy planning construction of the 67,000-ton *Yamato* class which would out-range and out-gun any warship afloat. With eighteen-inch guns, they would be the largest, most powerful and deadly battleships ever built.

When Ohio inventors and bicycle repairmen Orville and Wilbur Wright managed to fly their odd-looking machine at Kill Devil Hill near Kitty Hawk, North Carolina in December 1903, the event attracted relatively little interest. Mankind's first successful attempt at powered flight did not impress the American government of the time. Still, the Wrights went on with their aerial experimentation, attracting far less attention than they deserved. After rejection by their own government, they offered their invention to Britain, where the War Office and Admiralty turned them down three times. In France during 1908, however, they met a very different reaction when they put their flying machine through an exciting one-and-a-half-hour display. By then, Britain,

Russia and much of Europe had awakened to the military potential of aircraft.

On 14 November 1910, an American aviator named Eugene Ely coaxed his 50-horsepower Glenn Curtiss bi-plane from a short platform built on the cruiser *Birmingham,* in history's first "carrier launch" of an aircraft. Two months later, Ely executed the first carrier landing on the 120-foot deck platform of the cruiser *Pennsylvania*. Less than a year later, he died in a crash during one of his demonstration flights. Of his achievements, the British magazine *Aeroplane*, 25 January 1911, commented: ". . . this partakes too much of the nature of trick flying to be of much practical value. A naval aeroplane would be of more use if it 'landed' on the water and could then be hauled on board. A slight error in steering when trying to alight on deck would wreck the whole machine." By 1911, following many trials, aircraft were being successfully launched from flimsy tracks erected on the forward turret of British battleships.

In 1912, the Royal Flying Corps was established in Britain, with the intention of providing both military and naval aviators and aircraft to support their respective services in a war. Experimentation into the possible offensive use of naval aircraft for the delivery of bombs and torpedoes soon began. In 1913, British trials involving a Short seaplane dropping a torpedo were successfully carried out, and in America, Glenn Curtiss was achieving considerable accuracy in dropping bombs on "warship" targets from his planes.

Britain's naval air capability steadily increased from 1914 onwards. When the First World War started the Royal Navy was operating one seaplane carrier, 39 aeroplanes and 52 seaplanes; by the end of the war in 1918, her naval and land air forces mustered eleven carriers, 3,000 land and seaplanes and more than 50 non-rigid airships, with 55,000 personnel.

Hitler's Plan Z was due to be completed in 1944. It was to be the ultimate battleship, never to be surpassed. At an unbelievable 144,000 tons, the unnamed monster was to be more than twice the size of the Japanese giant, *Yamato*. Armed with eight twenty-inch guns, the German behemoth was to be capable of 34 knots. Like so many of the Führer's dreams, it would not come true.

In the experimental bombing runs by aircraft under the command of General Billy Mitchell, who used these tests to support his ideas that the battleships were obsolete in the face of air power, the first USS *New Jersey* (BB-16) was sunk off Cape Hatteras, North Carolina on 5 September 1922.

"The long day finished with us slinging our hammocks, holding the 'nettles' [strings] open at our head-end with a short stick, unfolding our heavy woollen blankets lengthways across our hammock before swinging our bodies in; a comfortable bed, with our boots and clothing made into a pillow. We soon got used to it, as we did to the ever-present hum of fan motors pushing stale air from one compartment to

German air strength by the end of the war included nearly 700 seaplanes, 190 land planes and seven airships. Entering the war with only a handful of aircraft and personnel, the United States Navy emerged from it with nearly 1,900 flying boats and seaplanes and more than 50,000 men. The first aerial attack on warships occurred on Christmas Day 1914 when German seaplanes and Zeppelins dropped bombs on British ships which had attempted an attack on the Zeppelin sheds at Cuxhaven in northern Germany. Neither the planes nor the Zeppelins succeeded in hitting a ship.

In all of the First World War, no warships were seriously damaged or sunk in attacks by aircraft and only a few merchant ships were destroyed or seriously damaged in such attacks.

Proponents and opponents of naval aviation after World War I engaged in a debate that had begun after the Battle of Jutland and would continue throughout the 1920s and 1930s. The British Admiralty was not at all enthusiastic about developing a naval air arm. It viewed the aircraft carrier with suspicion just as it had regarded the submarine a decade earlier. The first aircraft carriers, existing vessels converted to launch and recover aircraft, were perceived as too slow to keep up with the capital ships of the Fleet. It was not until 1923 that HMS *Hermes*, the world's first purpose-built aircraft carrier, was completed. Even then, few in the Royal Navy were keen about expanding the role of aviation for their service. This lack of enthusiasm in naval circles had contributed to the government decision to form an independent Royal Air Force in 1918. Relatively few naval people accepted that aviation served any useful naval function beyond reconnaissance duties.

The Navy and War Departments of the U.S. government were separately administered and were heatedly involved in the debate. The prime advocate of strategic bombing by fixed-wing aircraft as an ultimate war-winning policy was Brigadier

General William 'Billy' Mitchell. In his opinion, if aircraft were "allowed to develop essential air weapons," [they could] "carry war to such an extent . . . as almost to make navies useless on the surface of the water." Mitchell wanted to prove to the Navy, the nation and the world that accurate aerial bombing of an enemy's capital ships was feasible and that aircraft would play a decisive role in future naval warfare. A series of trials was agreed with the Navy and scheduled to begin in 1921. Former enemy warships were to be the targets of Mitchell's bombers and the ships were to be boarded between bombing tests so that the damage caused by the bombing could be assessed. Mitchell wanted to make the trials as high-profile as possible, for maximum publicity value, and was less concerned with a scrupulous adherence to the rules of the tests than with his planes sinking battleships. Though he established an early precedent when his 2,000-pound bombs quickly sank the *Ostfriesland*, this only proved that an old German battleship at anchor, with no active anti-aircraft guns and no damage control, could be sunk by bombers.

The argument continued. The conventional conservative wisdom in the British and American navies held that, whether or not Mitchell was correct, a navy's first responsibility was to be prepared to fight wars in the present and not to concentrate all their resources on preparing for the future. Mitchell and his supporters, on the other hand, argued that, it having been shown, at least to the satisfaction of some, that bombers could sink battleships, it followed that in the next war, all the battleships involved would be sunk by bombers, as would all the aircraft carriers. Both sides were, of course, wrong. Battleships would prove to be dangerously vulnerable to bombers, but the bombers that did most of the damage came not from land bases but from carriers. In fact, during World War II, very few battleships succumbed to attack by shore-based bombers. In excess of 200 aircraft carriers participated in that war and only one was actually sunk by shore-based bombers.

THE·WONDER·BOOK·OF THE·NAVY

the next, and the subdued roar of machinery. The lights were not dimmed until lights out at 10 o'clock. The first night, fitful sleep came to most after a lot of wriggling about, trying to keep our blankets wrapped around us at the same time, and attempting to ignore the bright overhead light. Our long troubled night, broken by odd bumps underneath as passers-by 'headed' our hammocks, as they went about their duties, was ended by the switching on of all lights and raucous shouting of the duty Petty Officer. The time being 5.30 gave us little time to lash up and stow our hammocks, get dressed and find our promised cup of Kye [cocoa] and ship's bisquit. The established mess mates had turned out early to draw the rations, lash up their hammocks, and dispose of the rations in comfort. We were only caught the once, as like all things learned the hard way, only fools get caught twice. The next day we mustered at 6 o'clock, still trying to crunch the hard ship's biscuit before someone robbed us of it. On mustering, the Duty Officer gave the usual orders to scrub the decks. That morning, in the unusually cold weather for Portsmouth, the sea water turned to icy slush as it was hosed on to the deck."
— a sailor in HMS Hood, from *The Royal Navy In The Second World War* by Julian Thompson

IN 1912, at the age of eighteen, Hans Wilhelm Langsdorff enlisted in the Imperial German Navy. He saw front-line action four years later in the Battle of Jutland and soon afterward was placed in command of a minesweeper. In the 1920s, he commanded a flotilla of torpedo boats and then, in the early '30s, served for four years in Berlin at the Ministry of Defence. By 1938 he held the rank of Kapitän zur See and was given command of the pocket battleship *Admiral Graf Spee*.

Admiral Graf Spee, and her sister ships *Admiral Scheer* and *Deutschland*, were the pride of the new German Navy in the 1930s. With their high-speed diesel-powered performance, and their eleven-inch guns, they commanded considerable respect from the world's other naval powers. Their relatively light belt and deck armour, however, made them more vulnerable than they seemed. In their design they appeared to conform to the restrictions of the Versailles Treaty, but they clearly exceeded the treaty-imposed weight restrictions.

Graf Spee sailed from her berth in Wilhelmshaven on 21 August 1939, a few days before the outbreak of war with Britain, for the South Atlantic. The voyage would be known as her 'raider cruise'. Her assignment was to hunt, attack and sink merchant vessels plying the vital shipping lanes to Britain. From 30 September to early December, she sank nine British freighters—a total of 50,000 tons.

Unlike many commanders who followed him, Captain Langsdorff was a strict adherent to the dictates of the Hague Conventions. He ensured that *Graf Spee* displayed her battle ensign when she encountered a ship to be attacked, and signalled a clear warning to the merchant crew: STOP. DO NOT USE WIRELESS OR WE WILL FIRE. He saw that the merchant crew were taken off their vessels before his crew sank them. Not one of the 62 prisoners he took from the merchant ships sunk by *Graf Spee* was harmed.

On the morning of 13 December 1939, a lookout in *Graf Spee* sighted a ship in the distance and Captain

THE BATTLE OF THE RIVER PLATE

The elderly German battleship *Schleswig-Holstein* entered the Polish harbour of Danzig on what had been billed as a friendly visit in late August of 1939. Six days later, her gun crews opened fire on the Polish fortifications near the harbour. The surprise attack marked the opening shots of the Second World War.

left: The German pocket battleship *Admiral Graf Spee* in 1939. above: Kapitän zur See Hans Langsdorff, commanding officer of the *Admiral Graf Spee*.

Langsdorff ordered his helmsman to pursue the vessel to identify it. They were about 200 miles off the estuary of the River Plate, which separates Uruguay and Argentina on the east coast of South America. As the pocket battleship closed in on the potential prey, it was identified as the French liner *Formose*. Just then another ship was sighted from *Graf Spee*. It was the Royal Navy cruiser HMS *Exeter*, which had heard radio distress calls from *Formose* and was steaming to her assistance. The *Exeter* signalled two light cruisers which were then hunting for *Graf Spee*, HMS *Ajax* and HMNZS *Achilles*, which hurried to join her. As the cruisers approached the area, *Graf Spee* turned on a southerly course. *Formose* had changed course and departed.

Captain Langsdorff, his ship low on fuel, preferred to avoid combat with the British warships and altered course to evade them, but he soon noted that the *Ajax* and *Achilles* were approaching and cutting off his escape route from *Exeter*. His only option was to stand and fight. He hoped to destroy *Exeter* before the other cruisers arrived, and began firing his eleven-inch guns before the British ship with her eight-inch guns was in range to return fire. One shell struck *Exeter*'s bridge with devastating effect, killing all present but the captain, another officer and one midshipman. Seriously damaged, with fires below decks, three feet down by the bows and shipping water forward, *Exeter* was a ruin, but she was soon within range and began firing salvos at the German warship. Another shell from *Graf Spee* caused her to slow dramatically, but she maintained position to block any attempt by the German ship to escape to the north. By mid-day, however, the badly damaged British cruiser had to retire from the action, leaving it to *Ajax* and *Achilles*.

In his book *Langsdorff of the Graf Spee, Prince of Honour*, Joseph Gilbey writes: "There is little to compare to the hellish brutality of a sea battle. Men are entrapped in a tight steel box, a warship. They are beyond sight of land, floating in untold fathoms of sea-water. Separated by miles of rolling ocean, combatting warships throw tons of high explosives at each other. It seems an unreal fantasy. Eventually, like a thunderbolt, a shell pierces the ship. A deafening explosion sends lethal particles of shrapnel and flying debris ricocheting off the ship's interior panels. Unfortunate men are cut down instantly in death or mutilation. Fire, fumes and flooding in darkened confined spaces summon terror to the survivors. Exercises can never equal the real thing."

Ajax and *Achilles*, both armed with six-inch guns, had sandwiched *Graf Spee* and, under cover of smoke screens, were firing at the German warship from both sides, causing considerable damage. Captain Langsdorff decided to break off the action and headed out to sea, but the British cruisers gave chase and, leaving the smoke screens behind, closed to within a mile of the German vessel. *Graf Spee* was being savaged by the close-range attack and turned westward, laying a smoke screen as she manoeuvred. Langsdorff signalled the German Admiralty: "I HAVE TAKEN 15 HITS. FOOD STORES AND GALLEYS DESTROYED. I AM HEADING FOR MONTEVIDEO." The *Graf Spee* was followed closely by *Achilles*. Both British cruisers had suffered in the action and few of their bigger guns were still functioning. *Ajax* and *Achilles* took up positions off the estuary that evening as *Graf Spee* entered the harbour.

Captain Langsdorff requested that the authorities in Montevideo grant him fifteen days to repair his ship and make her seaworthy again. They gave him 72 hours, during which his 60 wounded were treated and the 36 dead were taken off the ship for burial. The British Admiralty, meanwhile, had dispatched a fourth cruiser, HMS *Cumberland,* to join the other three and to await the German's next move.

Langsdorff believed, incorrectly, that the Royal Navy aircraft carrier *Ark Royal* and the battlecruiser *Renown* had come to the aid of *Ajax* and *Achilles*. He sent the following signal to Admiral Raeder in

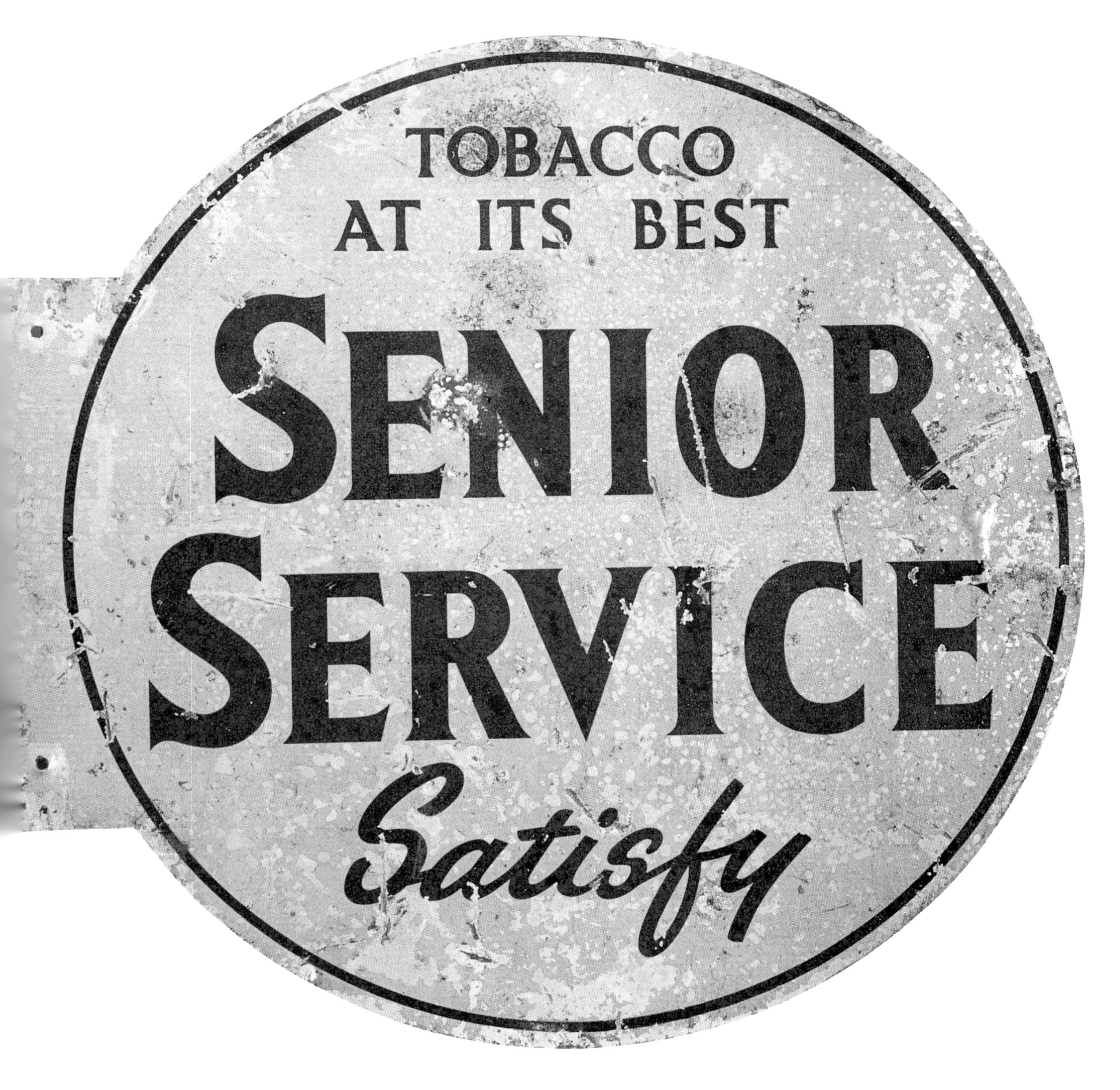
TOBACCO
AT ITS BEST
SENIOR
SERVICE
Satisfy

Berlin on 16 December: "APART FROM THE BRITISH CRUISERS AND DESTROYERS, THE AIRCRAFT CARRIER ARK ROYAL AND THE BATTLE CRUISER RENOWN HAVE JOINED THE NAVAL FORCES TO TIGHTLY BLOCK OUR ESCAPE ROUTE. NO PROSPECT OF BREAKING OUT INTO THE OPEN SEA OR REACHING HOME. PROPOSE EMERGING AS FAR AS NEUTRAL WATERS LIMIT AND ATTEMPT TO FIGHT THROUGH TO BUENOS AIRES USING REMAINING AMMUNITION. BREAKOUT WOULD RESULT IN CERTAIN DESTRUCTION OF GRAF SPEE WITH NO CHANCE OF DAMAGING ENEMY SHIPS. REQUEST DECISION WHETHER TO SCUTTLE DESPITE INADEQUATE DEPTH OF WATER OR ACCEPT INTERNMENT." After conferring on the matter with the Führer, Raeder signalled Langsdorff that the *Graf Spee* was to remain at Montevideo for as long as authorities there would allow; a breakout to Buenos Aires was approved, but internment in Uruguay was not. If scuttling was necessary, everything in the ship was to be thoroughly destroyed. From *Langsdorff of the Graf Spee, Prince of Honour*: "As the hours ticked away, the world waited. A blood-bath seemed certain. Tension mounted at 6.45 pm when a black cloud of smoke puffed out of *Graf Spee*'s funnel. Slowly, amid the rattle of heavy chains, the forward anchor rose out of black, sucking mud. Idling diesels revved into powerful life. *Graf Spee* swung round and moved slowly into the exit channel. Two battle flags waved lazily from their halyards high on the ship's masts. A makeshift steel patch on the port bow covered a large hole suffered in the previous battle. Nonetheless, the damaged warship presented a powerful, beautiful picture as she moved gracefully toward her fate."

In the late afternoon of 17 December, Langsdorff headed the battleship back down the estuary towards the British warships. When *Graf Spee* reached a point just beyond the three-mile limit, Captain Langsdorff halted her. The Captain, his officers and crew, then promptly abandoned their ship, leaving in launches. At eight that evening, three time-bombs exploded, ruining the warship and starting a massive fire. *Graf Spee* soon settled in the shallows, scuttled by her crew, her superstructure still above the water. The German merchant ship *Tacoma* rescued some of the crew. For several days the hulk continued to burn.

Again, from *Langsdorff of the Graf Spee, Prince of Honour*: "At 10 am, Monday, December 18, two seagoing tugs, *Colaso* and *Gigante*, with the barge *Chiriguana* in tow, approached Buenos Aires. Close to 1,100 weary sailors crowded into every corner of the little ships. Most of the crew wore tropical whites while the officers stood out in their blue uniforms. Men overflowed onto the gunwales and clung to the rigging trying to find breathing space. Exhausted and hungry, their uniforms sweaty and crumpled, the 'shipwrecked' sailors had escaped potential disaster in Montevideo. On the black headbands of their white hats, printed in Gothic gold letters, blazed the name of their ship—*Panzerschiff Admiral Graf Spee*."

Captain Langsdorff spent the next few days writing letters to his wife and son in Germany and to the German ambassador in Buenos Aires. On the morning of 20 December he shot himself in the head with a pistol borrowed from the German Embassy and was found dead in his room at the Naval Arsenal in Buenos Aires, wrapped in the ensign of his ship.

For his actions during this, the first major naval victory for the British in World War II, Commodore Henry Harwood, commander of British cruiser Force G from HMS *Exeter*, was knighted and promoted to Rear Admiral. British casualties in the battle totalled 72, with 61 killed in *Exeter*, seven in *Ajax* and four in *Achilles*. Winston Churchill called the action a great victory which "in a cold and dark winter warmed the cockles of our hearts."

The burnt-out wreck of *Graf Spee* lies in the shallows off Montevideo harbour. Her foretop can still be seen on clear days.

The German supply ship *Altmark* was sailing through Norwegian waters en route to her home port on 16 February 1940, carrying 299 British prisoners of war. They were merchant navy and lascar seamen whose ships had been sunk in the South Atlantic by the pocket battleship *Graf Spee*. The *Altmark* was a 12,000-ton auxilliary warship disguised as a tanker. The British destroyer *Cossack*, skippered by Captain Philip Vian, spotted *Altmark* among the fiords and gave chase. *Cossack* caught up with *Altmark* at Jossingfiord near Bergen. It was evening and the crew of the German ship tried to blind the *Cossack* crew with a searchlight. They then charged the British warship astern at full speed, powering through a channel in the ice. *Cossack* skilfully avoided major damage in the encounter. *Altmark* was then boarded by crewmen of *Cossack* who rescued the British sailors. A Lieutenant-Commander Turner led the boarding party and famously shouted to the men he had rescued, "The Navy's here!" The incident caught the imagination of the British public which, at that time, was desperate for any sort of victory. They quickly made Vian a national hero and *Cossack* a household word.

left above: The burning, scuttled *Admiral Graf Spee*, left below: Crew members of *Graf Spee*.

A DATE WHICH WILL LIVE IN INFAMY

In joint army and navy war games of February 1932, carrier-based bombing and strafing aircraft of the United States Navy carried out simulated attacks on army and air base facilities on Oahu, Hawaii. The attacks were staged just after dawn of a Sunday morning, in two waves, and all of the targets were taken by surprise in an ominous demonstration of carrier air power. The Japanese attack on Pearl Harbor nearly ten years later was nearly identical in most respects to that of the 1932 war games.

On Sundays, the sailors of the USS *Arizona* breakfasted on beans, cornbread and coffee. The Navy allotment for food in the 1920s was 40 cents per man per day.

right: Japanese envoys Admiral Kichisaburo Nomura (left) and Saburo Kurusu (foreground) in Washington to negotiate with U.S. Secretary of State Cordell Hull in 1941.

" 'High-altitude bombers overhead!' a lookout with binoculars reported. I squinted up. Heavy smoke from dozens of fires was darkening the sky. Above it, patches of blue showed amid the drifting cumulus. The planes were at 10,000 or 12,000 feet, looking smaller than birds. They were flying over the battle line in a single long column from the seaward side.

"At last, several of our five-inch, twenty-five caliber anti-aircraft guns had ammunition. (It had been passed up by hand from the magazines at great sacrifice, I later learned.) They opened fire with an ear- piercing *crack*! The sky was dotted with black puffs of exploding shells from the *California* and many other ships, mostly below the Kates.

"Bombs began to fall— metallic specks that reflected the sunlight fitfully as they wobbled down. The specks grew larger and more ominous. I felt totally helpless. These might well be the last few seconds of my life. Whether they were or not depended on the skills of an enemy pilot and bombardier, not on anything I could do."
— Ted Mason, USS *California*

right: Waikiki Beach, Honolulu, Hawaii in 1941, below: Downtown Honolulu shortly before the 7 December 1941 Japanese attack on the American naval facilities at nearby Pearl Harbor.

above left: USS *West Virginia* sailor Richard 'Mac' McCutcheon in 1941, above: Hula dancers in Honolulu, 1941, left: President and Mrs Roosevelt chatting with Britain's King George VI and Queen Elizabeth during their 1939 visit to Washington. overleaf above right: The photo album of Mac McCutcheon from his service aboard the USS *West Virginia*, BB-48, below right: The Thanksgiving Day 1941 dinner menu of the *West Virginia*, then moored in Pearl Harbor, far right: The USS *Arizona, BB-39,* in drydock at Pearl Harbor during 1939.

Thanksgiving Day
--MENU--

U.S.S. West Virginia

20 November, 1941
Pearl Harbor T.H.

CREAM OF TOMATO SOUP

SALTINES

FRESH SLICED TOMATOES   SWEET PICKLES

ROAST YOUNG TOM TURKEY

GIBLET GRAVY   SAGE STUFFING

CREAMED MASHED POTATOES   GLAZED SWEETS

FRENCH PEAS

HOT SOUTHERN ROLLS   BUTTER

PUMPKIN PIE   ICE CREAM

COFFEE   CIGARETTES

"Properly 'buttoned up,' the *California* could have shrugged off two or even three torpedoes with minor listing that would have been quickly corrected by counter-flooding the starboard voids. Instead, she had assumed a port list of fourteen or fifteen degrees. The list was still increasing. Suddenly, I found myself sliding toward the low side of the birdbath, which brought me up sharply against the splinter shield. My earphones were jerked from my head. Before replacing them, I looked down. A hundred feet below me was nothing but dirty, oil-streaked and flotsam-filled water. Lifeless bodies from the *Oklahoma* floated face down. Motor launches were criss-crossing the channel, picking up swimming sailors.

"If the *California* capsized—and that, I could see, was a distinct possibility—I had at least a fighting chance to join the swimmers. My shipmates below decks had none.

"I planned to climb to the opposite side of the splinter shield as the ship went over and launch myself in a long flat dive when the maintop touched the water. If I could avoid getting fouled in the yardarm rigging or the radio antennas, I just might get clear."
– Ted Mason, USS
California

far left: Pearl Harbor and Battleship Row before the attack, centre above: Admiral Isoroku Yamamoto, above left: Admiral Chiuchi Nagumo, left: Japanese rehearsal model of Pearl Harbor.

69

right: Japanese Zeros ready to attack from their carrier on 7 December. right centre: Battleships *Maryland* (inboard), *Oklahoma* (capsized), *Tennessee* (inboard), *West Virginia* and *Arizona*, far right:The forward ammunition magazine of *Arizona* explodes in the Sunday morning attack, below: A Japanese torpedo bomber attacking in a still from the film *Pearl Harbor*, below right:The aftermath of the attack recreated in another still from the film.

"On December 6th 1941, a lot of us were out sunning ourselves on the upper deck, until it got so hot that you had to run down and jump in the showers. A typical Saturday in Pearl. It was good duty. A calm, regular day. On Sunday morning, we had breakfast and I had the duty. My station was to handle a fire extinguisher. That day a third of the ship's company had liberty on shore. The bugle sounded 'Fire and Rescue' and I ran off to get my white hat from my locker. The Officer of the Deck at this point thought that there had been some kind of strange explosion over by Ten-Ten dock. A torpedo had passed under a ship there and hit a cruiser and they both sank. And then we were ordered to General Quarters. Then I realized it was the Japs. I started running aft. I went up two decks, heading to the turret. On the way, I saw a plane and wondered what he was doing. He turned and went toward the *California* and as he turned, I saw the red ball on the wing. Before I got to the turret, there was a tremendous explosion somewhere below us. It was a torpedo. The whole ship was shaking and, by then, the ladder was full. I went around to another ladder and got up to the top deck. From there I went up to the boat deck and under the overhang of the turret to my battle station in the turret.

"The explosions continued; the ship would shake and the blast covers would clang, and then we started listing slowly to port, very slowly and I was watching that and thinking that we might have to get through that hatch door in the bottom of the turret pretty soon. Meanwhile, the damage control officer managed to counter-flood to keep the ship from capsizing. She eventually just settled to the bottom.

"The hatch cover was still open and someone stuck his head up and yelled 'Abandon ship! Abandon ship! We got out and there was no big rush. The *Tennessee* was inboard of us and we made it to the fo'c'sle, took our shoes off and jumped into the water and swam to Ford Island. When we got to shore the first thing we heard was 'Get down, get down! Strafing.' I got down by a truck at the edge of the golf course as a plane turned toward us and began firing. The tracers seemed to be coming right at me. Only one of his guns was firing. I got under the truck and the tracers turned away from me.

"About then a woman came down from one of the houses there, carrying clothes. I wandered over to see what was going on and she fitted us out with dry clothes."
– Richard McCutcheon, USS *West Virginia*

right: (l to r) The *West Virginia*, *Tennessee* and *Arizona* burning after the 7 December attack.

"Ahead of the *Nevada*, a large pipeline snaked out from Ford Island in a semicircle ending at the dredge *Turbine*. Since it blocked more than half the channel, the line was always disconnected and pulled clear when the battleships were scheduled to stand out. This morning, of course, it was still in place. But the sailor conning the *Nevada* squeezed her between the dredge and the dry-dock area without slowing down.

"The flames were now shooting up past her anti-aircraft directors nearly to her foretop. She had been hit repeatedly, and Pearl Harbor was pouring into her hull; her bow was low in the water. If she were to sink in the channel, she would plug up the entire harbor like a cork in a bottle. With bitter regret, we watched her run her bow into shallow water between the floating dry-dock and Hospital Point. The current carried her stern around, and she finished her evolution pointing back up the channel she had tried so valiantly to follow to freedom."
— Ted Mason, USS *California*

far left above: Ford Island hangars and aircraft ablaze, far left below: The USS *Nevada* ca. 1943, above centre: The Nevada burning after the raid, above right: The ruined galley of *Nevada*, left: USS *California* has settled to the harbour bottom in this photo taken the day after the surprise attack.

At the height of his business career Kazuo Sakamaki became the head of Toyota's Brazilian operations. In December 1941, Sakamaki was a 23-year-old ensign in the Japanese Navy and one half of the crew of a midget submarine struggling to enter Pearl Harbor. His mission was to sneak into the harbour unobserved, ahead of the main attack by the aircraft of the Imperial Japanese Navy and be ready to sink one of the target battleships at the appropriate moment. It was a suicide mission involving five such midget subs. But the gyrocompass of Sakamaki's boat failed and the other four subs were either lost or destroyed during the attack. Sakamaki's boat became stranded on a coral reef down the coast and he was forced to abandon it. He was later discovered, unconscious, by an American soldier and became the first Japanese prisoner of war of World War II. He recalled feeling deep shame with the failure of his mission, for letting his sub fall into enemy hands, and for surviving when his comrades had all died in the attempted raid. In time though, he gradually overcame the guilt he felt and went on to help his fellow Japanese prisoners in POW camps in the United States.

above right: A civilian casualty of the strafing attack, in his car near the Pearl facility, right: President Roosevelt signing the Declaration of War with Japan, far right: Efforts to right the *Oklahoma* were not successful until 1943.

above: An American sailor killed during the raid. centre right: Ford Island mooring of the *West Virginia* in 2003. far right: The hull of the *Oklahoma* after being refloated on 8 March 1943.

ACCORDING TO Mike Holloman, a powder hoist operator for the sixteen-inch fifty-calibre centre gun of turret number three on the USS *Missouri* in 1985: "It really isn't terribly noisy inside the gun room during firing, but the feeling and excitement are something else. The big guns are always fired off the side of the ship; shooting straight along the beam is too hard on her. The ship acts as a part of the recoil. You feel her sway from top to bottom after firing a broadside, and then she settles out. Some say that firing a broadside pushes the ship back about 30 feet, but this is debatable. When the guns are fired, there is a faint smell of rotten eggs, from the black powder primer charge.

"From the gun room level, down to the ammunition magazines, it takes about 70 men to operate one of the sixteen-inch gun turrets on an *Iowa* class battleship. A really good crew can shoot two rounds per minute per gun. The range is a little over twenty miles."

There are three guns in each of the three big gun turrets of an *Iowa* class battleship. Each of the turrets weighs 160 tons. Holloman: "Each gun has its own powder hoist which brings up 660 pounds of powder per shot, in six 110-pound bags. The bags are made of silk so they will completely burn away on ignition and contain about 480 grains of smokeless-powder (SP) charge. The powder bags are subject to detonation under shock, because of a black-powder ignition pad (identified by the red-coloured end of the bag) quilted to the back of each bag to ensure instant ignition on firing. Once, while moving powder cans on the overhead rail system down in the magazines (each can contained three of the 110-pound bags), a can suddenly dropped about two feet to the deck. We all froze and then looked up to see that a section of the railing was missing. The event caused a lot of hearts to beat faster.

"The gun room itself has five men working in it. They are: the Gun Captain, who is in charge of the gun, the powder hoist operator; the projectile operator, who also works the rammer; the primer man, who cleans the primer hole and puts the primer in; and the powderman, who helps handle the powder.

"All varieties of the projectiles weigh 2,700 pounds, except the armour-piercing type, which weighs 1,900 pounds. When a projectile comes up from the projectile deck, it is rammed into the breech, or chamber section of the gun, while the gun is primed. Next come three powder bags which are rammed into the breech after the projectile. Three more powder bags are placed in the loading tray and a foil pack to reduce fouling, is inserted between the fifth and sixth bags. The remaining powder bags are pushed gently into the breech to avoid setting off the black-powder base. The last bag to go in is positioned next to the breech plug. The primer man then puts a primer the size of a shotgun shell into the firing lock of the breech. The breech is then closed and the gun goes into 'battery" and is ready to shoot. Everyone in the gun room must pay careful attention to where they are standing, especially the primer man. Just before the gun is fired, three tones are sounded. It fires on the third tone.

"After the initial firing of a big gun, it returns to the loading position. Before the breech is opened, a 16psi blast of air is manually sent through the barrel to clear out any burning embers. After the first shot is fired, the gun clears the barrel on its own. Once the breech has been opened, the face is wiped by the Gun Captain to clean it and ensure that no burning powder remains on it which could ignite the next powder bags prior to re-closing the breech."

Tony Alessandro, another powder hoist operator on *Missouri* (in 1944 and 1945): "By the time we shot the guns it was automatic because we had practiced so much. When you fire for real, it's like starting a football game; you just get ready to receive the kickoff. The firing became routine, except when we went to the Japanese home islands."

BIG GUNS

There are strange hells within the minds war made Not so often, not so humiliatingly afraid / As one would have expected— the racket and fear guns made. / One hell the Gloucester soldiers they quite put out: / Their first bombardment, when in combined black shout / Of fury, guns aligned, they ducked low their heads And sang with diaphragms fixed beyond all dreads, That tin and stretched-wire tinkle, that blither of tune: 'Apres la guerre fini', till hell all had come down, Twelve-inch, six-inch, and eighteen pounders hammering 'hell's thunders.
— from *Strange Hells* by First World War poet Ivor Gurney

"I always wanted to be a gunner's mate so, I asked around to find out how I could get reassigned, and was told to see a turret captain. I went to see him and he had to check with the division officer and they took me in the turret and put me to work on the number two gun. Each man there had a part of the inside of the turret he had to take care of and wipe down and clean and shine, every day."
— Richard McCutcheon, USS *West Virginia*

left: USS *New Jersey* gunner packing powder bags in a 16-inch gun, November 1944.

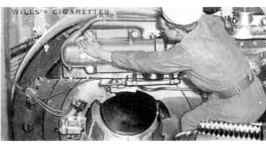

12-in. Shells on Quarter-deck of a Battleship.

Off Honshu, we didn't know what to expect. We didn't want to be like a duck in a shooting gallery."

Herb Fahr was a member of the *Missouri* crew in 1954: "The only gunnery practice I had seen was with the five-inch and the 40 millimeters. I wasn't prepared for the shock that goes through the ship when those sixteen-inch guns go off. We could feel it in the bowels of the ship, like thunder in a cave. The barbershop was the only place in the ship that had four-foot flourescent lights, and when the sixteen-inch guns were going to be fired, those flourescent tubes had to be removed or they would

"A hard pounding this, gentlemen. Let us see who can pound the longest."
— Wellington at the battle of Waterloo

far left: Looking aft from the bow of the USS *Mississippi*, BB-23) at her main guns, in 1908.

83

In the days of lace-ruffles, perukes and brocade Brown Bess was a partner whom none could despise— / An out-spoken, flinty-lipped, brazen-faced jade, / With a habit of looking men straight in the eyes— / At Blenheim and Ramillies fops would confess / They were pierced to the heart by the charms of Brown Bess.

Though her sight was not long and her weight was not small, / Yet her actions were winning, her language was clear; / And everyone bowed as she opened the ball / On the arm of some high-gaitered, grim grenadier. / Half Europe admitted the striking success / Of the dances and routs that were given by Brown Bess.

When ruffles were turned into stiff leather stocks, And people wore pigtails instead of perukes, Brown Bess never altered her iron-grey locks. / She knew she was valued for more than her looks. 'Oh, powder and patches was always my dress, / And I think I am killing enough,' said Brown Bess.
– from *Brown Bess* by Rudyard Kipling (Brown Bess was the nickname for the army musket)

have shattered.

"I wanted to see those guns go off, so I got permission. The best place to observe was up on the 07 or 08 decks where the lookout and gun trainers were. What a sight that was! A broadside brought a flash of fire and smoke a hundred yards out, and the sound was incredibly loud. The water adjacent to the ship would get foamed-up from the concussion and the sideways motion of the ship from the recoil. Watching those guns go off was one of the most thrilling moments of my life."

The big guns of the *Iowa* class battleship represent the ultimate refinement of a weapon, the naval gun, which was first deployed some 600 years ago when the English king, Edward III, known as the 'King of the Sea', had a few guns fitted to some of his ships prior to the Hundred Years' War. The first use of 'big guns' in battle at sea was at the battle of Sluys in 1340, though little resulted from employment of the guns. The British prevailed over their French enemy thanks to the superiority of their archers. But this trial spawned the beginnings of naval gun power. By the end of the sixteenth century, a wide range of naval gun types had been fitted into a variety of ships.

While there is disagreement among historians about the origins of gunpowder, the consensus favours China. Early Chinese literature tells of ninth-century Thang alchemists who, while trying to develop the 'elixir of immortality', accidentally invented what they referred to as 'fire drug' or 'fire chemical'. The earliest known reference to the composition of gunpowder was made in 1004, but no specific formula was provided.

By the eleventh century, the Chinese had had considerable experience using gunpowder in fireworks and they employed that background to develop the world's first bombs and grenades. Their interest in the potential military uses of gunpowder led them to strictly control their

production of saltpetre and sulphur and to ban the sale of these ingredients to foreigners. Just how the knowledge of gunpowder and its composition was acquired by Westerners is not known, but by the mid-fourteenth century the first guns had appeared on the battlefields of Europe.

In 1625, the difficulty of producing saltpetre in Europe caused King Charles I of England to publish the following order: "Loving subjects . . . inhabiting within every city, town and village . . . shall carefully and constantly keep and preserve all the urine of man during the whole year, and all the stale of beasts which they can save and gather together whilst their beasts are in their stables and stalls, and that they be careful to use the best means of gathering together and preserving the urine and stale, without mixture of water or other thing put therein. Which our commandment and royal pleasure being easy to observe, and so necessary for the public service of us and our people, that if any person do be remiss hereof we shall esteem all such persons contemptuous and ill affected both to our person and estate, and are resolved to proceed to the punishment of that offender with what severity we may."

In their defeat of the Spanish Armada in the English Channel in August 1588, the English navy had elected to engage the enemy at a great range rather than at close quarters. It was the advent of the new era in naval warfare. But the naval gun battles of that time generally yielded more sound and fury than actual damage. In those days, naval guns were clumsy and troublesome weapons, requiring much time and effort in loading, and they had to be retracted from their firing positions to be reloaded. Gunpowder at that time was expensive and, at sea, was subject to dampness. Quality control in its manufacture was uneven at best, and when the weapons were fired, the limited spaces of the gundecks were shrouded in filthy black smoke. There was little precision in the manufacture of cannon, making them unreliable and

greatly limiting their accuracy and effectiveness in damaging enemy vessels.

The eighteenth-century HMS *Victory*, among the most famous of all warships, brought a formidable striking power into battle. An excellent description of the firing preparation for the big cannon of the English warship is provided on the HMS *Victory* website: "The Royal Navy trained hard and well [in the days of Admiral Nelson] and could reload the 32-pounder cannon in 90 seconds. This was quite a remarkable time, given the considerable amount of manhandling required to move the 3.5 tonne gun backwards and forwards, and far shorter than that achieved by French or Spanish crews. It is little

wonder that the most common injury to gun crews was abdominal rupture.

"When the gun was fired it recoiled inboard, restrained by the large ropes attached to the rear of the gun barrel. A sponge was dipped in water and thrust down the barrel to remove any traces of burning powder. The new charge and wad were then inserted into the barrel and rammed hard against the rear of the gun. The wad held the charge in place and ensured that the powder was tightly compressed. Next, the rammer was removed and the ball inserted, held in place by a further wad rammed hard down the barrel. A pricker was inserted into the breech hole to open the

"I was a powder car man, running an electric hoist back and forth down to the upper handling room. There was nothing but powder in that room. It was directly under the projectile room where the shells were kept. We all trained so that we knew every job around the turret."
– Richard McCutcheon, USS *West Virginia*

overleaf: Believed to be the USS *Missouri* firing a broadside during the 1991 Gulf War.

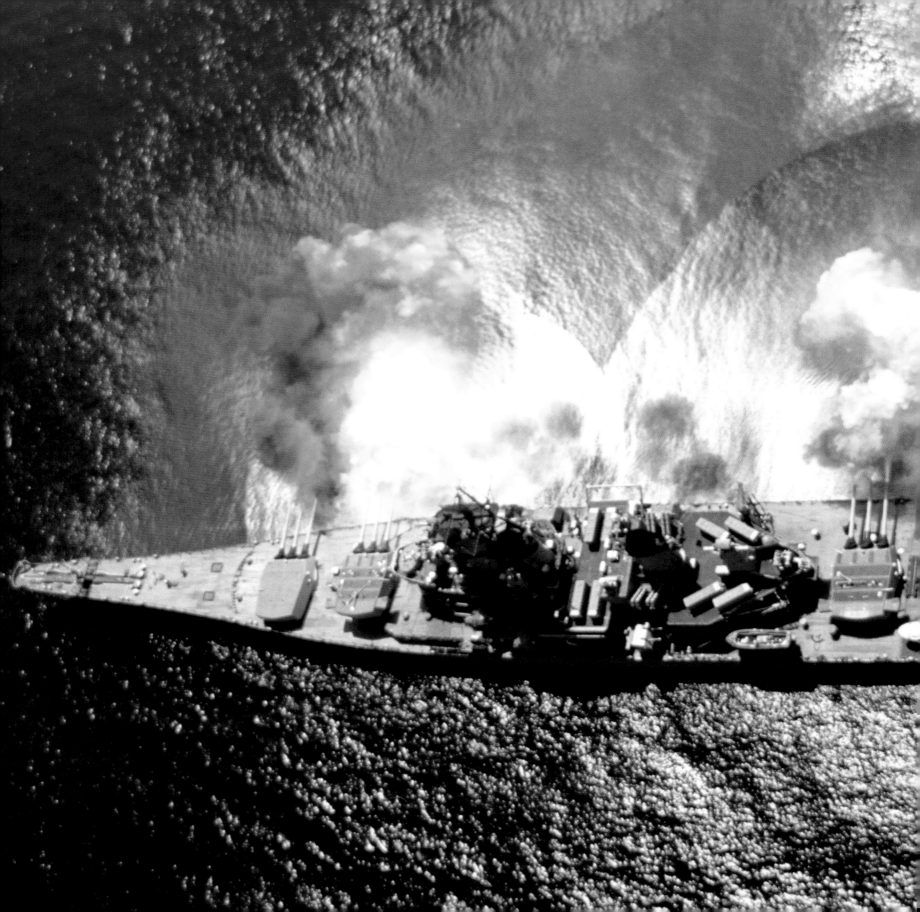

gunpowder charge and then a small quantity of fine powder was poured down the firing hole and into the flint lock pan. The flint lock was cocked and the gun was ready to fire.

"The gun was served by a six-man crew, known by numbers to make orders easier in the noise of battle. Number 1 was the Gun Captain, who aimed and fired the gun. Number 2 used a long spike to turn and raise the barrel; Number 3 loaded the gun and rammed the shot and powder home. Number 4 sponged out the gun, ensuring that no burning powder or waste was left to cause premature ignition of the new charge. Number 5 worked opposite number 2, to move the gun, whilst Number 6 was the smallest and youngest member of the crew—the powder monkey. Often a young boy, perhaps only 10 or 12 years old, the powder monkey collected the gunpowder charges from the magazine deep in the hold of the ship and carried them to the gun.

"The whole 3.5 tonnes was now run out, with the crew straining on the carriage ropes to pull the gun muzzle through the gun port in the side of the ship. When the gun came to bear on the target, the Gun Captain pulled the lanyard to the flint lock. As the flint scraped across the pan, a shower of sparks ignited the fine powder, which ignited the main charge and the gun fired, ejecting its iron ball with a forward velocity of some 500 metres per second. The gun would recoil backwards at some 2 metres per second, and the process of cleaning and reloading began again.

"The gun could be loaded with a variety of shot—from the plain cannon ball to bar shot, chain shot and grape shot. Bar and chain shot whirled around in flight and was intended to cut through enemy rigging, bringing down masts, sails and spars and disabling the ship. Grape shot was an anti-personnel weapon, firing a quantity of smaller balls in a cluster. These spread out and created a murderous hail of metal across an enemy deck. The 32-pound cannon ball was effective in punching holes through the wooden walls of the enemy, creating a huge spray

"We were loading ammo and I was standing near a vestibule on the powderflats as a high-explosive round was being lowered. I was on the sound-powered phones with the guy who was lowering the round from the main deck. I told him to stop lowering the round, which weighed 2,700 pounds, but it kept coming down. I yelled into the phones to stop, but the round just kept on coming. I tried to squeeze into the vestibule. I was cornered, with nowhere to go as the projectile kept coming toward me. Then, just as it was about to pin me against the bulkhead, the tip of the projectile warhead caught on a 1/2" pipe and came to rest about 4" from my hip. You can imagine the relief I felt." — Mike Holloman, USS *Missouri*

"Do battleships move sideways when they fire their big guns? What looks like a side-ways wake is just the water being boiled up by the muzzle blasts. The ship doesn't move an inch or even heel from a broadside. The guns have a recoil slide of up to 48 inches and the shock is distributed evenly through the turret foundation and the hull structure. The mass of a 57,000 ton ship is just too great for the recoil of the guns to move it. But because of the expansive range of the overpressure (muzzle blast), a lot of the rapidly displaced air presses

against the bulkheads and decks. Those structures that are not armored actually flex inwards just a bit, thus displacing air quickly inside the ship and causing loose items to fly around, sort of like having your house sealed up with all windows and vents closed and when you slam the front door quickly, the displaced air pops open the kitchen cabinets."
— R.A. Landgraff

The sixteen-inch big guns of the *Iowa* class battleships were called "bag guns", as the propellant charge used to fire them was packaged in cylindrical bags loaded separately from the projectile. The guns used six 110-pound bags of the smokeless powder (SP) to make the projectile achieve the required initial velocity. The powder bags were made of silk so they would burn away completely when the charge was ignited.

Every time one of the sixteen-inch guns was fired, the rotating band of the round eroded the liner of the barrel as it passed through the bore. A sixteen-inch/50 calibre Mk 7 gun was designed to fire 290 rounds before the barrel had to be relined, assuming that all of the shots used the 2,700-pound armour-piercing projectiles.

of deadly flying splinters. At close range, the 32-pound ball was capable of penetrating wood to a depth of 2 $\frac{1}{2}$ feet.

"With the enemy holed and disabled and the crew killed or wounded with grape shot, the attacking ship could now close the enemy and board the vessel to secure victory. Boarding with close-quarter hand-to-hand fighting was often the deciding factor in battle."

As the battleship was gradually transformed from a wind-powered wooden vessel to a steam-driven ship of steel, her weaponry was greatly improved, and so was her armour, to counter the effects of the improved weaponry of the enemy. The great naval powers were all determined to build high-speed battleships with powerful armament and theoretically invulnerable protective armour. But attempting to combine these qualities inevitably resulted in a conflict. Protection could only be achieved at the expense of speed, and vice versa; the heavier the guns, the less the protection and/or the speed. Naval armour is heavy and the amount of it needed to provide proper protection for a giant warship was immense. Coping with the threats of heavy shells, mines, torpedos and, ultimately, aerial bombs, was a supreme challenge for naval architects. The whole ship could not possibly be clad in armour of uniform thickness, instead the armour had to be concentrated where it was most needed, in horizontal armour belts that protected the engine and boiler rooms, and the magazines, from torpedoes and shell fire, and on the turrets which housed the ship's main armament. The thickness of this protective belt increased over the years in response to the improving armour-piercing capability of big naval guns; the most extreme example being the 1881 masted turret ship *Inflexible*, with her compound iron armour which varied from 16" to 24" in thickness. No thicker armour has ever been employed in a battleship.

left: Lowering one of the great sixteen-inch guns into a turret of the USS *North Carolina*, BB-55 during her fitting-out.

"[In war] the latest refinements of science are linked with the cruelties of the Stone Age."
— Winston Churchill

When Vulcan forged the
bolts of Jove / In Etna's
roaring glow, / Neptune
petition'd he might prove
Their use and power
below; / But finding in the
boundless deep / Their
thunders did not idly sleep,
He with them arm'd
Britannia's hand, / To guard
from foes her native land.

Long may she hold the
glorious right, / And when
through circling flame
She darts her thunder in
the fight, / May justice
guide her aim! / And when
opposed in future wars,
Her soldiers brave and
gallant tars / Shall launch
her fires from every hand
On every foe to Britain's
land.
— *The Origin of Naval
Artillery*
by Thomas Dibdin

right: The breech of a
sixteen-inch gun aboard
the Japanese battleship
Nagato in August 1945.
above: Sixteen-inch shell
on the USS *Missouri*.

The advances in metallurgy that had made
improved ship armour possible had also led to
development of the armour-piercing shell, which in
turn led to a further evolution in protective armour.
Improved steel-making techniques had resulted in
metals of extraordinary hardness and strength.

It was not until late in the nineteenth century that
the major problems with naval guns were finally
resolved. By the 1820s, Russian warships were
mounting guns that could fire explosive shells as well
as grapeshot and case-shot. In the 1850s, gun-barrel
rifling—spiral grooving which caused the projectile
to spin as it was fired (for greater accuracy)—was in
use and breech-loading was beginning to replace
muzzle-loading, significantly improving a gun's rate
of fire. Spring or hydraulic recoil mechanisms were
replacing ropes and crude, slow-burning fuses were
replaced, initially by clockwork devices and later by
percussion and concussion fuses. Near the end of the
century, forged steel shells were developed—the first
shells capable of striking and penetrating armour
without disintegrating. The projectile had evolved
from a sphere to a cylindrical shape and, by the
1890s, its explosive ingredients had changed from
gunpowder as both propellant and filler, to cordite
and other smokeless powders for the propellant and
nitroglycerine compounds for the filler. Muzzle
velocity, or the speed at which a shell leaves the gun
barrel, was increased with the development of new
explosive propellants and the range of shells was
improved as the big gun barrels were lengthened
and, increasingly, rifled.

Methods for sighting the big guns were crude and
relatively ineffective until the introduction of the
optical rangefinder near the end of the nineteenth
century, to aid in locating the target and calculating
its distance from the ship. These rangefinders would
eventually reach nearly 50 feet in length and were
mounted on the highest part of the battleship
superstructure, where the equipment could function
to optimum capability. This capability, together with
advances in the predictors which allowed a gun to be

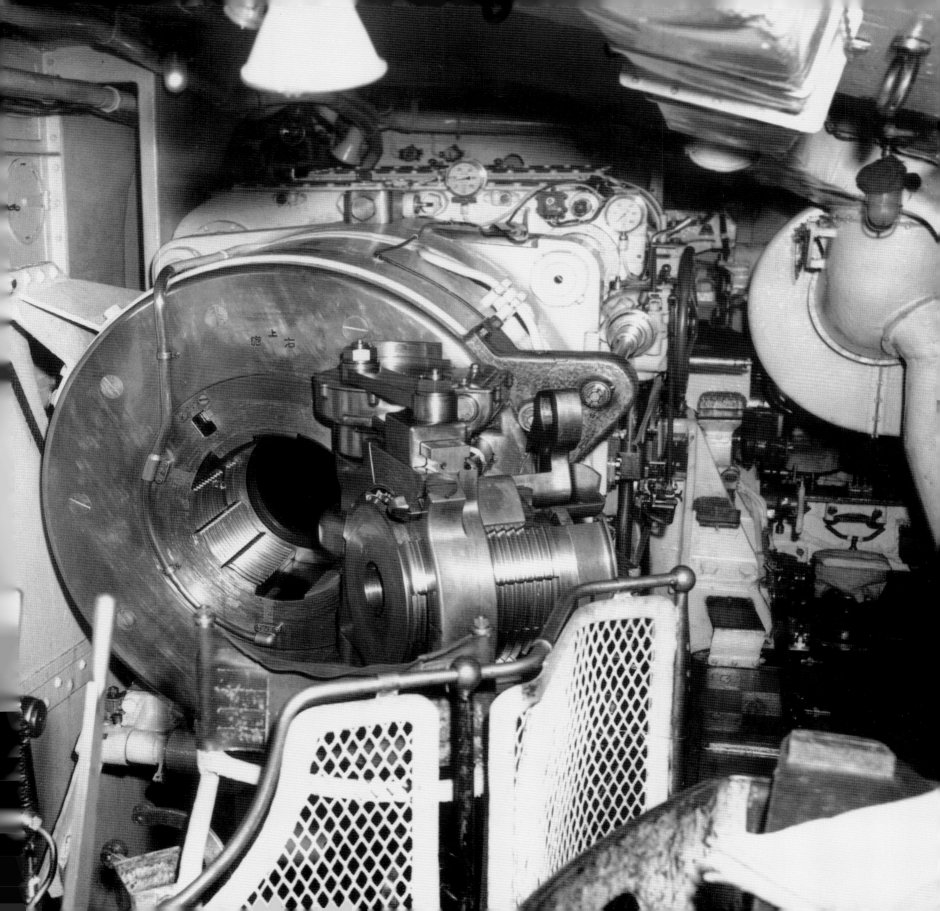

kept on target despite the speed and roll of the ship, and the possible movement of the target during the time it took for the shell to reach it, dramatically improved the effectiveness of battleship big guns.

Big naval guns reached their ultimate evolution with the design and construction of the largest and most powerful warship ever built, Japan's *Yamato*. The eighteen-inch main guns of *Yamato* and her sister ship *Musashi* were capable of sending shells to a maximum range of nearly 33 miles with great precision. They were the only guns of this calibre ever mounted in a ship. The three-gun turrets for these weapons weighed 2,774 tons each, and each armour-piercing projectile for the guns weighed half again as much as its counterpart for the sixteen-inch guns of *Iowa*, the ultimate American battleship class. In creating these weapons for the *Yamato* class ships, Japan's naval weapons planners determined to produce the most powerful battleships in the world, battleships that even the industrial strength of the United States could not hope to equal.

When interviewed for a 1989 New York *Daily News* article, gunners serving in the USS *Wisconsin* spoke of the pride they felt in their jobs. Billy Owens of Corpus Christi, Texas: "This is a gunner's mate's ultimate dream—to be on the biggest guns, where you can climb right up through 'em if you want. For us gunner's mates it doesn't seem noisy when they go off. To hear 'em go off, well, that's part of it. Little guns, you get a bang. This one, you get a boom." Gunner's Mate Chief Robert Durham of Deridder, Louisiana: "It's the lure of the battleship, the lure of the gunner's art. I feel that we're firing something that's a piece of history and that damn well is going to make more history." And Gunner's Mate Chief Robert Loos of Youngstown, Ohio: "It's a rare assignment to come aboard a battleship at all. To be attached to the turret, well, that's the top of the list. I don't know anyone who wouldn't like the chance. It's just the pure awesome power."

We did the thing that he projected, / The Caravan grew disaffected, / And Sin and I consulted; / Blood understood the Native mind. / He said: 'We must be firm but kind.' A mutiny resulted. I never shall forget the way That Blood upon this awful day / Preserved us all from death. / He stood upon a little mound, / Cast his lethargic eyes around, And said beneath his breath: 'Whatever happens we have got / The Maxim Gun, and they have not.' – *The Maxim Gun* by Hilaire Belloc

Richard Landgraff of the Long Beach [California] Naval Shipyard, was aboard the USS *Missouri* for her second sea trials. The exercise was mainly for testing the ship's weapons and combat systems. After the 16-inch guns were fired, Landgraff went all through the ship looking for damage resulting from the shock, always a matter of concern. "But the ship had come through the firing exercise beautifully. The worst that happened was that some of the old World War II light fixtures shook and broke the bulbs, some paint flakes 'snowed' from the overhead and the 'dogs' (latches) on the life jacket lockers rattled loose, allowing a couple of the locker doors to swing open."

left: Main guns from the USS *South Carolina, BB-26,* are scrapped in 1923 at Philadelphia.

THEY WERE THE BIGGEST and most sophisticated battleships in the world when they were launched in early 1939. Adolf Hitler himself launched the 41,700-ton *Bismarck* at the Blohm & Voss shipyard, Hamburg, on 14 February; her sister ship *Tirpitz* was launched at Wilhelmshaven in April. The great warships were a propaganda bonanza for Germany and the Nazis took full advantage of it. The Allies would not learn the actual dimensions and specifications of the *Bismarck* class battleships until after the end of World War II.

These warships were planned expressly to attack and destroy the vital commerce of Germany's enemies on the Atlantic sea lanes. It was the intention of Admiral Erich Raeder, Commander-in-Chief of the German Navy, that *Bismarck* and *Tirpitz*, in company with the battlecruisers *Scharnhorst* and *Gneisenau*, should be sent into the Atlantic on their mission of disruption and destruction as soon as the big battleships had completed their sea trials in 1941. It was not to be. *Gneisenau* had sustained heavy damage while at St. Nazaire when the Brittany port was bombed by the RAF in April, and *Scharnhorst* required a refit. *Tirpitz*, meanwhile, was still out conducting her trials. Only *Bismarck*, of the four vessels, was ready for action that spring.

Raeder then formed a new hunting battle group of *Bismarck* and the heavy cruiser *Prinz Eugen*, under the command of Vizeadmiral Günter Lütjens. Its task on deployment was to work together in attacks on enemy merchant shipping. *Bismarck* would attract the attentions of the British warships escorting the merchant vessels in convoy, while *Prinz Eugen* would attack the merchant ships. On 19 May, the two heavily armed and armoured German warships sailed from the port of Götenhafen, heading west between Sweden and Denmark, around the south coast of Norway to Bergen. Their progress was recorded by an RAF photo-reconnaissance Spitfire and was reported to the Commander-in-Chief of the Royal Navy's Home

Fleet at Scapa Flow, Admiral Sir John Tovey. In Scapa lay the proud new battleships *Prince of Wales* and *King George V*, as well as the new aircraft carrier *Victorious* and the battlecruiser *Hood*. Tovey dispatched *Prince of Wales* and *Hood* to Iceland on 21 May, where they were to guard that approach into the Atlantic. He had the heavy cruiser *Norfolk* on station in the Denmark Strait and she would soon be joined there by her sister ship, the *Suffolk*. Late that night, *Bismarck* and *Prinz Eugen* made their way out of Bergen to the open sea, turning northwest towards Iceland.

All day on the 22nd the weather in that part of the world deteriorated, making further photo-reconnaissance flights by the RAF impossible. Tovey got no additional reports on the movements of the German warships until late in the day when conditions improved and he learned that *Bismarck* and *Prinz Eugen* had left Norwegian waters. The next morning he left Scapa in his flagship, *King George V*, accompanied by the carrier *Victorious*, four cruisers and six destroyers.

The two German warships approached the northern edge of Iceland on 23 May and turned southwest into the Denmark Strait. The first sighting of *Bismarck* by a lookout on *Suffolk* came at 7.22 p.m. when the two ships were about seven miles apart. Patches of heavy mist and fog shrouded the area and *Suffolk* quickly entered the safety of one. She was soon joined by *Norfolk*, but not before the latter had been spotted by *Bismarck*, which fired several rounds at the cruiser. Sheltered in the mist, the two British warships settled in to keep track of their adversaries while Admiral Tovey's battle squadrons hurried to the scene. Vizeadmiral Lütjens was aware of the enemy cruisers, but not of Tovey's approaching vessels.

Prince of Wales and *Hood* were, at this point, approximately 500 miles due south and proceeding at high speed on course to intercept *Bismarck* and *Prinz Eugen*, expecting to encounter them early in the morning of the 24th. Now the weather became

BISMARCK

"Thank you for showing me all of mankind's lofty ideals. Now let me introduce you to the basement."
– Sigmund Freud

". . . this war of groping and drowning, of ambuscade and stratagem, of science and seamanship . . ."
– Winston Churchill

left: A Royal Air Force reconnaissance photo of the German battleship *Bismarck* in the Grimstadtfjord on 21 May 1941. above: Vizeadmiral Günter Lütjens, in command of the *Bismarck-Prinz Eugen* hunting group.

below: HSM *Hood* in
1932, right: *Bismarck*,
the pride of the German
Navy, in profile.

worse, with snow and reduced visibility. The
British cruisers lost contact with the German ships,
but regained it just before 3 a.m.

Prince of Wales was a new 36,750-ton battleship
which had been rushed into service before a
proper period of sea trials could be carried out.
Work on her main armament continued even as
she steamed towards *Bismarck*. Her armour was
far superior to that of *Hood*, with a fifteen-inch-
thick armoured belt and five- to six-inch deck
plating. She mounted ten fourteen-inch guns.

The 41,200-ton battlecruiser *Hood* had been
designed during World War I. She was old but
powerfully armed with eight fifteen-inch guns, and
was still fast and formidable. Her armour was
suspect, however, being relatively thin on her after
deck; a worrisome prospect against a ship like
Bismarck, which was capable of lobbing her fifteen-
inch shells at a high angle from a long range.
Britain's largest battlecruiser, *Hood* had been an
icon of British naval power for many years. In
command of *Hood* and *Prince of Wales* was Vice
Admiral Sir Lancelot Holland, on board *Hood*.

At 5.25 a.m. *Bismarck* and *Prinz Eugen* were

sighted by the lookouts of *Prince of Wales*. Now, both *Hood* and *Prince of Wales* were steaming on a heading that allowed them to use only their forward guns, while Lütjens in *Bismarck* was able to bring all of his main guns to bear on his adversaries. It is likely that Vice Admiral Holland had positioned his ships in this way to protect the vulnerable *Hood* from the plunging, long-range fire of *Bismarck*.

Holland gave the command to open fire on the German ships at 5.52 a.m. He directed that his ships lay their fire on the lead enemy vessel, which he had mistakenly identified as *Bismarck*, but was actually *Prinz Eugen*. The Germans immediately returned fire, dropping many heavy shells in close to *Hood*. Shells from *Bismarck* began to straddle *Hood*, and now the gunners of *Prinz Eugen* also concentrated on *Hood*, sending a salvo into her which started an ammunition fire. *Prince of Wales* was now directing all of her firing onto the *Bismarck*.

In a few moments, the British warships began adjusting their positions in order to bring more guns to bear on their targets. Shortly after 6 a.m., a new salvo from *Bismarck* found its mark on *Hood*, briefly

"A great Empire will be destroyed, an Empire which it was never my intention to destroy or even to harm . . . I consider myself in a position to make this appeal since I am not the vanquished begging favours, but the victor speaking in the name of reason."
– Adolf Hitler addressing the Reichstag, 19 July 1940

illuminating the sullen sky as the battle cruiser's aft ammunition magazines exploded, destroying much of her stern. The great ship immediately listed to starboard up to twelve degrees before righting herself. Then she began leaning to port and continued to do so until, at more than 30 degrees of list, she could not recover. In less than three minutes, she was down by the stern, slipping rapidly beneath the surface. From her entire crew, there were only three survivors.

The gunners of *Bismarck* and *Prinz Eugen* now shifted their attention to *Prince of Wales*, whose compass platform was soon destroyed, killing all personnel there except Captain Leach. Much of his armament was now inoperative and he discreetly chose to withdraw his ship from the action. Vize-admiral Lütjens decided against pursuing the wounded *Prince of Wales*, in order to take his battleship to St. Nazaire for repairs to the damage

she had incurred in the battle. *Prince of Wales* joined the cruisers *Norfolk* and *Suffolk* in shadowing *Bismarck*. Before leaving the area, Lütjens ordered *Prinz Eugen* to continue out into the Atlantic on her assigned duty.

"Sink the *Bismarck*, at any cost," ordered Winston Churchill on 24 May when news of *Hood*'s loss reached the British people. With that, Admiral Tovey re-directed vessels of the Home Fleet, including the 33,950-ton battleship *Rodney*, to the hunt for the German ship. *Rodney* mounted nine 16-inch guns and would ably complement Tovey's flagship, *King George V*, the battle cruiser *Repulse* and the carrier *Victorious* in their pursuit of *Bismarck*. While rushing to intercept the German battleship, Tovey ordered several Swordfish and Fulmar aircraft from *Victorious* to mount a torpedo attack against *Bismarck*, but the results were negligible.

far left: Hitler's only visit to *Bismarck*, left: A still from the 1960 Twentieth-Century Fox film *Sink The Bismarck*.

Commander Alan Swanton, Fleet Air Arm, died aged 85 in January 2003. Swanton was one of the Swordfish pilots who attacked the German battleship *Bismarck* on 26 May 1941, northeast of Brest. He had taken off from the carrier *Ark Royal* in appalling weather conditions, believing it to be the final air strike of the day. Initially, his squadron erroneously attacked the British cruiser *Sheffield*. After returning to the carrier to rearm and refuel, Swanton and fourteen other Swordfish pilots and crews took off again and most of them were immediately separated in the thick cloud. Swanton and his flight managed to keep together in the murk, located the *Bismarck* and attacked from her port side. Approaching through extremely accurate radar-controlled German flak, both Swanton and his air gunner were wounded, but he was able to continue the attack and get back to *Ark Royal* where he landed safely. There he learned that the squadron's torpedoes had jammed the rudders of the German battleship, crippling her and leaving her a sitting duck in further British attacks.

right: Survivors of the battleship *Bismarck* struggle in the sea while awaiting rescue.

Vizeadmiral Lütjens ordered a course change during the early morning hours of 25 May and soon managed to lose the shadowing *Norfolk, Suffolk* and *Prince of Wales*. Tovey, with no reliable information coming in on the whereabouts of *Bismarck*, guessed Lütjens' intentions. He turned his group of hunters northeast towards Iceland, while Lütjens continued to head southeast towards St. Nazaire. It was early evening before Tovey knew he had guessed wrong and altered course again to the southeast. But Lütjens, too, guessed wrong. He believed that the British were still tracking *Bismarck* on radar when, in fact, they were not. He thought he had nothing to lose in sending a lengthy signal to his overseers in France, reporting that he was still being shadowed by three British warships, describing *Bismarck*'s action against the *Hood*, and giving his ship's present position, for which the British, who were intercepting the signal, were undoubtedly grateful.

The crew of an RAF Catalina flying boat piloted by U.S. Navy Ensign Leonard Smith on a routine patrol, aided by Ultra intercepts from Bletchley Park in England, spotted *Bismarck* at 10.30 a.m. on 26 May and radioed her position to Admiral Tovey. The admiral's only real chance of catching the German battleship now lay with Force H which was north of Gibraltar and heading towards *Bismarck*. Force H was composed of the aircraft carrier *Ark Royal*, the battlecruiser *Renown* and the cruiser *Sheffield*. *Sheffield* was the first to locate *Bismarck* and took up the job of shadowing her.

In the mid-afternoon, fourteen Swordfish torpedo bombers left *Ark Royal* to attack *Bismarck*, but mistakenly launched their torpedos at *Sheffield*. Luckily for the British cruiser, the new-type fuses in the Swordfish torpedoes failed to function and *Sheffield* was unscathed. The Swordfish of *Ark Royal* tried again at just after 7 p.m. Fifteen of the bi-planes launched from the carrier, with old-style fuses in their weapons, reached *Bismarck* in two hours and began their attack. Two torpedoes struck the battleship, one hitting the armoured belt amidships and doing no significant damage. The other hit aft near the ship's rudders, jamming them. The pride of the German Navy was now unable to steer, a sitting duck. Her crew soon lost all hope of escaping the British pursuers. They were harassed through the night by five Royal Navy *Tribal* Class destroyers which continued to attack *Bismarck* with torpedoes, though none of them hit their target.

King George V and *Rodney* steamed into view of the German battleship at first light on 27 May. The firing began at 8.47 a.m. *Rodney*'s big guns fired first, but as soon as the distance between the two battleships had narrowed to less than twelve miles, they both opened fire. By *Bismarck*'s third salvo, her gunners had straddled *Rodney*. It should have spelled the end for the British ship, but *Bismarck*'s inability to manoeuvre had sealed her fate. In thirteen minutes, shells from the two British warships heavily damaged *Bismarck*, ruining 'Anton' and 'Bruno', her forward turrets, her forecastle and her bridge. Though a flaming mess, she remained afloat but no longer able to fight from her main fire control station. Her remaining firing capability came from her after director and that was soon put out of action. Over the next hour both *Rodney* and *Norfolk* continued their efforts to sink the sturdy *Bismarck*, now with torpedoes, but to no avail. Then, in mid-morning, the Royal Navy cruiser *Dorsetshire* moved into the area from the west where she had been escorting a convoy. At 10.25 a.m., she fired three torpedoes at *Bismarck*. The helpless battleship rolled in the waves, with much of her main deck awash. At 10.39 a.m., she rolled over and lay on her side. In seconds she went down and was gone. The largest, finest warship in the history of the German Navy sank on the ninth day of her maiden voyage. Of her crew of more than 2,200 men, just 115 survived, rescued by the *Dorsetshire*, the destroyer *Maori* and the U-boat *U-74*.

Relative warship strength of
the principal naval powers at
the start of World War II:

BRITAIN
Capital ships	15
Aircraft carriers	6
Pocket battleships	0
Heavy cruisers	15
Light cruisers	49
Destroyers/TBs	183
Submarines	57

GERMANY
Capital ships	2
Aircraft carriers	0
Pocket battleships	3
Heavy cruisers	2
Light cruisers	6
Destroyers/TBs	34
Submarines	57

FRANCE
Capital ships	7
Aircraft carriers	1
Pocket battleships	0
Heavy cruisers	7
Light cruisers	12
Destroyers/TBs	72
Submarines	78

UNITED STATES
Capital ships	17
Aircraft carriers	8
Pocket battleships	0
Heavy cruisers	18
Light cruisers	19
Destroyers/TBs	165
Submarines	106

ITALY
Capital ships	4
Aircraft carriers	0
Pocket battleships	0
Heavy cruisers	7
Light cruisers	15
Destroyers/TBs	133
Submarines	102

JAPAN
Capital ships	10
Aircraft carriers	10
Pocket battleships	0
Heavy cruisers	18
Light cruisers	20
Destroyers/TBs	102
Submarines	64

BATTLESHIP SAILORS

But the standing toast that pleased the most / Was— The wind that blows, the ship that goes, / And the lass that loves a sailor!
– The Round Robin

below: Battleship sailor Tony Iacono served aboard the USS *New Jersey* from 1943 until 1946 as a gun pointer on a five-inch mount.

"BATTLESHIP SAILORS, we get the big head. We're the best. In any competition with another ship, we come out on top. We work hard, and the work is tedious. But when we pull into port, we look good. We know that."
– Ernest Ervin, Reidsville, North Carolina

"I actually had some connection with all the *King George V* battleships. When I first left Dartmouth in January 1941, I was appointed to the *Prince of Wales*. In fact, I never joined her because my father, who was then Director of Naval Ordnance, came home at Christmas time for a short weekend and, although he wouldn't say where he was going, I had guessed correctly that he was going to become captain of the *Prince of Wales*, and so I couldn't go there. I had a month in the *Rodney*, and I joined *Duke of York*, as a Sub-Lieutenant in the late summer of '42. I was president of the Gun Room Mess. My action station was in the fourteen-inch transmitting station (computer room, as the American Navy called it), where I was on a thing called the spotting plot. The fall of shot was observed from the director control tower, right up aloft, passed by telephone to me on the spotting plot, and it fell to me to apply the necessary corrections to either continue to straddle the target, or to move so that you did straddle the target."
– Admiral of the Fleet Sir Henry Leach, HMS *Duke of York*

"I served aboard the 'Big Mo' from October 1948 to August 1950, in the Deck Division as a hot-shellman on the left gun of five-inch mount Number 10. That was on the port side. Early in 1949 I transferred to the Radar Division, where I stood watches in Radar, learning the job, operating different radars, radar navigation and plotting. After going to radar school, I returned to the 'Mo' and was ordered to stand my first watch on the conn, or bridge.

"The radar watch on the bridge stood right next to the Captain's chair on the starboard side and operated a radar repeater. This watch functioned as the Captain's 'eyes', ready to answer questions from the Captain or the Officer of the Deck, about other vessels, navigation points, range and bearings, and questions to and from Radar or the Combat Information Center. The uniform of the day was whites and I had made sure that I looked sharp in my starched whites and nicely shined shoes. It being my first watch, I was nervous.

"On the bridge, it was all business. Nobody talked unless it was necessary. Nobody smoked or drank coffee except the Captain or the Officer of the Deck.

"Our skipper at the time was Captain Harold Page Smith, Jr., a really good man, the type of man most sailors wanted for a skipper. One of his mottos was 'A clean ship is a happy ship.' We were the happiest ship in the fleet. When I assumed my watch on the bridge, the skipper was not yet there, but early into my watch he came and sat in his chair.

"Captain Smith was a smoker. So was I. He lighted a cigarette and when he exhaled, I inhaled. It did not take the skipper long to notice this action on my part. The skipper asked me if I smoked and I replied, 'Yes, sir.' He then reached into his shirt pocket, withdrew a pack of Camels, shook a cigarette out and asked me if I wanted one. Dying for a smoke, of course I wanted one, and I took it. The Captain was even kind enough to give me a light. Moments later he left his chair. I thought we really had a good skipper who looked out for his men. Crewmen were not supposed to smoke on the bridge and here was the Captain giving me a cigarette. Moments after the skipper left his chair, while I was enjoying my cigarette, the Officer of the Deck spotted me smoking. He screamed my name and asked me 'What the hell do you think you're doing smoking on the bridge?' All I could say was, 'But, but, but . . .' After a few minutes of real good ass-chewing, the skipper came back to his chair, laughing. He told the OD that he gave me the cigarette. Of course, by that time I had stomped on

below: Visitors Day at the Great Lakes Naval Training Station near Chicago, Illinois, 1918.

There was a man lived quite near us; / He had a wooden leg and a goldfinch in a green cage. His name was Farkey Anderson, / And he'd been in a war to get his leg. / We were very sad about him, Because he had such a beautiful smile / And was such a big man to live in a very small house. When he walked on the road his leg did not matter so much; / But when he walked in his little house It made an ugly noise. Little brother said his goldfinch sang the loudest of all birds, / So that he should not hear his poor leg / And feel too sorry about it.
— *The Man with the Wooden Leg*
by Katherine Mansfield

Each ship has its own baseball cap. It is a working cap, but has transcended its origin to become a non-official part of the uniform.

the cigarette. Captain Smith asked me if I had learned anything. I think I was too dumbstruck to reply, but after the watch I made up my mind to never accept a smoke on the bridge, not even from an admiral. There were no hard feelings from the Captain. He had just played a joke and had a little fun with a member of his crew."
— Ted Pederson, USS *Missouri*

"It was January 1991. We had been in the Persian Gulf a few weeks and the war between the U.S. and Iraq had just started. I was Boatswain's Mate of the watch, midnight to four a.m. I had all of my men placed on the other watches and had made sure they were there on time to relieve the off-going watches.

"I was standing at my station on the port side of the bridge and was recording an entry into the Boatswain's Mate book. I had sent my runner below decks for something.

"I noticed that there was someone wearing a black pea coat standing beside me. It was a cold night and we were all wrapped up good and warm. I saw this person from the corner of my eye as I wrote in the book. I figured he was one of the quartermasters just hanging out, wanting to strike up a conversation. I had a feeling of 'comfort' the whole time he was there. It was a feeling like you had when you were a kid and your dad was really proud of you for something.

"I turned towards the figure standing beside me . . . and he wasn't there. I wasn't frightened at all. It was eerie in a way, though, but in a good way.

"After the watch that night, at about four in the morning, I was going below decks from the bridge, behind the quarter-master's area. I was about to open a hatch to pass through, when the hatch door opened by itself. I thought that someone was on the other side and coming my way. I stepped through the hatch and there was no one there. Then the door shut behind me and dogged itself."
— John E. Shelton, USS *Missouri*

"My GQ station turned out to be in the first compartment forward on 'Broadway' which is a long corridor down the middle of the ship right above the main engine and fire rooms. The 'Mo' had four fire rooms to make steam for the four engine rooms. Therefore, there were eight compartments along Broadway and mine was the first forward over the number one fire room. Entry to 'After Diesel' was just aft of the number four engine room, so, when GQ sounded, I had all eight compartments to run through to get to my battle station. Aboard ship, compartments are separated by watertight doors, which are kind of oval-shaped. The doors have a rubber strip around them and, when closed, match up with a 'knife-edge' going around the doorway. Along Broadway, the bottom of the doors was about eighteen inches above the deck, and when you were moving to your GQ station, you were moving fast and sometimes your shin would not quite make it over the bottom of the door, and, bam-scrape, another hatch scar. I still have those scars today."
— Herb Fahr, USS *Missouri*

"Few officers on assuming command realise to what extent their personality is mirrored in the ship. Every word which you say on the bridge is noted by the ship's company. Every word which you say in the wardroom is marked by the officers. A display of unwarranted temper on the bridge, an unjust or over-hasty reprimand, a careless piece of shiphandling, an uncloaked show of anxiety, all these incidents will be reflected by your officers and men just as the planets reflect the light of the sun. Similarly, a disregard of danger on the bridge carries courage to every corner of the ship.

"Experience in the Fleet has shown that a large number of serious offences could have been avoided if the Captain's Standing Orders, particularly those concerning rum, and the inspection of libertymen returning from leave, had been more concisely written, and more rigidly applied.

"The supply and issue of rum needs a Commanding Officer's keenest supervision. It is essential that an officer attends daily issue, and checks most carefully the supply and opening of new casks. Supply Ratings will only fall to the temptation of misappropriation or the falsifying of accounts if they know that the officers are out of touch with the situation."
— from *YOUR SHIP, NOTES AND ADVICE TO AN OFFICER ON ASSUMING HIS FIRST COMMAND, 1944* [Royal Navy]

In the mid-1930s, a little fox terrier named *At'Em* was made a member of the crew of the USS *Arizona*. He was issued his own Navy serial number and liberty card.

Nineteen-year-old Seaman First Class Tony Iacono was a gun-pointer in mount four, a five-inch gun mount on the battleship USS *New Jersey* in 1944: "We used to have a gunshack on the port superstructure, for the gunner's mates on the port side. It was right next to a vent that sucked hot air out of the bowels of the ship. We used to plug that up with blankets so that the chefs would sweat. Then the chefs would come up and say 'Hey, what's happening? And we would trade with them. We would take the blankets out of the vent in exchange for their bringing us a tray of cake.

"When we came into port, either at Ulithi or Mog Mog, we would get a ration of 3.2 beer. We would go ashore and play baseball. The winning side would drink all the beer, which was warm."
— Tony Iacono, USS *New Jersey*

"We had been in and out of Guantanamo Bay, Cuba, during the stormy season and were on our way back to Guantanamo. I was on watch on the bridge and overheard this exchange. We were on a direct

The dragon-green, the luminous, the dark, the serpent-haunted sea.
— from *The Gates of Damascus, West Gate* by James Elroy Flecker

below: A sailor on the USS *Pennsylvania*, BB-38, writes a letter to a loved one 1940

I've tried for many an hour and minute / To think of this world without me in it. I can't imagine a new-born day / Without me here . . . somehow. . . some way. / I can not think of the autumn's flare / Without me here . . . alive . . . aware. / I can't imagine a dawn in spring / Without my heart awakening.

These treasured days will come and go / At swifter pace . . . but this I know . . . I have no fear . . . I have no dread / Of that marked day that lies ahead. / My flesh will turn to ash and clay But I'll be here . . . somehow . . . some way.
— *Somehow*
by Don Blanding

right: Cigarette cards, a matchbook cover, and a postage stamp celebrate the sailor's life.

106

heading for the bay entrance and going at a pretty good clip of around 25 to 30 knots. The wind had increased to a high velocity. We had picked up a line of US Navy destroyers off our starboard side at about 10,000 yards or five miles. They were on a collision course with us, which is where the bearing remains constant and the range continues to decrease. I informed the skipper, Captain H.P. Smith. When the range between us and the lead tin can had reached about three and a half miles, Commander George Peckham, the Executive Officer, came on the bridge and stated rather loudly, 'Captain, there is a fleet of tin cans off our starboard bow on a collision course.' The skipper replied, 'I see them, George.' A few minutes later, the Exec returned to the bridge and announced, 'Captain, the fleet of tin cans on our starboard bow is still on a collision course.' The skipper replied, 'I see them, George.' The Exec then left the bridge.

"Moments later, the lead destroyer was about 2,500 yards away and the Exec returned to the bridge to announce quite loudly, 'Captain, we are on a collision course with that lead tin can. The Executive Officer recommends we reduce speed and change course to avoid!' The skipper looked at the Exec and replied, 'George, you tell the Executive Officer that I am the skipper of this ship and I outrank every skipper on those tin cans, and and besides that, I'm bigger!' We did not change course or speed. The tin cans backed down, not us. Word got around the ship about this exchange. The crew liked our skipper a lot more."
– Ted Pederson, USS *Missouri*

"Life in the old Navy was no picnic. Below decks, the short battleship [USS *Maryland*] looked like a beehive, with over 2,000 men in the ship's company. Crewmen could not have cameras and they could not go topside. For most of the four years that I was on board the *Maryland*, crew members could only be at their living quarters, their General [combat] Quarters, or perhaps have the luxury of a pass to

visit the ship's barber. On the *Maryland*, the crew slept in hammocks. They had bins for mess tables and they ate in the same compartment where they slept."
– Harold Porter, USS *Maryland*

"We never took our clothes off at sea, except odd times when we would sneak a quick wash all over. For sleep, any locker, table top or mess stool—one could sleep on anything, even if only about four inches wide."
– R.V. Racey, RN, from *Battleship, Cruiser, Destroyer* by Gregory Haines and Commander B.R. Coward, RN

"We knew about the war coming and we painted the ship a dull black, instead of the gray. They tried that out. The plan of the day would come out and it would say ALL HANDS REPORT FOR PHYSICAL DRILL FOLLOWED BY GUNNERY DRILL. We had that every day except Saturday and Sunday."
– Richard McCutcheon, USS *West Virginia*

"The final and most important temptation which confronts every Commanding Officer is the same as that which has brought so many dictators to the ground. 'Power corrupts' is a dictum which does not only apply to politics. Bernard Shaw has recently enlarged on this by stating 'Power corrupts the weak and dements the strong.' As a Commanding Officer you are an autocrat pure and simple, and you are subject to the same temptations as an autocrat. No one in your ship can check your excesses, or point out your eccentricities; no one can question your more downright assertions; everyone must endure your temper or any other foible you may develop. You are treated with the deference and ceremony not always granted to a cabinet minister.

"All this has the effect of accentuating your weaknesses, unless you watch yourself most carefully. Only some candid and regular

Shh! Don't talk too much.
Shh! Don't know too much.
Jack, don't be too hip,
'Cause a slip of the lip
Might sink a ship.
– unattributed

He has not even seen you, he / Who gave you your mortality; And you, so small, how can you guess His courage or his loveliness.

Yet in my quiet mind I pray He passed you on the darkling way— / His death, your birth, so much the same— / And holding you, breathed once your name.
— *War Baby*
by Pamela Holmes

right: A much-tattooed sailor aboard the USS *New Jersey* in December 1944.

introspection will keep you in command of yourself. The forces which turned Captain Bligh into a tyrant, though perhaps weaker, are still extant. Bligh was in many ways a good character; he was an efficient officer and a competent seaman; he possessed great courage and powers of endurance; but he had insufficient strength of will to repress two instincts, which are normally repressed in youth. He submitted himself to unbridled temper, and to sadism. The modern laws of the Navy rightly do not tolerate a practical application of the latter, but do not forget that it is within your power to cause considerable mental anguish to your younger officers by a consistent tone of sarcasm and contempt, and that, after the undue strain and fatigue of command in warfare, it is quite as simple to submit to such childish intolerance over small and petty irritations. And what is worse, *nobody* is going to tell you about them. In all officers, but above all in Commanding Officers, the words Officer and Gentleman should be entirely synonymous."
— from *YOUR SHIP, NOTES AND ADVICE TO AN OFFICER ON ASSUMING HIS FIRST COMMAND, 1944* [Royal Navy]

"I ate that chow for three years. We had beans Monday, Wednesday and Saturday, three times a day. We had a lot of Spam, a LOT of Spam. We had all the coffee we wanted, made in big urns. During General Quarters, there was no chow. When we were under attack, we didn't eat. When the attack was over, the first thing we had to do was clean up the guns, get rid of the hot cases and get ready for the next battle. After that, you ate when it was time for your side to eat.

"Some of that food, for a guy who came from a small town in the middle west, I couldn't eat it. It didn't even look good. But some of those guys just sloshed it down like it was good. Some of that stuff they used to make for us was streaky, watery, gooey stuff we used to call Slumgullion. It didn't

even look fit to eat. I wouldn't eat it. There was no ketchup, no butter and no ice on the table. They made their own bread, with a lot of weevils in it. We used to hold the bread up to the light and count the bogies in it. Sometimes there would be ten or twelve dead weevils in it. And then, when there was foul weather, and the cooks couldn't cook because the sea was too rough, we used to get 'horse cock' [balogna] sandwiches. I used to fill my locker up with sandwiches because I never got seasick. The chow on the ship was good when you were in port, but when you were at sea, it was . . . whatever you could get. There was one time when we were at sea for 60 days and we got beans all the time because they ran out of everything."

"We used to pick up Tokyo Rose when we were standing watch at night. She played all the nice music. Glenn Miller, Benny Goodman, Tommy Dorsey, all the good songs. You're on watch at four in the morning, you can't go to sleep, you can't even sit down. You've got to stand up. One night she said, 'Today we sank the Blue Dragon (the Japanese used to call our ship the Blue Dragon), and we'd laugh like hell. She was always saying things like, 'You know, your wife or girlfriend is out with your neighbour. She's cheating on you.' Always planting bad thoughts in your mind.

"I used to gamble and sometimes I'd win. Craps or cards. And, I'd send money home to my father because I knew that the house wasn't paid for. I said 'Pay for the house.' I didn't know how much I sent. So, when I came back from the service, he handed me a check book with over $3,000 in it. I said, 'What's this?' He said, 'That's your money. That's the money you sent your mother to pay for the house. Now this is *your* money, if you want to use it to get married, go to school or buy a car . . . nothing else. You can't waste it.' So, I wound up buying a car."
— Tony Iacono, USS *New Jersey*

"General messing—all catering being done by the Paymaster and his staff. The food in general was

108

Chief Petty Officer Robert Sambataro served aboard the USS *Missouri* as a medical corpsman during the Korean War. "Among the ships under United Nations command was HMCS *Cayuga*. I recall that they asked for medical supplies. What I didn't know then was that the medical officer was the famous imposter Ferdinand 'Fred' Demera. We both came from Lawrence, Massachusetts.

"There have been several accounts about the various careers of Demera. He took on several guises, among them zoologist, law student, teacher and assistant prison warden. But surely his crowning achievement was that of surgeon-lieutenant aboard the *Cayuga*.

"Demera studied all the medical books on board and performed dental surgery on the captain. He also looked after the wounded that were brought aboard. How did this come about? Well, he became a friend of a New Brunswick doctor, J.C. Cyr. He stole Cyr's medical certificates and used Cyr's name when applying to join the navy. The navy was eager to have him, and since there was no medical examination and no fingerprinting, he was accepted in no time flat.

"His exploits aboard the ship made great press, but the end came for Demera when Dr Cyr in New Brunswick said that *he* was the *real* Dr Cyr. Demera was given $1,000 in back pay and deported to the U.S. No charges were filed. He died in 1982, after having been ordained a Baptist minister."

On the Bridge of the Flagship.

COPYRIGHT 1942. MID-STATES PRESS, CHICAGO

Place One Cent Stamp Here

POST CARD

RY, MADAM, OUR ORDERS ARE TO SEARCH EVERYONE FOR JCEALED WEAPONS

NAVY YA

O'Toole

47637

very good, the only dish which few would eat was tripe and onions. It usually went straight from the galley to the gash."
— A.W.R. Brown, RN, from *Battleship, Cruiser, Destroyer* by Gregory Haines and Commander B.R. Coward, RN.

"We left Cuba and the order came down to put on flank speed, which was about 33 knots or 38 land miles per hour, the highest speed that the ship could steam. The fantail was awash with the four screws digging into the water with 180,000 horsepower on her shafts. Down in the after diesel, the four shafts passed through that space and were turning at a furious rate. We made Norfolk in about eight hours and got to our regular berthing space at pier 7 in time for liberty call. We were home again."
— Herb Fahr, USS *Missouri*

The Navy had installed a square white porcelain bathtub in the captain's in-port cabin [of the USS *Iowa*] for President Franklin D. Roosevelt's trip to Casablanca in November 1943. Roosevelt, crippled by polio, was unable to use standard shipboard showers. Seaman First Class Leo Sicard, was assigned to push Roosevelt around and help the president. "He was a real sailor, and knew his way around," remembered Sicard, who was frightened by his responsibility, but was comforted when Roosevelt said: "I'm a human being, just the same as you."
— from *Navy Times*

"As well as the individual acquaintance of your men, you must know the 'atmosphere' of the ship. You must be close enough in touch with your ship's company to know of any feeling or rumour in the ship which may be a bad influence; for it is your job to dispel such impressions.
  "That your men should know you is equally important. They must know you well enough to look upon you as the trustee of their welfare on

below: 20-year-old Robert Sambataro aboard the *Iowa*-class USS *Missouri*, BB-63, heading for combat in Korea, September 1950.

111

None of us ever doubted he was indeed the best of us, more skillful in the art of living than the rest of us.

His death was no pitiful drama laboriously enacted before our eyes. He died remotely beyond the horizon / as a comet or a meteor dies.
— from *20th Century Requiem*
by Patricia M. Saunders

Under the bludgeonings of chance / My head is bloody, but unbowed.
— *Invictus*
by W.E. Henley

board and in their homes. Men are proverbially shy about putting in requests to see officers, and particularly the Captain. You must make it clear to the men that not only their Divisional Officers, but you yourself will do all you can for their welfare. One of the instinctive desires in every man's mind is for security. If the sailors know that you are watching over their home security you will have gone a long way towards getting a happy ship.

"The men will also know you indirectly in the way you handle the ship and exert your influence to bring the ship to a high standard, but it is during your ship's company talks that each and every man will get to know you best. For that reason you must look upon your talks to the crew as one of the most important things you do. The first point to realise on these occasions is that you are talking to a body of men, a number of whom are quite intelligent, and that it is the intelligent ones, and not the dull ones, who are going to criticise your speech afterwards. Therefore, while talking in simple language, you must never talk down to the men. Neither imagine that you will get the best out of a crew which you never address at all.

"An intelligent man wants both information and inspiration. For this reason the Silent Skipper of last-century fiction, who in some way gained the devotion of his men by never uttering a word, will not be a success today. At the same time, a sailor does not want to be mustered on someone else's messdeck to hear a succession of vague and longwinded discourses on nothing in particular. Neither does he enjoy false heroics or "flannel." Like his tot, the sailor prefers his talks neat. For this reason, when you talk, do it at a convenient time when everybody will hear. Make certain, also, that you have something quite definite to say, and work out exactly how to say it beforehand. If Winston Churchill has to rehearse all his speeches, there is no reason why you should not.

"Bring in all you can about ships' movements without compromising security. If you have been

in action explain all you can, giving praise where due. If you have been in any large operation, use it to give the men a wider outlook, and foster a feeling of trust and admiration in the Commander-in-Chief and other senior officers.

"Finally, when addressing a ship's company, Be Yourself. You cannot consistently go on being someone else for the whole commission. The sailors want to be commanded by a character, not a character sketch."
— from *YOUR SHIP, NOTES AND ADVICE TO AN OFFICER ON ASSUMING HIS FIRST COMMAND, 1944* [Royal Navy]

"The two officers scrambled out on the gunwale. The vast flat steel wall of the battleships' side confronted them. It towered like a skyscraper and stretched away, seemingly for blocks, on either side, hiding the atoll. Maryk leaped to the landing platform, a small square wooden grille bleached by salt water at the bottom of the steep gangway ladder. Keefer followed. 'Lie off and wait for us,' the exec shouted to Meatball. They mounted the ladder, jingling the guy chains. The OOD was a short, round-faced lieutenant commander, grey at the temples, wearing very clean, very starched khakis. Maryk asked for the location of the flag officer. The OOD briskly gave him directions. The *Caine* officers left the quarterdeck and walked slowly aft, looking around at the majestic main deck of the *New Jersey*.

It was another world; and yet, somehow, the same world as the *Caine*, transfigured. They were on a forecastle, with anchor chains, wildcat, pelican hooks and bits, with ventilators and life lines. But the *New Jersey*'s pelican hook was as big as the *Caine*'s main guns; one link of the battleship's anchor chain would have stretched across the minesweeper's entire bow; and the main battery, the long, long cannons with their turrets, seemed bigger than the whole *Caine*. There were sailors and officers everywhere, the same crowd of blue

Servant of God, well done!
Well hast thou fought /
The better fight.
— from *Paradise Lost*
by John Milton

I have had playmates,
I have had companions,
In my days of childhood,
in my joyful schooldays—
All, all are gone, the old
familiar faces.
— *The Old Familiar Faces*
by Charles Lamb

above left: Bud Abbott
and Lou Costello
starred with the
Andrews Sisters in *In
The Navy*, a 1941
Universal Pictures film,
below left: A fighting
Kirk Douglas in a still
from *In Harm's Way*,
released by Paramount
in 1965.

below: Joseph M. Mellor served in the Royal Navy battlecruiser HMS *Repulse* from 30 August 1941 until 2 November of that year when he was sent on a course in Colombo. *Repulse* was operating with *Prince of Wales* off the east coast of Malaya on 10 December when they were sighted by a Japanese submarine. The ships were attacked by torpedo bombers and both were sunk with great loss of life. The telegrams at right were received by Mellor's wife. far right: American battleship sailors at sea during World War II.

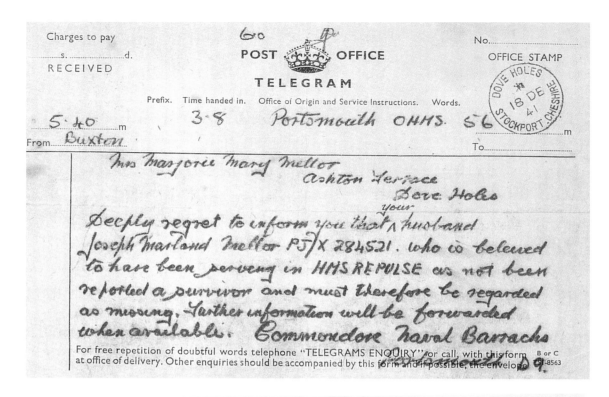

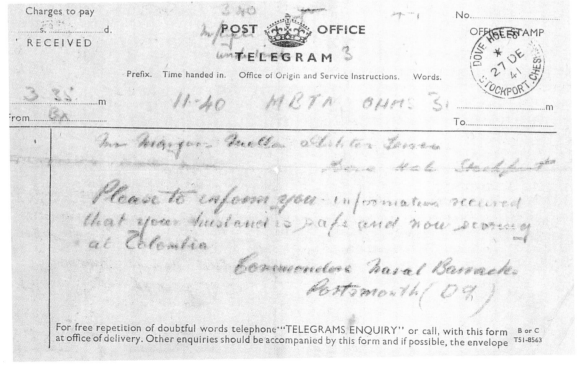

below: *Iowa*, *Colorado* and *West Virginia* gather in Japan, October 1945

and sprinkling of khaki, but the sailors were clean as Sunday-school boys, and the officers looked like their teachers, grown up and fussily neat. The great central cathedral of bridge and stacks jutted out of the deck skyward, a pyramid of metal, nervous with anti-aircraft batteries and radars; the deck dwindled aft beyond it for hundreds of feet. The *New Jersey* was awesome."
– from *The Caine Mutiny* by Herman Wouk

"Armoured hatches were a hazard in harbour, but could be even worse at sea when one waited for the roll of the ship to help bias the weight in favour of either closing or opening the hatches, which were actuated by massive springs. There were several nasty accidents to feet and hands."
– W. Burley, RN, from *Battleships, Cruisers, Destroyers* by Gregory Haines and Commander B.R. Coward, RN

"We stopped off at the Hollywood USO for some coffee and doughnuts, and chatted with some of the hostesses. One of them came up with some tickets for a TV show and we decided to go. It was the popular 'Truth or Consequences' show with Jack Bailey as MC. We got there early and got seats in the front row. As they do in these shows, they always have a sub-host come out and 'warm up' the audience. The show was to be taped for showing an hour later. It always opened with the audience laughing it up a lot. What were they laughing at? On this particular show, it was me. In order to get the audience to laugh, the sub-host picked out a soldier and a sailor from the audience to come down to the stage. We were asked our names and where we were from, and I got a word in about being stationed on the 'Mo' and that got a round of applause. We were then asked who we thought could get dressed faster, men or women. Of course, the GI and I both said men. So, to prove it, the sub-host brought out two suitcases. One held women's clothes, the other one, men's.

117

THE SEMAPHORE ALPHABET.

CHARACTERS	HAND FLAGS	CHARACTERS	HAND FLAGS	CHARACTERS	HAND FLAGS	CHARACTERS	HAND FLAGS
A		I		Q		Y	
B		J		R		Z	
C OR ANSWERING SIGN		K		S		ATTENTION	
D		L		T		FRONT	
E OR ERASE SIGN		M		U			
F		N		V			
G		O		W			

The USS *Missouri*, BB-63, is the last of a line of warships called Missouri. The first of these was a steam-powered wooden side-wheel frigate completed in 1842. She had two paddle-wheels and was armed with two ten-inch guns and eight eight-inch guns. On 26 August 1843, a crewman dropped a demijohn of spirits of turpentine in a store room. A fire ignited and spread so rapidly that containment was not possible. In a few hours, the burnt-out hulk sank. More than 200 of her crew were rescued by the British ship-of-the-line *Malabar*.

The second *Missouri* was an iron-clad center-wheel steam sloop of the Confederate States of America. She was launched in April 1863 and was used mainly to transport workers around the coast of Louisiana. At the end of the Civil War, she was surrendered to the U.S. Navy.

BB-11, the first warship to bear the name *Missouri*, was launched 28 December 1901 and was a 12,362-ton battleship with a complement of 40 officers and 521 men. She was armed with four twelve-inch guns, sixteen six-inch guns and a variety of smaller weapons. While engaged in target practice on 13 April 1904, a flare-back from one of her guns ignited a fire causing more than a thousand pounds of gunpowder to burn. Many of the ship's spaces quickly filled with deadly gas which suffocated five officers and 29 men.

In December 1907, BB-11 was among sixteen white-painted battleships to pass in

We were to see how fast we could get dressed. We each chose a suitcase. I got the women's clothes.

"Now it was a matter of timing. The show was about to begin. The announcer was getting ready when the GI and I got the signal to start dressing, and that was all that was needed. I attacked the suitcase and threw on some panties about six sizes too large and, with a prompt from the sub-host, I started pulling a girdle over my head. This brought howls from the audience, and that was what was being taped when the show was being introduced. The GI and I were shuffled under the seating area, took off the clothes we had put on and, with a well-done from the sub-host, we were both handed an envelope and escorted back to our seats. When the show was over my buddies gathered around me to find out what was in the envelope. I opened it and there were four one-dollar bills, a note and a gift certificate. The note said the four dollars was to pay the taxes for the prize on the gift certificate which was for a Zenith Transoceanic Portable radio (the envy of everyone during the '50s). The radio could be picked up at the studio tours gift shop, which at that time was closed.

"So, we left the studio and went across the street to a bar where we asked the bartender to put the TV on for us so we could watch the show we had attended, and I bought the beer with the four dollars. When the show came on, I saw the audience laughing at the GI and myself, and as the camera panned around, my buddies showed up, laughing with the rest of them.

"The next day we toured the beaches in the hope of seeing some stars. We enjoyed the sight of thousands of bodies in skimpy bikini's. We hit all the famous beaches and the municipal pier at Santa Monica. I also ran up to the TV studio and picked up my prize radio. I was to enjoy it but a short time as it was stolen soon after. Anyway, it was a fun and relaxing liberty."
– Herb Fahr, USS *Missouri*

In April 1924, a woman named Madeline Blair managed to stow away aboard the USS *Arizona*, (BB-39), when the battleship was berthed in New York City. While the ship was under way to her next port of call, San Pedro, California, a scandal erupted when the stowaway was discovered. It transpired that the lady had been providing favours to the sailors who helped to conceal her presence for nearly a month. Twenty-three sailors were tried and sentenced to naval prison terms of up to ten years. Blair was transferred to a commercial vessel which returned her to New York.

far left: The brig in the USS *Missouri,* below left: Maynard Loy served aboard the *Missouri* in 1952 during the Korean War, left: Mac McCutcheon's 1941 belt buckle.

review before President Theodore Roosevelt at Hampton Roads, Chesapeake Bay. The Great White Fleet then departed on a celebrated fourteen-month world cruise. She later served as a training ship and, in June and July 1912, helped protect American lives at Guantanamo Bay during the Cuban Revolution. She served as a training vessel with the Atlantic Fleet during World War I, as well as transporting troops to and from France. She was scrapped in January 1922, under the terms of the Washington Naval Arms Limitation Treaty.

The final battleship *Missouri*, BB-63, was commissioned on 11 June 1944. Speaking at her launch ceremonies, Senator Harry S. Truman said: "The time is surely coming when the people of Missouri can thrill with pride as the *Missouri* and her sister ships, with batteries blazing, sail into Tokyo Bay."

A BATTLESHIP CONSTRUCTION PICTORIAL

below: The German battleship *Tirpitz* in her fitting-out berth.

The gloomy hulls, in armour grim, / Like clouds o'er moors have met, / And prove that oak, and iron, and man / Are tough in fibre yet.

But splendours wane. The sea-fight yields / No front of old display; / The garniture, emblazonment, / And heraldry all decay.
— from *The Temeraire* by Herman Melville

U.S.S. ALABAMA (BB-6
BOW VIEW ON BLDG W
NORFOLK NAVY YARD PORT
PHOTO SERIAL 10-10-3-6

right: USS *Alabama,* BB-60, on the building ways at the Norfolk Navy Yard, Portsmouth, Virginia, right centre: *Alabama* in her fitting-out berth, below right: The USS *North Carolina,* BB-55, nearing completion in the New York Navy Yard, April 1941.

As he laboured, his mind ran o'er
The various ships that were built of yore,
And above them all, and strangest of all,
Towered the Great Harry, crank and tall,
Whose picture was hanging on the wall,
With bows and stern raised high in air,
And balconies hanging there,
And signal lanterns and flags afloat,
And eight round towers, like those that frown
From some old castle, looking down
Upon the drawbridge and the moat.
— from *The Building of the Ship*
by Henry Wadsworth Longfellow

U.S.S. Alabama (BB60)
Bow view at fitting out pier
Norfolk Navy Yard, Portsmouth VA
Photo Serial 10-174-50 July 31

AMERICAN PRODUCTION

far left above: The launch of *Bismarck* at Hamburg, February 1939, left: *Alabama* on her sea trials, far left below: Launching the USS *North Dakota*, BB-29, at Quincy, Massachusetts in 1908, below: The completed USS *North Carolina* in the New York Navy Yard, 1941.

THE NEW CAPITAL SHIP

"IF WE REBUILD the battlefleet and spend many millions on doing so, and then war comes and the airmen are right, and all our battleships are rapidly destroyed by air attack, our money will have been largely thrown away. But if we do not rebuild it and war comes, and the airmen are wrong and *our* airmen cannot destroy the enemy's capital ships, and they are left to range with impunity on the world's oceans and destroy our convoys, then we shall lose the British Empire."
— Royal Navy Admiral E. Chatfield to Lord Halifax

The Commander-in Chief of the Combined Japanese Fleet, Admiral Isoroku Yamamoto, had been educated at Harvard University in Boston, Massachusetts. He had served Japan as its Naval Attaché in Washington and was well informed about the military strengths and capabilities of the United States. As the beginning of World War II in the Pacific loomed, Yamamoto had no illusions about America as an adversary and did not favour such a war, but accepted its inevitability. He also believed that Japan could not win a long, drawn-out war with the United States. Yamamoto was convinced that Japan must "give a fatal blow to the enemy at the outset, when it was least expected". He was certain that anything less than the total destruction of the U.S. fleet "would awaken a sleeping giant".

Hector Bywater, a British naval authority, had published a book, *Sea Power in the Pacific*, in 1921, and by the following year it had become required reading at Japan's Naval War College and her Imperial Naval Academy. Bywater believed that distance, and the effort connected with secondary fuel and supply consumption, meant that the Japanese home islands were essentially protected from direct assault by American forces. With impressive foresight, he predicted that the only workable strategy for an American assault on Japan would require a massive island-hopping campaign, through the Marianas and on to Guam

right: F4U Corsairs, returning from a combat mission over North Korea, circle their aircraft carrier, the USS *Boxer* as they wait for planes in the next strike to be launched from her flight deck on 4 September 1951.

126

and the Philippines. Following the success of *Sea Power in the Pacific*, Bywater published a second book called *The Great Pacific War*, in which he argued that Japan could achieve the goal of making her empire invulnerable by mounting a successful surprise attack on the U.S. fleet, followed by an invasion of Guam and the Philippines and the fortification of its mandate islands. Bywater and Yamamoto met for an evening at London's Grosvenor House during the admiral's 1934 trip to Europe. In the meeting Yamamoto expressed his profound interest in Bywater's theories and their possible implications for Japan.

The creation of the Greater East Asian Co-Prosperity Sphere—that was how the Japanese referred to their intended conquest of South-East Asia in the late 1930s. They had already conquered Manchuria and then invaded mainland China. These adventures caused the United States to impose an embargo on Japan which covered war materials, scrap iron, steel, and aviation fuel. All Japanese assets in the U.S. were frozen as well. Japan had few natural resources and now her sources for strategic commodities were drying up. Her militarist rulers knew that to survive and to win in China, they had to have the tin, bauxite, rubber and oil of Malaya and the Dutch East Indies. They saw war with the British Empire, the Dutch government in exile, and the United States as inevitable, and began planning attacks on American air bases in the Philippines and the U.S. Pacific Fleet at Pearl Harbor, Hawaii. The complete destruction of these targets would be necessary to clear the way for Japanese forces to conquer Malaya, the East Indies and China. They called upon Admiral Yamamoto to devise, plan and implement the spectacular early Sunday morning surprise attack on the American battleships and facilities in Pearl Harbor on 7 December 1941. The admiral was known as "the father of Japanese naval aviation", and had led the campaign to develop his nation's aircraft carrier fleet. In January 1941 he began planning the Pearl Harbor raid.

Rear Admiral Heijiro Abe, Imperial Japanese Navy (Ret), retained a souvenir of his visit to Pearl Harbor on 7 December 1941, a yellowing photograph he had taken from his Nakajima bomber as the squadron he commanded dropped their armour-piercing bombs on the vessels in battleship row. On his first run over the harbour, Abe encountered heavy smoke from an earlier attack by Japanese torpedo bombers. The smoke obscured his target, the USS *West Virginia*, forcing him to lead the squadron around for a second run. When he released his single bomb he watched it strike what believed must have been the ship's powder magazine. He recalled seeing the great ship shake convulsively and belch flames from many openings. He recorded that instant with his German-made camera and returned to his carrier where he had four prints of the photo made—one for the carrier task force chief, one for the skipper of his ship, one for Imperial Headquarters in Tokyo and one for himself. His print is the only one known to have survived the war. He has guarded the photo carefully over the years. His greatest wish has been to one day return to Pearl Harbor "to offer prayers for the repose of the souls of the fallen Americans there. I have to do it before I die".

left: Eugene Ely making one of the first aircraft deck landings, on the USS *Pennsylvania* at San Francisco, 1911.

129

Yamamoto's lingering misgivings about attacking the United States resurfaced as the date of the raid approached. He realized that a number of the U.S. Navy's key warships would not be in port at Pearl, as they were either in transit between the U.S. west coast and Hawaii, or re-fitting on the west coast. Additionally, the American aircraft carriers in the Pacific, *Lexington* and *Enterprise,* were operating at sea, and *Saratoga* was in port on the west coast. Yamamoto now knew it would not be possible to wipe out the U.S. Pacific Fleet in a single blow and that an essential second strike on the remains of the enemy fleet would have to be mounted within six months of the Pearl attack.

Admiral Yamamoto was inspired by the successful Royal Navy air attack on battleships and other warships of the Italian Navy at Taranto in November 1940. Bomb and torpedo-bearing Swordfish bi-planes had crippled much of their enemy's fleet with one strike in the shallow waters of that port facility. The admiral noted similarities between the facilities at Pearl and Taranto and considered them in his initial planning of the raid. He determined that, for such an attack to succeed, he would require a 31-warship task force including six aircraft carriers, *Akagi, Kaga, Soryu, Hiryu, Shokaku* and *Zuikaku,* to approach within 200 miles of the Hawaiian Islands where they would likely encounter heavy enemy defences in the form of at least 100 fighter aircraft and the anti-aircraft guns of up to 68 warships.

Pearl Harbor lies adjacent to the large airfield complex of Hickam Field and the Honolulu Airport. The harbour itself is a relatively shallow basin surrounding a small airfield known as Ford Island and there is only one narrow channel leading from the harbour to the Pacific Ocean. On the eastern shore lay a submarine base, oil storage tanks and drydocks. At anchor on the southeast side of the harbour on the day of the attack, were eight battleships of the American fleet, *Arizona, California, Maryland, Nevada, Oklahoma, Tennessee, Utah*

and *West Virginia.* Another battleship, *Pennsylvania,* lay in a nearby drydock where she was being repaired. These warships would become the principal targets of the Japanese air strike.

Yamamoto's plan called for the Imperial Japanese Fleet to be assembling near the Kurile Islands north of Japan on 22 November. On that day Japan's two special envoys in Washington, Admiral Kichisaburo Nomura and Saburo Kurusu, reported that they had made no progress in their attempts to resolve the differences between the two nations. Japan's militarists decided, therefore, that diplomacy had failed and directed their task force to head east from the Kuriles on 25 November. Escorted by battleships, cruisers, destroyers and submarines, the six Japanese carriers crossed much of the western Pacific, observing strict radio silence in an effort to reach the area north of the Hawaiian Islands without being detected by the enemy.

On 7 December 1941, the Japanese Ambassador to Washington asked for an appointment to see the American Secretary of State, Cordell Hull, at 1 p.m. The Ambassador later telephoned and asked that the appointment be postponed to 1.45 p.m. as he was not quite ready for the meeting. He arrived at 2.05 p.m. and was received by the Secretary at 2.20 p.m.

The Japanese Ambassador stated that he had been instructed to deliver at 1 p.m. the document which he then handed to the Secretary, and said that he was sorry that he had been delayed owing to the need for more time to decode the message. The Secretary asked why the Ambassador had specified one o'clock. The Ambassador replied that he did not know, but that that was his instruction. The Secretary noted that he was receiving the message after two o'clock.

After reading the first few pages, the Secretary asked the Ambassador whether the document was being presented under the instructions of the Japanese Government. The Ambassador replied that it was. As soon as he had finished reading the document, the Secretary turned to the Japanese Ambassador and said: "I must say that in all my conversations with you during the last nine months, I have never uttered one word of untruth. This is borne out absolutely by the record. In all my fifty years of public service I have never seen a document that was more crowded with infamous falsehoods and distortions—infamous falsehoods and distortions on a scale so huge that I never imagined until today that any Government on this planet was capable of uttering them." The Ambassador then left the room without comment.

THE JAPANESE GOVERNMENT REGRETS TO HAVE TO NOTIFY HEREBY THE AMERICAN GOVERNMENT THAT IN VIEW OF THE ATTITUDE OF THE AMERICAN GOVERNMENT IT CANNOT BUT CONSIDER THAT IT IS IMPOSSIBLE TO REACH AN AGREEMENT THROUGH FURTHER NEGOTIATIONS.

One week before the document was given to Secretary Hull, the following final warning message was issued to key American and British personnel by the U.S. Chief of Naval Operations: "This despatch is to be considered a war warning. Negotiations with Japan looking toward stabilization of conditions in the Pacific have ceased and an aggressive move by Japan is expected within the next few days. The number and equipment of Japanese troops and the organization of naval task forces indicates an amphibious expedition against either the Philippines, Thai[land] or K[o]r[e]a peninsula or possibly Borneo. Execute an appropriate defensive deployment preparatory to carrying out the tasks assigned in WPL46. Inform District and Army authorities. A similar warning is being sent by War Department. Spenavo inform British."

The Japanese task force commander, Vice Admiral Chiuchi Nagumo, received a signal from Yamamoto on 2 December which read "Niitaka Yama Nabora" or "Climb Mount Niitaka", the authorization to begin the operation against Pearl. Admiral Nagumo had positioned his fleet exactly 230 miles north of the

PLEASE DRIVE CAREFULLY
MY BUMPERS ARE ON THE SCRAP HE[AP]

Hawaiian island of Oahu on 7 December and his carriers began launching their bomb and torpedo-laden aircraft at 6 a.m. that day. 50 A6M2 Zeke (Zero) fighters accompanied 40 Nakajima B5N2 Kate low-level torpedo-bombers, 50 high-level Kates and 50 Val dive-bombers. At 7.53 a.m. the first wave of Japanese planes passed Barber's Point and approached their target. They would be followed an hour later by a second wave of 170 bombers.

Skirting the Oahu coastline at an altitude of 9,800 feet, the raiders began their descent towards the harbour which that morning was sheltering 94 American warships of various types. The ships were not protected by anti-torpedo netting as the Navy did not believe they were vulnerable to attack by Japanese forces so far from Japan. The first targets to be struck by the raiders were the Pearl Harbor Naval Air Station on Ford Island and Hickam Field, as nine

dive-bombers from *Shokaku* blasted the hangars and aircraft on the Ford Island apron. Then 18 more dive-bombers from the same carrier struck the hangar line and aircrew barracks at Hickam. Meanwhile, dive-bombers from *Zuikaku* were busy pounding Wheeler Field as fighters from *Soryu* and *Hiryu* were establishing Japanese control of the airspace over Wheeler. But the greatest airfield damage was sustained at Kaneohe Naval Air Station, where most of the station's aircraft were destroyed by planes from *Shokaku* and *Zuikako*.

Next, lumbering torpedo-bombers from *Akagi* and *Kaga* began their run on the warships moored northwest of Ford Island, as other torpedo aircraft homed in on the vessels of Battleship Row and those at Ten-Ten Pier.

The battleships *Arizona*, *California*, *Nevada*, *Oklahoma* and *West Virginia* were all struck by

As her lines were cast off, and the nuclear-powered aircraft carrier USS *Harry S. Truman* and the ships of her battle group got under way on her January 2003 deployment, the following announcement was heard over the ship's intercom (1MC), PEACE ON EARTH TO MEN OF GOOD WILL . . . ALL OTHERS—STAND BY.

right: An OS2U Kingfisher spotting plane flying over Angaur in the Palau Islands group during allied landing operations in September 1944.

torpedoes. A direct bomb hit down the funnel of *Arizona* caused her forward ammunition magazines to explode. She broke in two and capsized, taking the lives of more than a thousand of her crew. Many crewmen from *Tennessee* and *Maryland* died when their vessels were bombed and they tried to escape by leaping into the water which was covered with a heavy layer of burning oil. In her drydock, *Pennsylvania* was enveloped by a cloud of thick black smoke which may have protected her from greater damage. In another drydock, the destroyer *Shaw* was hit and, in the most spectacular explosion of the entire attack, was blown apart, her demise captured on film in one of the most dramatic photographs of the war.

Nevada was now endeavouring to run through the carnage and make her way out the narrow channel to the open sea. She came under a renewed attack, but was successfully beached out of harm's way. The burning, badly damaged *West Virginia* had settled onto the bottom of the harbour. Within days, *California,* the victim of three torpedo hits, would do the same. *Oklahoma* lay overturned, her masts in the mud of the bottom. *Maryland* suffered relatively minor damage, *Utah* had capsized and *Tennessee* had taken two major bomb hits. Thirteen smaller vessels were sunk or damaged, including the destroyers *Cassin* and *Downes* in drydock near the *Pennsylvania*.

The attack was over by 10 a.m. In addition to the many U.S. Navy ships damaged or sunk, 188 aircraft had been destroyed and five more planes from the inbound carrier *Enterprise* were shot down by mistake. In all, more than 2,400 U.S. personnel were killed in the various attacks on American military installations on Oahu that day. The Japanese lost just 29 aircraft of the 360 that participated in the raids.

In the attack, the oil tank farm facility and the dockyard installations were mostly undamaged. Of the targetted battleships, only four were actually sunk and much of the damage done was reparable. The battleship *Nevada* later participated in the D-Day invasion of Normandy and the Battle of Iwo Jima. Of the battleships at Pearl on 7 December, five were repaired and active within the next three years. The damaged airfield facilities were soon repaired.

The American aircraft carriers were unaffected by the attack and, shortly, they and their successors would become the nucleus of the new U.S. Navy striking force, the new capital ships.

The primary effect of the elaborately planned and carefully executed Pearl Harbor raid was, as Admiral Yamamoto had feared, to wake a sleeping giant. Jolted from their isolationism by the shocking surprise attack, stunned and disbelieving, the American people soon rallied. They were united in their determination to avenge "the date which will live in infamy," as President Franklin D. Roosevelt referred to it in his declaration of war address to the U.S. congress on 8 December. That same day Britain, at war with Germany since September 1939, declared war on Japan. The Pearl Harbor attack had caused the United States to enter the war and ally with Britain, initially against Japan, and then against Germany and Italy as well. By 11 December what had been essentially a European conflict had become a world war.

The Japanese armed forces controlled Manchuria, French Indochina and parts of China by 7 December when they began their new offensive in Southeast Asia and the Pacific. They moved swiftly to invade the Philippines, Hong Kong, Thailand, Guam, Singapore, Malaya, British Borneo and the Dutch East Indies. They aimed to drive the British, Dutch and Americans out of Asia; to implement their "co-prosperity sphere"; increase their power base and secure for themselves the natural resources they required for their effort to conquer China; and, ultimately, to weaken and demoralize the United States and force her to negotiate for peace on Japan's terms.

In pursuit of these aims, the Japanese also took Burma within a year of the Pearl Harbor raid and began seizing bases and facilities in the Solomon Islands, New Guinea and the Aleutian Islands. But

In a move calculated to boost civilian morale in the United States, as well as to begin to pay the Japanese back for their raid on Pearl Harbor, the U.S. Army Air Force planned and carried out a bold bombing attack on Tokyo in spring 1942. Led by Lieutenant Colonel James Doolittle, a force of sixteen B-25 Mitchell bombers took off from the flight deck of the carrier USS *Hornet* on the morning of 18 April. They flew 550 miles west to bomb various targets in the Japanese capital city. While the damage done was relatively small, the point had been made. It was a tiny taste of the whirlwind Japan would reap before she would finally be forced to surrender in the summer of 1945.

Isn't God upon the ocean
Just the same as on the land?
— from *Ballad of the Tempest*
by James T. Fields

I was born on an Irish sea of eggs and porter, / I was born in Belfast, in the MacNeice country, / A child of Harland & Wolff in the iron forest,
My childbed a steel cradle slung from a gantry.

I remember the Queen's Road trams swarming with workers, / The lovely northern voices, the faces of the women, / The plane trees by the City Hall: an *Alexander- platz*, / And the sailors coming off shore with silk stockings and linen.

I remember the jokes about sabotage and Dublin, / The noisy jungle of cranes and sheerlegs, the clangour, / The draft in February of a thousand matelots from Devonport,
Surveying anxiously my enormous flight-deck and hangar.

I remember the long vista of ships under the quiet mountain, / The signals from Belfast Castle, the usual panic and sea-fever
Before I slid superbly out on the green lough
Leaving the tiny cheering figures on the jetty for ever.

Turning my face from home to the Southern Cross, / A map of crackling stars, and the albatross.
– HMS *Glory*
by Charles Causley

right: F9F Panther carrier-launched jet fighters being readied for sorties over Korea in October 1950.

the key to Japan's ultimate success in the Pacific, as outlined by Admiral Yamamoto, would be Midway Island. There, the admiral believed, "The success or failure of our entire strategy in the Pacific will be determined by . . . destroying the United States fleet, more particularly its carrier task forces . . . by launching the proposed operations against Midway, we can succeed in drawing out the enemy's carrier strength and destroying it in decisive battle."

The Battle of Midway lasted from 3 to 6 June 1942. It was among the greatest battles of the war. In it carrier aircraft of the Japanese and American fleets clashed near the central Pacific island, with the Japanese losing 250 planes and four of their six carriers. Just as Midway was the beginning of the end for Japan in the war, so it was the beginning of the end of the battleship's reign as the principal capital ship of the world's naval powers.

Rear Admiral Chester C. Woods, Commandant of the U.S. Third Naval District, stated at the decommissioning of the USS *Wisconsin* on 8 March 1958: "We have seen the end of the trail for this magnificent breed of ship. The battleship is finally turning over her mantle of naval primacy to new and more effective weapons, a primacy which has been held by the battleship, or line-of-battle warship, for many hundreds of years of sail and a hundred years of steam. The battleship is still the heavyweight of all the ships in the world which utilize only their built-in power to inflict damage to the enemy. But when the hitting power of a ship could be extended far beyond the range of the guns of a battleship, as in the case of the carrier and its embarked aircraft, then the supremacy of the battleship was doomed. The new 'king' is the carrier. But some day it too will pass on, giving way to another king of that future era—the guided-missile ship or something else which we cannot now know."

Aircraft carriers had become the dreadnoughts of our time.

SCHARNHORST AND GNEISENAU

20-year-old Pat Kingsmill was flying one of six Swordfish torpedo-bombers attacking the German battlecruisers *Scharnhorst* and *Gneisenau* and the heavy cruiser *Prinz Eugen* off Calais on 21 February 1941. Kingsmill and the other members of Fleet Air Arm Squadron 825 had had no combat experience before this assignment. As the elderly bi-planes of 825 approached the German warships at 90 knots, Kingsmill was following his leader, Lt.-Cdr. Eugene Esmonde, when the latter was shot down as the flight neared the target ships. Then a second Swordfish became a fireball as Kingsmill watched. At a distance of 2,000 yards from his target, the *Prinz Eugen*, he banked onto a direct line to the vessel and received a bullet wound in the back. Flying on through heavy smoke and shell bursts, Kingsmill's observer was wounded in the leg and his telegraphist-gunner had to straddle a huge hole in the fuselage to keep from falling into the sea. Now the aircraft was hit again, starting a fire on one wing and damaging the engine. The pilot had to struggle with

right: The ice-covered German battleship *Scharnhorst* in the Baltic, January 1940.

THERE WAS A sense of urgency in the planning of Germany's next generation of pocket battleship or *Panzerschiff* in 1932. The new French *Dunkerque* class battleship was causing great concern among the German design staff, which held that the next *Panzerschiff* must be a more powerful warship than the soon-to-be-launched *Dunkerque*. The three existing *Panzerschiffs* already exceeded the 10,000-ton maximum imposed on German warships by the Versailles Treaty. Now the designers no longer pretended to honour the limitation as the Germans sought to achieve a vessel superior to the French threat in one of 26,000 tons, which would grow to 38,900 tons, fully loaded, by the time the two ships of the *Scharnhorst* class were completed in 1939.

By retaining high-pressure steam for their power, instead of the newer diesel technology, the creators of *Scharnhorst* and *Gneisenau* produced a warship capable of 31.5-knots. Armament consisted of nine eleven-inch guns, twelve 5.9-inch guns, fourteen 4.1-inch guns and sixteen 37mm guns. Much debate surrounded the decision to go with eleven-inch main guns, as larger guns were clearly desirable to counter the thirteen-inch weapons of *Dunkerque*. Eleven-inch guns were selected, however, with provision being made for the possible installation of larger guns at some future date. The armour belt tapered from a maximum of 13.8 inches to 6.7 inches and two-inch armour covered the upper deck surface. Although the Allies would continue to describe the two ships as battle cruisers, the Kriegsmarine always rated them as battleships.

Gneisenau was completed before *Scharnhorst* and, during initial sea trials, it was found that too much water was coming aboard forward, so a new clipper or 'Atlantic' bow was added in late 1938. Repositioning the anchors further reduced excessive spray, and smoke around the bridge was reduced with the addition of a large funnel cap. Radar was installed in 1938 and augmented in

1942 and the catapult and aircraft hangar were also modified. *Scharnhorst* was given an Atlantic bow and the large funnel cap in 1939. Her first sea trial sortie into the Atlantic came in late March 1939. *Gneisenau* and *Scharnhorst* had passed their sea trials by 22 August and, when World War II broke out in September, both were at anchor in the River Elbe near Hamburg. In early October, *Gneisenau* sailed to Wilhelmshaven. She then departed on a North Sea operation in the company of a cruiser and nine destroyers. *Scharnhorst,* meanwhile, was undergoing repairs to her superstructure, damaged during a target-practice exercise.

On 21 November, *Scharnhorst* and *Gneisenau* left Wilhelmshaven to harass the British Northern Patrol, a line of cruisers stretched across the Iceland-Faeroes Gap. They were accompanied by the light cruisers *Köln* and *Leipzig* initially, but continued on their own after their second day at sea. Vizeadmiral Wilhelm Marschall was in command of the German warships. The group had not been detected by British reconnaissance aircraft or submarines and the Admiralty did not know of their presence in the area, or even that they were at sea.

On the 22nd, *Scharnhorst* claimed her first victim of the war, the 16,600-ton armed merchant cruiser HMS *Rawalpindi*, a converted passenger liner, under the command of Captain E.C. Kennedy. She mounted eight six-inch guns and two three-inch anti-aircraft guns. *Rawalpindi* was sighted by the *Scharnhorst* lookouts at 4.07 p.m. When the *Scharnhorst* ordered her to halt, Captain Kennedy ignored the demand and immediately signalled the Commander, Home Fleet, his position and that he had sighted "the enemy battle cruiser *Deutschland*", having mistakenly identified *Scharnhorst* as such. At this point, Kennedy tried to reach the safety of a nearby fog bank but was cut off by *Scharnhorst*, which fired a shot across the British vessel's bow. One of Kennedy's lookouts then sighted another ship in the distance, which he took to be part of the British Northern Patrol. Kennedy headed the *Rawalpindi* towards the distant vessel, seeking its support in the situation, only to discover shortly that the other ship was *Gneisenau*.

Altering course again, Kennedy prepared his ship to fight *Scharnhorst*. As he did so, Vizeadmiral Marschall ordered him to abandon ship. Kennedy responded with his six-inch guns and tried to shield his ship in smoke. The distance between the two enemies was shortening rapidly, and when it fell to less than 8,000 yards, *Scharnhorst* began firing on *Rawalpindi*. Except for Captain Kennedy, a Chief Petty Officer, and one sailor, everyone on the bridge of the British vessel was killed by the first German salvo. Now *Rawalpindi* was receiving fire from the distant *Gneisenau* as well. The German warships were scoring dramatic hits on the merchant cruiser, starting immense fires too furious to contain and disabling many of her guns and much of her power supply. Then, as Kennedy led a party of two ratings aft in an effort to put their smoke generator back into action, a shell burst nearby, killing all three of them.

Out of control and out of the fight, the flaming hulk of *Rawalpindi* began to sink. In eight minutes of firing, *Scharnhorst* and *Gneisenau* had put 141 heavy shells into and near the British vessel, and ceased their firing. *Rawalpindi* exploded at 5.30 p.m. Vizeadmiral Marschall gave the order to pick up survivors, a humane act that jeopardized his battleships which were brightly illuminated by the burning wreck of his target. At 7.14 p.m., he halted the rescue operation. The two German warships left the scene, carrying 27 survivors from *Rawalpindi*.

After their successful raiding mission, *Scharnhorst* and *Gneisenau* sailed back to Brest for repairs. This suited the British, who made plans to keep them bottled up in the French port. Over the next the controls which were becoming more and more sluggish as he tried circling to evade harassing enemy fighters. He attempted to align on the *Prinz Eugen* to drop his torpedo, but the German warship manoeuvred violently and Kingsmill's torpedo narrowly missed astern of the vessel. The Swordfish was then hit again, its wings severely damaged. Kingsmill fought to keep the plane from stalling before he could ditch it in the sea. That accomplished, the pilot crawled back along the fuselage and assisted his crew from the sinking aircraft. Their small dinghy had been damaged by the gunfire and was useless. But, within ten minutes, they were rescued by an RAF motor torpedo boat. All of the 825 Squadron Swordfish were shot down that day. For his part in the action, Kingsmill was awarded the Distinguished Service Order.

left: The *Scharnhorst* conducting firing exercises.

from left to right: HMS *Jamaica*, HMS *Formidable*, HMS *King George V*, HMS *Anson*, and HMS *Duke of York*.

several months the RAF conducted a series of air raids on the German battleships at Brest, causing considerable damage and delaying their scheduled return to their assigned duties. In their efforts to destroy *Scharnhorst* and *Gneisenau*, the RAF flew 3,599 bombing sorties to the French port. 2,692 of these sorties completed their attacks, dropping a total of 4,118 tons of bombs on the town, the harbour and the ships. They lost 53 aircraft in the attacks.

On 13 November 1941, German Navy Commander-in-Chief Admiral Raeder tried to persuade Hitler to agree to a series of short strikes by *Scharnhorst* and *Gneisenau* against enemy operations in the Atlantic beginning in February 1942, when the two ships would again be fully ready for sea duty. Hitler was preoccupied with events in Russia and

responded by asking Raeder if he could get the two battleships back to Germany by means of a surprise dash up the English Channel. On Christmas Day the Führer decided that the continuing threat to the battleships in Brest was intolerable and that they were to be brought back to Germany and then re-deployed to Norway. Raeder and the senior German admirals opposed the idea as too risky. Finally, Hitler gave Raeder the choice of either bringing the battleships back to Germany via the Channel, or scrapping them. On 12 January 1942, Raeder accepted the high-risk option, which became known as Operation Cerberus.

The plan called for the two warships, in company with *Prinz Eugen*, to leave Brest at night and, hopefully, surprise the British by passing through the Dover Narrows in daylight; the Germans believing that the British would expect the passage

to occur in darkness. With *Scharnhorst* in the lead, the vessels, under the command of Vizeadmiral Otto Ciliax, left Brest at 10.25 p.m. on 11 February, after yet another raid on the harbour by the RAF with no appreciable result. They had slipped out of port and into open water undetected.

At high speed the three warships headed past the Somme estuary towards the Channel narrows, under the protective cover of a Luftwaffe escort. It was then that an RAF fighter patrol spotted the German aircraft and the warships they were guarding. The patrol reported the sighting and the position. At midday, the German vessels passed Cap Gris Nez, within sight of British shore-based gun batteries, which fired on but failed to hit the warships. In the next few hours the German ships came under attack by Fleet Air Arm Swordfish biplanes out of RAF Manston in Kent, destroyers from Harwich, RAF Beauforts and motor torpedo boats, all to no avail.

As the vessels passed north of Ostend, through the coastal shipping lanes that had been heavily mined by the Royal Air Force, *Scharnhorst* struck and detonated one of the magnetic mines, causing some damage and slowing her temporarily. But she was soon able to make 25 knots again. Ciliax was running his charges off the Dutch coast and the weather was deteriorating. The RAF then sent nearly 400 bomber sorties against the German warships. Only ten per cent of them even located their targets and none hit them. In the futile attacks, the RAF lost three Wellingtons, three Beauforts, nine Hampdens, two Blenheims, two Hudsons, three Whirlwinds, four Spitfires and six Hurricanes. The Royal Navy lost six Swordfish.

The warships continued eastward and, off the island of Terschelling, both *Scharnhorst* and *Gneisenau* struck mines. *Scharnhorst* lost most of her power and shipped more than a thousand tons of water. She struggled to continue, but finally made port in Wilhelmshaven. *Gneisenau* and *Prinz Eugen* arrived safely in the River Elbe early in the morning of 13 February. The Germans had

succeeded in executing their Channel Dash; Britain was embarrassed, but neither *Scharnhorst* nor *Gneisenau* would ever reach the Atlantic again.

Badly damaged by RAF bombs in a raid on Kiel in February 1942, *Gneisenau* would see no further action in World War II. She was moved to Götenhafen to be rearmed with fifteen-inch guns, but that work was halted in January 1943. On 27 March 1945, *Gneisenau* was scuttled for use as a blockship at Götenhafen, and would be broken up for scrap between 1947 and 1951.

By November 1943, Germany's war with Russia was going badly for the Reich and pressure was put on the German Navy to disrupt and destroy the Allied supply convoys to Murmansk. For the winter of 1943-44, *Scharnhorst* moved to Norway tasked with countering any attempted Allied landing in Norway, Jutland or northern Finland, attacking Allied arctic convoys, mining and/or bombarding enemy routes and bases, and, by her presence, tying up enemy warships.

On 18 December 1943, the German Navy,

left: *Gneisenau*, sister ship of the *Scharnhorst*, manoeuvres in a mild swell, below: Admiral of the Fleet Sir Henry Leach, Royal Navy Ret.

below: HMS *Duke of York* firing her big guns in rough seas off Scapa Flow.

monitoring British radio traffic, learned that a major new convoy was being readied for the run to Murmansk. It was convoy JW 55B, consisting of nineteen merchant ships due to leave Loch Awe, Scotland on 20 December. *Scharnhorst* was made ready for sea and departed Altafiord together with five destroyers on the evening of Christmas Day. The small force, under the command of Vizeadmiral Erich Bey, departed in a fearsome gale and sub-zero temperature.

Sailing with the convoy and providing protection were two British warship groups: Force 1 made up of the cruisers *Belfast*, *Sheffield* and *Norfolk*, and Force 2, under the command of Admiral Sir Bruce Fraser, consisting of the battleship *Duke of York* and the cruiser *Jamaica*. Fraser knew, via Ultra decrypts, that the German warships were under way. The British and German forces were sailing into a force 8 gale, in extremely heavy seas. The weather was worsening, with increasing sleet and snow. Through the night both forces continued towards Bear Island and in the early morning of the 26th, *Scharnhorst*'s destroyer escort spread out in search of the convoy. The two enemy forces approached each other, and a radar operator in *Belfast* had the first contact with *Scharnhorst* at 8.40 a.m. The battleship was then just 30 miles south of the convoy and closing rapidly. At 9.30 a.m., *Norfolk* opened fire, landing two shells on *Scharnhorst* and destroying her main radar. Vizeadmiral Bey ordered the battleship on a new course to the south, easily outdistancing the British cruisers giving chase. After 25 minutes Bey again changed course, heading *Scharnhorst* northeast towards the convoy. The British cruisers also altered course in order to position themselves between *Scharnhorst* and the convoy they were shepherding. They had lost radar contact with the German battleship, but by noon, *Belfast* regained it. In a few

"War involves in its progress such a train of unforseen and unsupposed circumstances that no human wisdom can calculate the end. It has but one thing certain, and that is to increase taxes."
– Thomas Paine

At 4 p.m. on 8 June 1940, lookouts of the German battleship *Scharnhorst* sighted the British aircraft carrier HMS *Glorious*, which was being escorted off Norway by two Royal Navy destroyers. *Glorious* had no air reconnaissance patrols airborne at the time and was caught by surprise when the enemy battleships arrived. Gunners of *Scharnhorst* began firing at *Glorious* at 4.32 p.m. from a distance of 28,500 yards. Six minutes later a shell from the battleship struck *Glorious*, starting a large fire on the flight deck. At 4.42 p.m., the sister ship of *Scharnhorst, Gneisenau* opened fire. One of her shells hit the carrier's bridge, killing the captain and most of the personnel there. At 4.56 p.m., a smokescreen from the escorting British destroyers caused the two German battleships to cease firing. One of the destroyers, HMS *Ardent*, then launched a series of eight torpedoes but made no hits on the German warships, which then began firing on *Ardent*. They quickly sank the destroyer. The battleships then resumed firing on *Glorious* and hit her in the centre engine room. At 5.30 p.m., the destroyer HMS *Acasta* launched a torpedo which struck *Scharnhorst*, tearing a massive hole in her hull and causing her to take in 2,500 tons of seawater. Her after main gun turret was put out of action as well, and 48 of her crew were killed. The British aircraft carrier was severely

moments, the enemies were in sight of each other and Bey again tried to take *Scharnhorst* away from a new confrontation with the cruisers which pursued her. Sporadic gunfire was soon being exchanged and in the action, *Norfolk* lost her radar and one of her turrets. Both *Scharnhorst* and *Sheffield* received hits but only minor damage resulted. Now, Bey cut off the exchange and turned *Scharnhorst* away and back at high speed towards the safety of Altafiord. He could not know that Admiral Fraser was bringing British Force 2 in the direction of the fiord to cut off the German battleship.

It was late afternoon and quite dark when the two capital ships came within sight of each other. In an early exchange of fire, one of the forward turrets of *Scharnhorst* was put out of action, but the other gunners of the German battleship were soon able to straddle *Duke of York* with their shells. The British battleship replied with several shots that landed on *Scharnhorst*. A hit pierced her armour belt and exploded in the Number One boiler room, causing a partial loss of power to her main turbines. *Scharnhorst* was no longer able to summon the great speed which had enabled her to outrun her adversaries. The range between her and the enemy warships began to shrink. The great German warship was now prey to both British forces which were closing on her. She was soon struck by four torpedoes, on both sides of her hull. All of the British warships pressed their attacks on the German battleship and she received a total of fourteen torpedoes in the action. Fires raged in her, lighting up the arctic night. Her ordeal finally ended when horrific flashes signalled the explosions of her ammunition magazines at 7.45 p.m.

The future Royal Navy Admiral of the Fleet Sir Henry Leach was a young Sub-Lieutenant assigned to the spotting plot in the fourteen-inch gun transmitting station of HMS *Duke of York*. He recalls the action against *Scharnhorst*: "Such was the strength of the Germans, based off Norway, and

such was their ability to interfere with Russian convoys, that the convoys were ceased. The game simply wasn't worth the candle because the losses were too great, particularly during the summer months. In those waters in winter it's always dark and in summer it's always light. In winter you got a sort of twilight between about midday and three in the afternoon; in summer you didn't get any twilight at all. The Russians squealed a bit about this [stopping the convoys], of course, and it was decided, partly to pacify the Russians and partly to draw out the *Scharnhorst* which posed a great threat to the convoys, to restart the convoys, but under a heavy, heavy escort.

"The *Belfast* and other ships were covering a southbound convoy, and the *Duke of York* and the *Jamaica*, a six-inch cruiser, were standing in the deep field, broadly covering three convoys. It was around Christmas Eve 1943. A signal came from Admiral Burnett, who was commanding the second cruiser squadron in the *Belfast*, that the southbound convoy had been attacked by the *Scharnhorst*.

"The weather was absolutely foul. *Scharnhorst* had made a pass at that convoy, and was beaten off by the *Belfast* and another cruiser, so at least we knew then that the *Scharnhorst* had left her shelter and was at sea. Now, Bruce Fraser in the *Duke of York*, the C-in-C, had to decide what the German battleship would do. Would she try to break out into the Atlantic as the *Bismarck* had done, or would she, once the convoy had passed and she had done little damage to it, return to her Norwegian base? In fact, *Scharnhorst* made a second attack on the southbound convoy and was again beaten off. Bruce Fraser guessed that, under the weather conditions at the time, she would probably return to base in Norway and he set course accordingly.

"On Christmas Day, we increased speed, so far as we could in the weather at the time. The *King George V* class were 'wet ships'. They had a fairly low freeboard and going into a heavy sea, they kicked it right up, and the forward turret was virtually under water. They were fine ships, but they were wet.

"In the evening of Christmas Day, we went to action stations. The policy in those days, and it was a very sensible one, was that you went to action stations when it got dark, if you were in a particular threat area, and all hands slept, insofar as they could, at their action stations. Because it was the very early days of radar and it was not at all reliable; this meant that if you got jumped in the middle of the night, instead of the inevitable confusion of going to action stations once the enemy had been detected, you were there already and all you had to do was roll over and do your stuff. So, everybody went to action stations and then the not inconsiderable problem was, how do you feed them? In those days, you had individual messing as opposed to cafeteria messing, which didn't come for decades after that. The quality of food was pretty dreadful because they had to cart it long distances in unheated containers, so it was cold and greasy and generally pretty unpleasant. And in those weather conditions everybody was feeling seasick anyway because even a ship that size was bucketing around.

"It wasn't until late afternoon of the day after Christmas when word was broadcast that the *Scharnhorst* had been driven off from the convoy and was last detected steaming south, more or less straight towards us.

"We were all cold and hungry and tired, but everybody wanted to get into this action and clobber the enemy. Fraser's plan was that, unless the enemy opened fire first, we would hold our fire until the range was 12,000 yards, because radar was uncertain and so was night action; you depended on star shells for illuminating the target and that sort of thing. Sitting there in my rather wet suit in the forward part of A turret, I could watch the range counter ticking down and ticking down until [it showed] 12,000 yards, and at 12,000 yards the five-two-fives opened fire with star shell and the fourteen-inch also opened up. When the star shells burst on the far side of the *Scharnhorst* she was jumped. She simply didn't know that we were there.

She was heading straight for us. Her turrets were trained fore and aft and she wasn't ready.

"As soon as the star shell burst, she turned away. She was capable of greater speed than the *Duke of York* and she turned, really, to make her base back in Norway. We altered course to follow her. The weather conditions were foul. We fired a number of salvoes but as the distance between us increased to 20,000 yards or so, our firing was checked. I can't tell you how galling that was, that after all this effort, and having caught her with her trousers down, she was going to escape into the night. And there was nothing we could do about it. The destroyers were dispatched to carry out a torpedo attack, but again, under those weather conditions, they could hardly go faster than the *Duke of York*.

"Then, quite suddenly, I think around eight o'clock, the change of range ceased and the range counters started to click down again. The range was closing. This, I think was due to a hit. *Scharnhorst* had had to reduce speed enabling the destroyers and the *Duke of York* to catch up, and we opened fire again as soon as we got within effective range. Then the end came quite quickly. The destroyers scored torpedo hits. We closed right in to something like 2,000 yards and it was a dreadful sight. *Scharnhorst* was on fire from end to end. People were silhouetted against the fire, jumping over the side into the water. It was reckoned then that if you were in that cold water for more than three minutes, you didn't survive. And then she sank, and that was that.

"We were all very tired and I can remember feeling 'thank God that's over and we won, she's gone' . . . it was success and we had achieved a mega-victory, but tempered by a sadness that a very fine ship had gone to the bottom. I think that there were about 33 survivors who were picked up by the destroyers and transferred to us."

Scharnhorst sank, taking 1,803 of her crew with her and ending the Battle of the North Cape. Of Germany's great battleships, only *Tirpitz* remained.

damaged in the continuing attack and, at 6.10 p.m., she capsized and sank. Ten minutes later, the same fate befell *Acasta*. More than 1,500 Royal Navy sailors died in this action.

FAST AND LAST

THE FOUR FAST BATTLESHIPS of the *Iowa* class are the last battleships in the world. They are BB-61, the USS *Iowa*, BB-62, the USS *New Jersey*, BB-63, the USS *Missouri,* and BB-64, the USS *Wisconsin*. The last of the last is the *Missouri*. While construction of *Wisconsin* began later than that of *Missouri*, and she had a higher hull number, *Missouri* was, in fact, the world's last battleship to be completed, serve and survive.

The idea behind the "fast battleship" stems from a desire among the great naval powers to combine the best characteristics of their battleships and their battle cruisers in order to develop a warship with great speed, firepower and armoured protection. In general, battle cruisers had been faster than battleships, but had lighter armour protection and thus greater vulnerability to enemy attack. As major improvements in gun calibre, ballistic efficiency and fire control increased the fighting range of the battleship, the battle cruiser's speed advantage over her big sister was nullified.

Near the end of the 1920s, the U.S. Navy and the

U.S. Bureau of Construction and Repair were involved in design studies for a new battleship. They avidly followed the progress of the new British *Rodney* class battleships, *Rodney* and *Nelson*, which were expected to establish a new standard for capital ships to come.

Following the end of World War I, developing trade interests in the Pacific caused the United States to concentrate much of her warship fleet on the U.S. west coast for the protection of those interests and American possessions. By 1935, it was clear to U.S. naval strategists that the nation's next war would be with Japan. Japanese naval planners, meanwhile, were bridling under the terms of the 1922 Washington Naval Treaty, which they perceived as a conspiracy to confine them to the role of a secondary naval power. They reacted by starting a major programme of warship modernization and radical reconstruction to develop the most formidable naval fighting force possible. One example of that effort was the refitting of their 1911-1913 *Kongo* class battle cruisers, which

The happiest hour a sailor sees / Is when he's down At an inland town, / With his Nancy on his knees, yo ho! And his arm around her waist!
— from *The Mikado* by W. S. Gilbert

below: The USS *Iowa*, BB-61, a broadside view in New York Navy Yard, July 1943

Writing in the U.S. Naval Institute magazine *Proceedings* about handling a battleship, Lt. Scott Robinson observed that the ship is conned from the 0-4 bridge level, where space is cramped and visibility astern limited. He notes that, when the main battery guns are fired, the windows on the bridge are rolled down, as they could not withstand the blast, and a "small gale" from the forward motion of the ship disrupts the deck watch's paperwork. When entering or leaving port, a separate team higher up, on the 0-8 level, controls the ship, for better visibility of the pier and other vessels or structures. Lt. Robinson noted that many surface warfare officers on the Iowa class battleships have had the opportunity to drive their magnificent ships, and he concluded: ". . . the battleship can be handled as well as any greyhound in the fleet. She offers the experienced conning officer an appreciation for large ship handling and the novice a forgiving platform on which to learn. The ship is powerful, graceful, and fun to drive. In many years of service the Iowa class battleships have indeed proven themselves one of the finest handling of all ships."

right: The USS *Iowa* off Korea firing her sixteen-inch guns at shore positions in 1950.

they twice modified on a large scale to re-create them as full-fledged battleships capable of 30.5 knots.

By the mid-1930s, U.S. intelligence was indicating that Japan was focused on developing an entirely new class of super battleship, posing an unacceptable level of threat to America's interests and her navy. In 1935, an intensive U.S. effort led to development and approval of designs for the new *North Carolina* class, a 37,000-ton battleship armed with nine sixteen-inch guns in three turrets and capable of a 28-knot speed. In armament she was comparable to the *Rodney* class battleships of the Royal Navy. But *North Carolina* had been planned with fourteen-inch guns and, when she was later up-rated to larger main weapons, the U.S. Chief of Naval Operations argued that her original armour left her under-protected and he opposed an allocation for two further *North Carolina* class warships in 1937. Instead, another new class of battleships was introduced that year. The *South Dakota* class featured a clever re-arrangement of the main spaces for machinery, operational plotting and ammunition magazines, in a shorter hull, together with a new armour layout, allowing considerable weight savings. These improvements on the *North Carolina* design, coupled with an additional 9,000 shaft horsepower, resulted in a highly successful, better protected battleship of roughly the same performance characteristics as the *North Carolina*s. Many aspects of the *South Dakota* design, in particular the approach to armour protection, were to be highly influential in the final fast battleship class.

The London Naval Conference of 1935, from which the Japanese had formally withdrawn, marked the point when they fully implemented *Yamato*, the battleship construction programme they had been planning since 1930. This fantastic new class capital ship would dwarf all existing, building, and planned battleships. At 69,500 tons,

1139-40
U.S.S NEW JERSEY (BB-62)
LAYING KEEL
NAVY YARD PHILA. PA.

above: Laying the keel of the USS *New Jersey, BB-62*, at the Philadelphia Navy Yard on 16 September 1940. right: An October 1945 photo of USS *Missouri* crewmen stripping paint from the sixteen-inch guns of their ship while returning to the Pacific coast of the United States.

Yamato was to be armed with nine eighteen-inch guns and was capable of 27 knots. The Japanese intended building seven of these giants—by far the largest and most powerful capital ships ever conceived and realized. Of the seven planned, four *Yamato* class vessels were laid down and, of these, two were actually completed—*Yamato* and *Musashi*. The *Yamato* programme proceeded at high-priority pace, and under the strictest security precautions. The vessels themselves were shielded from observation by enormous tarpaulins, and what little the U.S. Navy knew about *Yamato* was based largely on speculation. Accurate reports on characteristics and progress of the Japanese super ship from spies, diplomatic attachés, and analysis of Japanese radio traffic, were minimal. But American Navy speculation about *Yamato* was correct, though not actually proven so until the end of World War II.

It would seem that the members of the U.S. General Board and the Secretary of the Navy did not have access to any significant intelligence about the tonnage, gun calibre or capabilites of *Yamato* in 1938, or did not believe the reports they did receive. Their evaluation of "slow" and "fast" battleship studies did not result in a recommendation for a design that would achieve parity with what the U.S. Navy believed *Yamato* to be.

In October 1937, a special board was established to advise the U.S. Secretary of the Navy on the design, armament and construction of new battleships. Its analysis of the fast battleship studies caused the members to conclude that a new capital ship of 45,000 tons with a speed of 33 knots was feasible based on the *South Dakota* design. After various parallel studies were completed, the Bureau of Construction and Repair developed final requirements for the new American fast battleship and on 2 June 1938 submitted the preliminary design for a vessel designated hull number BB-61, the first ship of the *Iowa* class. The four sister ships of the new class would each be armed with nine sixteen-inch guns able to fire a 2,700-pound armour-piercing projectile 42,500 yards. Each would be 887 feet long with a beam of 108 feet and a draught of 36 feet. Eight Babcock & Wilcox boilers powered four General Electric turbine shafts which could make a speed of 32.5 knots. The standard displacement was 48,110 tons; fully loaded it was 57,540 tons. In addition to their main guns, the *Iowa* battleships went to war initially with twenty five-inch guns, 80 40mm guns, 49 20mm guns (except for the USS *Iowa*, which carried 60 40mm and 60 20mm guns) and three spotter aircraft. The initial crew complement was 1,921.

In the treaty resulting from a 1936 London naval arms limitation conference, the attending nations had agreed an "escalator clause" which would raise the imposed limit on capital ship gun calibre, and on displacement from 35,000 to 45,000 tons. The clause could be invoked by any of the naval powers attending, to match an increase by any nonparticipating nation. The United States had first invoked the escalator clause in mid-1937, increasing the gun calibre for future battleship construction to sixteen inches, to counter the Japanese. In 1938, the United States, Britain and France agreed to invoke the clause to raise the tonnage limit to 45,000, sparked by rumours and their limited information about Japanese battleship projects. Immediately thereafter, intensive design activity on the U.S. Navy's *Iowa* class of battleships began.

Three *Iowa* class vessels were planned initially, and a fourth was added to provide a back-up battleship which was to be deployed when any one of the other three *Iowa*s was unavailable for duty. The fourth *Iowa* type could also be used in the Atlantic, should it be required there. Funding for two further *Iowa* class battleships was included in the 1940 U.S. budget passed by the Congress. They were to be BB-65, the USS *Illinois*, and BB-66, the USS *Kentucky*. Ultimately, the *Illinois* would be cancelled in 1945. *Kentucky* was launched, went through several redesigns in the 1940s and 1950s to convert her into a missile-launching battleship, and was finally scrapped in 1958.

The *Iowa*s served through much of the final two years of World War II in the Pacific as part of the Fast Carrier Task Forces. When they were first deployed, their primary assignments included chasing and engaging commerce raiders, acting as commerce raiders themselves, engaging the Japanese *Kongo* class battlecruisers, and leading special strike forces.

IOWA CLASS BATTLESHIPS IN WORLD WAR II
USS *Iowa*

On 27 August 1943, the *Iowa* was sent to Argentia Bay, Newfoundland, to guard against the eventual breakout of the German battleship *Tirpitz*. She then carried President Roosevelt to Cairo and Tehran for war conferences with Prime Minister Churchill and Premier Stalin. On 2 January 1944,

BB-61 sailed to the Pacific as flagship of Battleship Division 7 in the Marshall Islands campaign. At the end of January she screened the aircraft carriers of Task Force 58 in air strikes on Kwajalein, Truk and Eniwetok Islands. In February, she supported carrier air strikes against Saipan, Tinian, Guam and Rota. Then, on 18 March, while bombarding Mili Atoll in the Marshall Islands, she was struck by two Japanese shells, sustaining only minor damage. In April, she operated in support of U.S. landings at Hollandia in New Guinea, followed by another screening of a carrier strike at Truk.

On 1 May, the *Iowa* bombarded the island of Ponape in the Carolines and on 13-14 June, she was sent to bombard Saipan and Tinian in the Marianas, going on to take part in the Battle of the Philippine Sea. In August, while part of Task Group 38, *Iowa* took part in strikes against Iwo Jima and Chichijima, followed by landings at Peleliu in September.

Still with TG38 on 10 October, *Iowa* supported

The bread gets better as the milk gets worse. Among food stores carried on board the *Missouri* in preparation for a cruise, a supply of fresh bread and milk was always welcome. During the initial weeks at sea, this stock was rapidly depleted and fresh milk was soon replaced with a longer-lasting substitute. This was the cue for the ship's bakery to commence full operations and soon the ship was filled with the unmistakable scent of freshly baking pies, biscuits and battleship bread.

below: Broadway in the USS *Missouri*, BB-63, now on public view in Pearl Harbor, Hawaii, right: The Truman chow line in *Missouri*, named for the former U.S. president, below right: In a main gun battery plotting room.

USS Missouri
17 August 1945
Dear Mom and Dad,
It's hard to believe, isn't it? A few days ago we were at war without much prospect of it finishing very soon. Now it's over, all except the occupation.

On the day the official word was received, the Missouri, with the other ships of Task Force 38, was in position for an air strike on Tokyo. The date, for us out here, was the 15th of August. When the message came, we already had air strikes on the way. Word was flashed to them to return and, after we gathered them all in, we retired to collect our wits and await any orders for our next move.

At eleven o'clock word went out to celebrate the occasion by breaking [out] the battle flags. All the ships blew their whistles and sirens in honor of this great occasion. We tooted our whistle with much gusto and the Mighty Missouri added her bit by getting the whistle stuck and continuing to toot until the engineers could get the steam secured and make minor repair.

That about constituted our celebration. We continued in an alert status because, although the war was over, we weren't really sure that the Japanese knew it.

Our last replenishment

period was spent in Leyte Gulf, Philippine Islands, where we found all our old friends, the tenders and supply ships from Ulithi Atoll.

After our replenishment we went to sea and proceeded directly to strike at Tokyo. From there we went to the north and struck Hokkaido and made the Muroran bombardment, that I wrote about before. From then till the end of the war we have made strikes all along the Japanese coast, so many that they are hard to remember.

Our bombardment group made a night bombardment on the Hitachi Arms Factory, Engineering Works and Copper Refinery near Minato on the east coast of Honshu. This was interesting because it was done on a night so black and in weather so bad that planes could not be used to observe the fall of shot. We didn't have any idea of the damage done until it was photographed by planes the next day and they sent us the pictures. To our surprise and gratification, we found that the damage was extensive and the targets were well covered. It is amazing what can be done with modern war equipment. We could hardly even see the next ship in column, much less the target which was fifteen miles away.

We are all proud that we have been able to help win this war. Let us all hope that this will be the last time that a war has to be won. Many of our friends have died with that hope. That hope has carried us through many a grinding, grueling day. Let

carrier air strikes on Formosa and the Ryuku Islands; she then went on to support strikes against Luzon in preparation for the Leyte Gulf landings of 20 October. The namesake of her warship class then returned to San Francisco for a refit, remaining there until March 1945.

On 15 April, *Iowa* arrived in the Okinawa area where she participated in screening the fast carriers in their support of U.S. Army operations on the island. U.S. forces were approaching the Japanese home islands at this point, and the *Iowa* was needed to cover carrier strikes against the southern mainland island of Kyushu between 25 May and 13 June. Thereafter, until the end of the war two months later, *Iowa* was engaged in the bombardment of Hitachi, Hokkaido and Muroran. She was present in Tokyo Bay on 2 September for the official surrender ceremony which took place on her sister ship, the USS *Missouri*.

USS *New Jersey*

The second battleship of the *Iowa* class was launched exactly one year after the Japanese attack on Pearl Harbor. The USS *New Jersey* went to war in January 1944, meeting her sister ship, USS *Iowa*, as part of Battleship Division 7 on 22 January. Her initial action came in a screening operation with Task Group 58 as the carriers *Bunker Hill*, *Cowpens* and *Monterey* launched air strikes against Eniwetok and Kwajalein. BB-62 was serving as flagship of Task Group 50 on 17-18 February, when her crew first fired her main guns at the enemy, engaging two Japanese destroyers and two other vessels. She sank a trawler that day. *New Jersey* remained with TG50 until April, participating in the bombardment of Mili and covering air strikes against the Palau Islands. She covered the landings at Hollandia in April and joined six other American battleships bombarding Ponape that month. In June, *New Jersey* took part in the bombardment of Saipan

and Tinian. She sailed into Pearl Harbor on 9 August, where she became flagship of the U.S. 3rd Fleet. She then went to Ulithi, operating from that Pacific fleet anchorage. For nearly a month, from 28 August, *New Jersey* worked, covering carrier air strikes against islands in the Philippines. During the battle for Leyte, she operated with a carrier group and joined TG38 in December in attacks on the island of Luzon. She spent the next month screening carrier air strikes against targets in Indo-China, Formosa, Luzon and Okinawa, and operated in the attacks on Iwo Jima from February through April and supported the landings on Okinawa. By early May, *New Jersey* was back in the States at Puget Sound Navy Yard for refit, which was completed at the end of June. She bombarded Wake Island on her way back to the western Pacific, arriving at Guam on 9 August, and became flagship of the U.S. 5th Fleet as the war ended.

Seaman First Class Tony Iacono: "I was on the *New Jersey* from 1943, before its commissioning, until 1946. I left it in Tokyo Bay when we were part of the occupation forces. Three years on one ship. We travelled to most of the Japanese-held islands during World War II and we took them all back, one by one. We were going into the Philippine Sea in June 1944. The whole fleet had gotten through the San Bernardino Straits in the dead of night, undetected. Then, we ran into a huge typhoon which we were in for six days and nights. We were going down to Hollandia to cover some operation. When we got down there, the Japanese started dropping high-altitude flares on us. You could literally read a newspaper on the deck at midnight. That's how bright it was.

"When we came back through the Philippine Sea, the Japanese were waiting for us with their Kamikazes, getting ready to sink us, which they couldn't do. We were shooting 20s and 40s and five-inch rounds at them. Then we got into the second Battle of the Philippine Sea, the Marianas

us pray that it carries those charged with formulating and preserving the peace to a successful accomplishment of their task.

Goodbye, now, and I hope to see you soon.
Love,
Bob
— a letter from Robert V. Shultz to his parents

above left: The first modern USS *New Jersey*, BB-16, in a camouflage paint scheme, 1918.
below left: Readying the USS *Iowa*, BB-61, for launching at the New York Navy Yard in 1942.

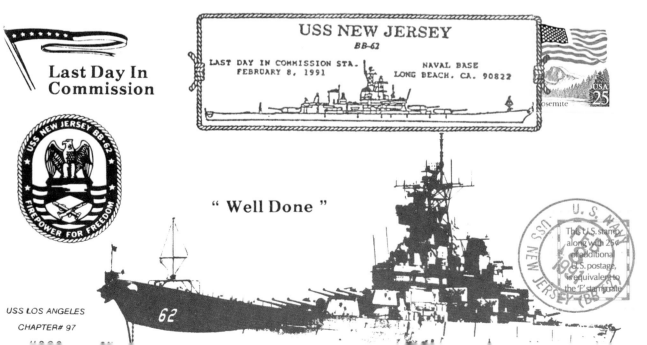

Last Day In
Commission

USS NEW JERSEY BB 62

FIREPOWER FOR FREEDOM

USS NEW JERSEY
BB-62

LAST DAY IN COMMISSION STA.
FEBRUARY 8, 1991

NAVAL BASE
LONG BEACH, CA. 90822

USA 25

Yosemite

" Well Done "

U.S. NAVY
USS
NEW JERSEY (BB

This U.S. stamp,
along with 25¢
of additional
U.S. postage,
is equivalent to
the 'F' stamp rate

USS LOS ANGELES
CHAPTER# 97

62

Turkeyshoot. After that, the Japanese Navy wasn't worth a nickel. They were devastated.

"The *New Jersey* was never hit by enemy fire. We might have got some shrapnel on the deck, but we never took an enemy hit of any sort. We did take a hit from one of our own ships. We were in port, in Palau, I think. It was a late Sunday afternoon and the guys were watching the movie on the fantail. The ships were coming in from target practice, shooting at sleeves. Some guy was on the first deck under the main deck taking a shower and a projectile came through the deck and cut off his leg. That was the only casualty we had on that ship while I was on it.

"It was near the end. We still had Iwo Jima and Okinawa to go, and Okinawa was holy hell. We pounded that island for a week . . . all the wagons . . . the *Iowa*, the *New Jersey*, the *Wisconsin*, the *Missouri*, the *North Dakota*, the *Washington*. We went around that island, around the clock, seven days. Every five minutes there was a beep and a salvo. Then, when we put troops on the shore there, all hell broke loose. The Japanese weren't about to give up that island without a fight. And the Kamikazes came out. They were out in full bloom. Every time we saw a little hole in the cloud, a plane would come out of it, straight down. That first or second day, we saved the *Bunker Hill* from Kamikazes three times. Then the Navy Department finally said, 'You can't keep up with the fleet. You're gonna have to go back.' They sent us back to Pearl with a cruiser and two destroyers, and then on to Bremerton. And there was the *Bunker Hill*, looking like a can-opener had hit it. It had taken several hits after we left Okinawa. A ferocious battle. The Navy took more casualties there than anybody."

In the preface to his excellent illustrated history, *Battleship New Jersey*, Commander Paul Stillwell, USNR, wrote: "To go to sea in the USS New Jersey . . . is to have the sense that she has managed to transcend the normal limitations of time. This feeling probably becomes most evident at night as she glides through the dark sea, the water making a swishing sound as it travels from bow to stern and leaves a luminescent wake beneath the starlit sky. With the coming of night, the eyes no longer focus on the details which command attention during daytime. Instead, the imagination conjures thousands of nights past when this majestic giant has also moved beneath these same stars. The darkness obscures the changes which have been wrought in order to make her again a potent weapon, as she was when she first took to the sea two generations ago . . .

"During the nocturnal walk about the forecastle comes the realization that there is much more to the ship than steel, guns, and missiles. Hundreds of Navy men breathe life and purpose into her inanimate elements. It is they who give her a soul and they who inherit the legacy from thousands of *New Jersey* men who have gone before."

USS *Wisconsin*

The *Wisconsin* reached the Pacific Fleet at Ulithi on 9 December 1944, following a successful work-up in the Caribbean that summer. As part of the 3rd Fleet, BB-64 participated in the attacks on Luzon in the Philippines in late December and then covered the fast carrier strikes on the Pescadores and Formosa. Operating with the 5th Fleet in February 1945, *Wisconsin* bombarded targets near Tokyo on the 16th, sailing from there to Iwo Jima to help in the bombardment prior to the landings on the 19th. From Iwo she went to the Japanese main island of Honshu to attack targets there. She took part in the Okinawa campaign with TF58 and then struck at targets near Kobe and Kure, before returning to continue a bombardment of Okinawa which lasted into May. She returned to Leyte for repairs and replenishment on 18 June, after which her final assignment of the war took her back to the Japanese home islands in support of further

At the end of the battle for Okinawa in June 1945, 12,520 Americans and 110,000 Japanese had been killed in the 81-day campaign.

above left: Campaign decorations of the USS *Missouri*, far left: A commemorative envelope issued on the last day in commission of the USS *New Jersey* in 1991, left: An instrument on the open bridge of the *Missouri*, above: The spotter helicopter of the *Missouri* during the Korean War, 1951.

"In June 1949 we made a midshipman cruise to Portsmouth, England. We were quite shorthanded in the Radar Division, way under normal and wartime standards. The trip up the English Channel was in very heavy fog. There were more than 1,300 hazards to navigation in the Channel at that time, most of them sunken vessels. On my watch in CIC [Combat Information Center], I rotated the operating dead-reckoning tracer (DRT), which was a large glass-topped table with a small 'bug device' under the glass. A chart of the Channel was placed on top of the glass and then covered with a sheet of tracing paper. The scale of the chart was dialed into the DRT machine, making the bug emulate the movements of the ship. We could, therefore, follow the progress of the ship up the Channel. As a precaution, we also double-checked our changing position by taking radar ranges and bearings. I recall that we stood a very long watch, more than twelve hours. When we were picked up by English tugs, the skipper called down and gave us a 'Well done!' He also informed us that the mess cooks had steak and eggs ready for us. H.P. Smith looked after his crew. We really enjoyed our stay in Portsmouth. We invited the local British naval personnel aboard for lunch and dinner, had children aboard and regular visits by the citizenry, and we were given a guided tour of HMS *Victory*, which was really appreciated by the crew."
– Ted Pederson, USS *Missouri*

carrier air strikes which continued until the end of the conflict in mid-August.

USS *Missouri*

The last of the breed of fighting ships, the battleship *Missouri*, spent the second half of 1944 in the Atlantic working up in her sea trials. Nineteen-year-old Margaret Truman, daughter of the then United States Vice President Harry S. Truman, who was from Missouri, had broken the traditional champagne bottle over the bow of BB-63 at the launching ceremony on 29 January. The *Missouri* became the fleet flagship of Vice Admiral Marc Mitscher at San Francisco and sailed to the western Pacific fleet anchorage at Ulithi in the Carolines, arriving there on 13 January 1945. Her first war assignment was as a part of Mitscher's Fast Carrier Task Force 58 in strikes against Tokyo and Yokohama on 16 and 17 February, respectively. She then supported the landings on Iwo Jima, returning to Ulithi before sailing to participate in a strike on the Japanese island of Kyushu on 18 March. She joined other American battleships in bombarding Okinawa on 24 March and continued in support of U.S. action there into May. On 7 April, *Missouri* was part of a carrier group that attacked and sank the *Yamato*, the largest battleship ever built.

Eighteen-year-old Seaman First Class Anthony E. Alessandro of Cincinnati, Ohio had been a crew member of the USS *Missouri* for just two months when the Japanese surrender was signed on his ship. He recalls: "*Missouri* sailed within a mile or two of three fleet aircraft carriers, along with destroyers and destroyer escorts. The ship's mission was to guard the fast carriers with plenty of anti-aircraft fire. Some of our fire missions were broadcast to the public back home. This action was announced throughout the *Missouri* over the 1MC (loudspeaker system).

"I was practicing being a first loader on a 40mm quad anti-aircraft gun. I remember thinking that I was really exposed up there by myself. If you have a misfire, you put a bag of sand over the gun breach. I am just a little guy and I didn't know if I could even lift the bag. Every time I put in a four-round clip I prayed, 'God, please don't misfire.'

"There were times when I was so tired, I didn't care what happened. We were out at sea for more than six months at a time and during one ten-month period we traveled over 100,000 nautical miles. We were in an Okinawa typhoon with 70-foot seas. I went out to the deck to take a look; all I saw was water above the mast. One of our kids was washed away and there was only one chance for a destroyer behind us to pick him up. Somehow, they got him and in a few days he was back on board with us. We lost two or three destroyers in that storm."

It was during this period, on 11 April, that BB-63 suffered a hit by a Kamikaze 'Zeke' aircraft which struck her starboard side at just below main deck level and abreast of her number three turret. Tony Alessandro: "He was wave skimming. We hit that plane with everything we had. I don't know how he got through all of that flak." It was mid-afternoon when the Japanese pilot guided his fighter into the *Missouri*'s flank, killing himself and starting a fire that was soon extinguished. No *Missouri* crew members were killed and damage to the ship was relatively minor. The ship's chaplain held a brief funeral service for the Japanese pilot the following day. Some of the crew wanted no part of a ceremony for the enemy. Less than a week later, the ship was again subjected to attack by a number of Kamikaze aircraft. One of them bore in on the battleship with great tenacity as his fighter was being riddled by anti-aircraft fire from *Missouri*. He managed to clip some machinery on the fantail of the big warship before plummeting into the sea in her wake. On impact his aircraft blew apart, sending bits of metal into the ship and wounding two sailors.

On 18 May, the *Missouri* was made Flagship,

previous page: USS *New Jersey* late in World War II, below: On the bridge of *Missouri*, right: Japanese students touring the *Missouri* in October 2002, below: Ship's communications on the bridge of the *Missouri*.

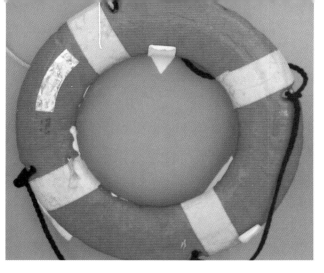

far left: A life ring on *Missouri*, left: A sailor's artwork still visible in Broadway, below left: The dent in the starboard railing of the Missouri where a Kamikaze plane struck on 11 April 1945, below: The commemorative plaque in the deck of *Missouri* marking the location of the Japanese surrender ceremony.

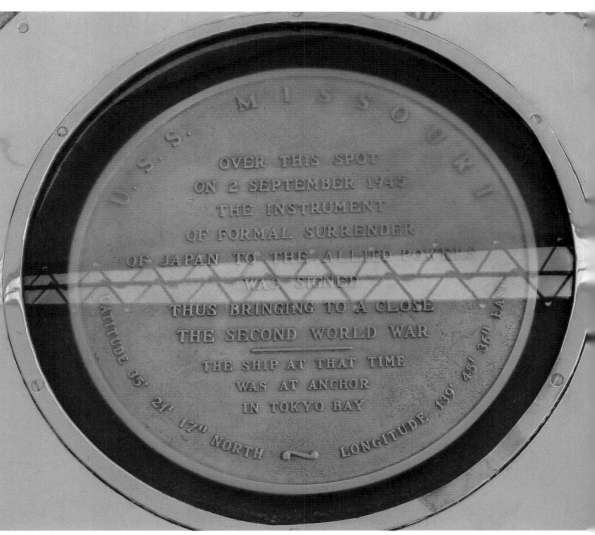

U.S.S. MISSOURI

OVER THIS SPOT
ON 2 SEPTEMBER 1945
THE INSTRUMENT
OF FORMAL SURRENDER
OF JAPAN TO THE ALLIED POWERS
WAS SIGNED

THUS BRINGING TO A CLOSE
THE SECOND WORLD WAR

THE SHIP AT THAT TIME
WAS AT ANCHOR
IN TOKYO BAY

LATITUDE 35° 21' 17" NORTH   LONGITUDE 139° 45' 36" EAST

right: The USS *Wisconsin*, BB-64, on view at the Hampton Roads naval Museum, Norfolk, Virginia.

U.S. 3rd Fleet and headquarters of Admiral William F. Halsey, Jr. At the end of the month she was busy again with TF38, screening carrier air strikes against Okinawa and later against Kyushu. After a brief stay in Leyte, she returned to Japanese home waters where she continued participation in carrier action and shore bombardment through the remainder of the war.

On 15 August, in the Oval Office of the White House in Washington D.C., President Harry S. Truman, surrounded by members of the press corps., stated: "I have just received a note from the Japanese government in reply to the message forwarded to that government by the Secretary of State on August 11. I deem this reply a full acceptance of the Potsdam Declaration, which specified the unconditional surrender of Japan."

The *Missouri* was selected as the site of the official surrender signing ceremony held shortly after 9 a.m., 2 September. In a brief address, General Douglas MacArthur stated: "We are gathered here, representatives of the major warring powers, to conclude a solemn agreement whereby peace may be restored. The issues, involving divergent ideas and ideologies, have been determined on the battlefields and hence are not for our discussion or our debate. It is my earnest hope and indeed the hope of all mankind that from this solemn occasion a better world shall emerge out of the blood and carnage of the past . . ." At the end of the ceremony General MacArthur said: "Let us pray that peace be now restored to the world and that God will preserve it always. These proceedings are closed." MacArthur used five different pens when he signed the surrender document. The pens were later presented to U.S. Army Lieutenant-General Jonathan Wainwright, Theatre Commander at Corregidor and a survivor of the Bataan Death March, British Army Lieutenant-General Arthur Percival, Commander of Malaya, the United States National Archives, the U.S. Military Academy, West

Point, and Mrs Douglas MacArthur. The signing was to take place at a fine old mahogany table provided by the crew of the British battleship, HMS *King George V*. However, the table was too small for the surrender documents, so an ordinary table from the enlisted men's mess of *Missouri* was substituted. It was covered with a green felt cloth from the officers' mess. It is now part of the collections of the Navy Museum at the U.S. Naval Academy, Annapolis, Maryland.

Tony Alessandro: "15 August 1945. News broke that the war was over. Everyone was blowing whistles and there was a lot of dancing and hugging going on—but the celebration eventually subsided. It was business as usual for the crew. Many of us were still apprehensive, and for good reason; five Japanese pilots had attacked the fleet that morning. All five were shot down by navy gunners.

"By 28 August, the *Missouri* was headed for Tokyo Bay. A lot of my buddies and I were pretty scared. We didn't know if it was a trap or if Japan really meant to surrender.

"I was on a working party with two other shipmates. We brought Japanese harbour pilots aboard from another ship while we were under way, before entering Tokyo Bay. They told us about the mine fields and harbour defences and on the morning of 29 August we passed into Tokyo Bay at Condition Two, a state of medium alert, and dropped anchor. The *Missouri* sailed into the bay without incident.

"At 7 a.m. on 2 September, 170 newsmen and cameramen boarded *Missouri* from the destroyer *Buchanon*, to cover the surrender ceremony. In the next hour, high-ranking military officials of all the Allied powers were received on board. Fleet Admiral Nimitz came on board shortly after 8 a.m. General of the Army Douglas MacArthur, Supreme Commander of the Allied Powers, came on board at 8.43 a.m. The eleven Japanese representatives headed by Foreign Minister Shigemitsu boarded at 8.56. I was looking down on the ceremony from

Pushing up through smoke from a world half-darkened by overhanging cloud— the shroud that mushroomed out / and struck the dome of the sky, the angry flames— black, red, blue— / dance into the air, / merge, scatter glittering sparks, / already tower over the whole city.

Quivering like seaweed, the mass of flames spurs forward. Cattle bound for the slaughterhouse avalanche down the riverbank; / wings drawn in, a single ash-colored pigeon / lies on its side atop the bridge. / Popping up in the dense smoke, / crawling out / wreathed in fire: countless human beings on all fours. / In a heap of embers that erupt and subside, / hair rent, / rigid in death, / there smolders a curse.
— from *Flames*
by Toge Sankichi

"The surrender would probably have been on the *Iowa*. The *Iowa* was President Roosevelt's ship—the one he took to different places. But when he died, Mr Truman became president. He's from Missouri, so *this* became his ship. When the surrender was scheduled, he said it would be on the *Missouri*."
— Albert Lee Kaiss, Captain USN Ret., the last commander of the USS *Missouri*

165

right: A galley aboard the USS *Missouri*, far left: A remotely piloted vehicle on the afterdeck of *Missouri*, below: A five-inch gun mount on the *Missouri*.

the fifth deck. At 9.02 a.m. General MacArthur stepped to the battery of microphones and the 23-minute ceremony was broadcast to the waiting world. Ten Allied and two Japanese officials signed the surrender document. By 9.38 a.m., the Japanese emissaries had departed the ship."

The USS *Missouri* left Norfolk, Virginia on 7 June 1954 as flagship of the Midshipman Training Cruise to Lisbon, Portugal and Cherbourg, France. About one day out, the *Missouri* was joined at sea by the

left: One of many hundreds of locator signs stencilled throughout *Missouri*'s decks. below: The *Iowa* at anchor.

right: Japanese prisoners of war being bathed, clipped, deloused and issued GI clothing aboard the USS *New Jersey* in December 1944.

USS *Iowa*, BB-61, the USS *New Jersey*, BB-62, and the USS *Wisconsin*, BB-64. The four vessels operated together for just a few hours, the first and only time the four greatest battleships of the United States Navy sailed together in the same task force.

Five feet tall and 115 pounds, Jack Delaney was just seventeen years old when he joined the crew of the *Missouri* in 1952 for her second deployment of the Korean War. He was assigned to Damage Control: "It's hard to believe it is more than fifty years since I served aboard the 'Mighty Mo.' Leaving my childhood orphanage in upstate New York behind, I reported aboard the *Missouri* with both excitement and apprehension about the adventure that lay ahead. Until then, my worldly travels were limited to the Great Lakes Naval Training Center, Illinois. The news was dominated by the Korean War and the ship was headed for action off the Korean coast.

"I was assigned to the Engineering Department and R Division. We were responsible for firefighting and damage control and, most importantly, for maintaining the water-tight integrity of the vessel. I soon became familiar with the layout of the ship, and was astonished at how many compartments a ship of that size contained. My duties required me to go into areas of the ship that most crew members never saw, from the Admiral's cabin to the shaft alleys, and fore and aft through 'Broadway,' the longest passageway on the ship. My boss was a First Class Petty Officer of fifteen years service, a tough man to work for, but easy to get along with if you did your job properly.

"We departed Norfolk, Virginia in September 1952, transiting from the Atlantic to the Pacific via the Panama Canal. We shoe-horned through the locks, requiring fenders along the sides of the ship to prevent damage to both the ship and the locks. What a tight squeeze! On the way to Korea, we relieved the USS *Iowa*, BB-61, off Yokosuka. It was a stunning sight, the two powerful battleships

lashed together from a single buoy in Tokyo Bay."

Missouri cruised up and down the Korean coast, shelling vital targets in support of Allied troops. Delaney: "For the next six months the days alternated between the excitement of hours at General Quarters, and the tedium of consecutive Mid-watches. The memory of spending half the night on those watches still makes me shudder. My watch had me taking soundings of the voids, to check the water-tight integrity of the hull. It meant roaming throughout the ship at all hours of the day and night. For a ship with a crew of 3,000 men, it was surprisingly quiet. I often had the eerie feeling that I was completely alone on board. With only red lights to illuminate her, the ship was almost entirely dark. In such subtle light, even crowded compartments full of sleeping men can appear empty."

Another *Missouri* veteran of that Korean War second deployment is Maynard Loy, a former Gunner's Mate. "We were either at General Quarters or standing watch most of our stay [off Korea]. Mail call was once, or maybe twice a month, when we would refuel or take on supplies from another vessel.

"On 22 December 1952 a most saddening event occurred. We lost our helicopter pilot, Ensign Robert Mayhew and his two observers, First Lieutenant Robert Dern and 1st Lieutenant Rex Ellison (USMC) while they were on a spotting mission. And, on our way back to the States, while approaching Sasebo Harbor, Japan, our captain, Warner Edsall, died on the bridge of a heart attack.

"One morning, while in Wonsan Harbor doing routine shore bombardment, the *Missouri* came under counter fire from enemy shore batteries. All three of our sixteen-inch gun turrets trained to our port side and fired a nine-gun salvo on broadside. This was a very rare occurrence as it put so much strain on the ship's superstructure, but we got the job done and pushed the enemy back so our ground forces could advance."

right: President Harry S. Truman in 1945, below: The Japanese representatives aboard *Missouri* at the formal surrender ceremony ending World War II on 2 September 1945.

Herb Fahr boarded the *Missouri* for the first time in March 1954. "I got to pier 7 at the Norfolk Navy Base and reported aboard the Mo to the Officer of the Deck in the time-honoured tradition of the Blue Jacket's Manual. First, salute the stern of the ship, where the American flag is flown when the ship is in port. Then salute the OOD while saying 'Permission to come aboard, sir. Fireman First Class reporting for duty.' I handed over my orders and a messenger took me to meet my division officer. At last, I was Ship's Company on a real ship. I met our division officer, an ensign who I did not know long as he was going off to submarine school. Another member of A Division took me down to the division compartment where I found a bunk and a locker, stowed my gear, changed into dungarees and got a very quick Cook's tour. My workstation was to be in 'after diesel', which was short for After Emergency Diesel, Compressor and Pump Room. It was at the very bottom of the ship, right next to the double bottom. The actual name for the space in between was the cofferdam."

The first decommissioning of *Missouri* was set for February 1955, and just before Christmas 1954, Herb Fahr received orders transferring him from the battleship to the general communications ship, USS *Eldorado*, based in San Diego. Before leaving the *Missouri*, Fahr made a brass commemorative plaque with the names of his A Division shipmates and the date of the upcoming decommissioning on it. He riveted the plaque to the braces that supported the cables coming out of the emergency diesel generator in the A Division compartment. He took a photo of the plaque with his five-dollar Brownie, but the picture didn't come out. Some time later he learned from the *Missouri*'s captain that some workers at the Pudget Sound Naval Shipyard had stripped out all the brass they could from the ship, including Fahr's plaque.

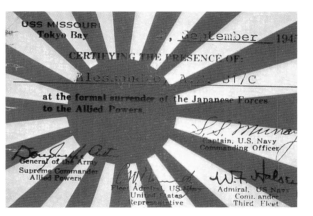

left: A card given to all attending the Japanese surrender ceremony aboard the *Missouri*, below: General Douglas MacArthur signing the surrender documents for the Allies, bottom: A flypast by U.S. carrier aircraft celebration of the official ending of the Second World War.

below: The *Missouri* in late 1945 prior to her return to the U.S. mainland from Pearl Harbor.

TIRPITZ

GRAND ADMIRAL Alfred von Tirpitz had won the favour of the Kaiser at an early stage in his career and with it his appointment to be Secretary of State at the German Navy Office. In 1897 he began shaping the Imperial German Navy's High Seas Battle Fleet. Tirpitz planned the fleet based on his 'risk-theory' which accepted that Britain would always be superior to Germany in fleet size, but would have to spread that larger number of vessels across the globe. The Germans, he felt, needed a battle fleet only large enough to deal effectively with that part of the British fleet that covered the English Channel and the North Sea. He estimated the size of the British Channel Fleet, and British shipbuilding capacity, and calculated that Germany would need to build 60 capital ships over the next twenty years. By June 1900, Tirpitz had secured authorization from the German Assembly to build a fleet of 38 battleships, 20 large and 38 smaller cruisers. By August 1914, when the First World War began, it was clear that the Tirpitz Risk Theory was incorrect. Germany's capital ship strength and capability then was less than it needed to be against that of the Royal Navy, and the gap was widening. Tirpitz soon lost the ear and the admiration of the Kaiser. He was being isolated from the naval decision-making process and in March 1916 he resigned.

In June 1935 an Anglo-German naval agreement was signed under which Germany agreed to restrict her fleet to 35 per cent of that of Great Britain. The Washington Treaty of 1922 and the First London Naval Conference Agreement were still in force. Under the terms of the latter agreements, capital ship displacement was limited to 35,000 tons. In 1936 Germany defied the agreed limitations, laying down her first genuine battleships since the First World War: *Bismarck*, which displaced 41,700 tons, and *Tirpitz*, displacing 42,900 tons.

From March 1942 onwards the mere presence of

"Everything turns upon the Battle of the Atlantic, which is proceeding with growing intensity on both sides. Our losses in ships and tonnage are very heavy and, vast as our shipping resources which we control, the losses cannot continue indefinitely without seriously affecting our war effort and our means of subsistence."
— Winston Churchill

left: *Final Assault*, a drawing by Robert Bailey, depicts the 12 November 1944 bombing of the German battleship *Tirpitz* by RAF Lancasters of No. 9 and 617 Squadrons

the battleship *Tirpitz* in Norwegian waters had caused the British to employ a large naval force to protect the Russian convoys in the North Atlantic, and to prevent the German warship from moving out into the Atlantic and becoming a greater threat. As Winston Churchill said: "She rivetted our attention." For more than two years she had not sunk a single enemy vessel or even fired on one.

When, in December 1941, Adolf Hitler became convinced that the British were on the verge of invading Norway, he demanded that Admiral Erich Raeder, Commander-in-Chief of the German Navy, redeploy his fleet there, where, according to the Führer, "the fate of the war will be decided".

Tirpitz proceeded to Trondheim on the Norwegian west coast, an ideal position from which to strike at the Russian convoys. In March of 1942, the battleship launched her first foray against a convoy, but Luftwaffe reconnaissance aircraft lost contact with the enemy convoy and *Tirpitz* was forced to withdraw to her hiding place in the

Foettenfiord, near Trondheim. On the way, she was attacked by a dozen torpedo-bearing Fairey Albacore aircraft from the Royal Navy carrier *Victorious*, but without effect. All of the torpedoes missed the battleship, which managed to shoot down two of the aircraft.

In a letter to the British Chiefs of Staff, Churchill stated: "The destruction or even the crippling of this ship [*Tirpitz*] is the greatest event at sea at the present time. No other target is comparable to it. A plan should be made to attack with carrier-borne torpedo aircraft and with heavy bombers by daylight or at dawn." But *Tirpitz* was well protected by the steeply rising mountains and cliffs where she lay in the fiord, and she was defended by torpedo netting on her more exposed side. The fiord was often covered in mist and, when it wasn't, *Tirpitz* was capable of shielding herself in a smokescreen of her own making. It seemed that a level-bombing attack was the only possible method for dealing with the battleship.

right: *Tirpitz* (and her sister ship *Bismarck*), were the first genuine German battleships laid down since World War I. The loss of *Tirpitz* marked the end of the German battle fleet.

In a series of futile attempts by RAF Bomber Command to destroy *Tirpitz*, the battleship was subjected to high-level attacks by Lancaster bombers using 4,000-pound blast bombs in March and April. They were augmented by Halifaxes dropping small mines in an effort to cause some of the mountainside to crumble down onto *Tirpitz*. These attacks were thwarted by the smokescreens. In three such raids, Bomber Command lost twelve heavy bombers, a rate of loss it would be unwilling to accept again for the next two years.

The very presence of *Tirpitz* in the area brought huge dividends to the Germans. In July she lay in Altenfiord on the northern tip of Norway, when the Russian convoy PQ17 passed by. British First Sea Lord Sir Dudley Pound believed (incorrectly) that *Tirpitz* was going to attack the convoy, which he ordered to scatter. In the chaos that followed, only eleven of the convoy's thirty-four merchant ships survived attacks by U-boats and Luftwaffe bombers.

When an attack on another convoy in January 1943 by the heavy cruiser *Admiral Hipper*, the pocket battleship *Lützow* and six destroyers, was foiled by the convoy escort, an enraged Hitler ordered that all of Germany's heavy warships be scrapped. He planned to have their big guns used on shore for coastal defence. Luftwaffe chief Hermann Goering applauded the decision, believing it to the advantage of his air force, but Admiral Raeder thought it folly and resigned over it. He was replaced by Karl Doenitz, Hitler's Admiral of Submarines. Doenitz initially supported the Führer's order, but soon changed his mind and, being more diplomatic than Raeder, was able to persuade Hitler, not only to reverse the order, but to dispatch both *Lützow* and the battlecruiser *Scharnhorst* to join *Tirpitz* in Norway. He felt that the three warships would pose a devastating new threat to the convoys. The Allies shared that view and suspended the Russian convoys through the spring and summer months, resuming them again under the protection of the increasing autumn darkness.

In September, the Royal Navy launched a daring raid by six midget submarines against *Tirpitz*. Three of the subs penetrated the netting surrounding the battleship. Of these, two were destroyed, but not before laying explosives which damaged *Tirpitz* sufficiently to keep her out of action for six months, during which *Lützow* was sent to the Baltic, leaving only *Scharnhorst* in the area. The circumstances would lead to her destruction on 26 December.

Once repaired, *Tirpitz* underwent trials in Altenfiord. There she was attacked in February by Russian bombers which did no significant damage. Now the British decided to utilize their growing carrier strength in a new assault on the battleship, in which two large carriers and four escort carriers would send out 146 aircraft of various types on 3 April 1944. Barracuda dive-bombers were to spearhead the raid, with Wildcats and Hellcats in a supporting role. Top cover was to be provided by Corsairs. The first wave of the strike took off at 3 a.m. and surprised the *Tirpitz* crew who were readying the ship for trials. With her guns largely unmanned and no time to put out a smokescreen, the battleship was extremely vulnerable. She received several hits in the attacks, and 300 of her crew were killed. But the damage was not great and *Tirpitz* was fully repaired within a month. She remained in northern Norway and continued to tie up Allied forces by her mere presence.

During August, aircraft of the Fleet Air Arm made five unsuccessful attempts to destroy the German battleship. Now the Commander-in-Chief of RAF Bomber Command, Sir Arthur Harris, was asked to do the job. He opposed any project that required him to divert bombers from his nocturnal area bombing campaign against the cities of Germany. But he finally agreed to provide No. 617 Squadron, which had gained fame by breaching the Möhne and Eder dams in the Ruhr Valley in spring 1943. 617 was under the command of Wing Commander

"We can do without butter, but, despite all our love of peace, not without arms. One cannot shoot with butter but with guns."
– Paul Joseph Goebbels

J.B. 'Willy' Tait. All he had to do was sink the *Tirpitz*.

The man who had designed the strange bouncing bombs used to break the Ruhr dams, Dr Barnes Wallis, was also the brains behind another innovative concept that the RAF hoped to employ against *Tirpitz*. Wallis had designed what he called a 'earthquake bomb': the Tallboy, 21 feet long and weighing six tons, was designed to penetrate deep into the ground before exploding and creating a shock wave that would demolish all nearby structures. It was thought it should be equally effective in penetrating the deck armour of a battleship. In September 1944, Bomber Command ordered two squadrons of Lancaster bombers, No. 9 and the previously selected 617, to fly their Tallboy bombloads from Lossiemouth in Scotland to Yagoderik near Archangel in Russia. The bombers did not have the range to carry Tallboys from their bases in Britain all the way to the Altenfiord, so the RAF elected to run the mission from a Russian base that was nearer the target. Six of the grossly overweight Lancasters were lost en route to Yagoderik.

The mission was flown on 15 September. RAF planners hoped that by having their bombers approach *Tirpitz* from an unexpected direction, the German radar operators would be confused briefly, delaying a reaction by the crew of *Tirpitz*. Such a delay, they believed, would delay the deployment of a smokescreen until it was too late to shield the battleship from the eyes of the Lancaster bomb aimers. But the *Tirpitz* crewmen did manage to lay a smokescreen before the Lancaster crews could drop their big bombs. Most of the Tallboys fell into the smoke pall, missing the battleship completely. Seven of the Lanc crews chose not to drop in the conditions, and brought their bombs back to base. The mission, however, was not a total failure. One Tallboy did hit *Tirpitz*, ruining her bow and flooding a forward section. A lengthy repair period was projected by damage assessors so, instead of opting for the major repairs required to make her fully seaworthy again, the German Naval Staff ordered the battleship to be utilized thereafter as a floating gun battery at Tromso for the defence of northern Norway.

The Germans intended to position *Tirpitz* in shallow water at Tromso, to guard against the possibility of her being sunk or capsized in a new attack. Her Tromso berth required some dredging, however, and for the time that work took, she would be more vulnerable. Her relocation also meant that, with certain modifications, RAF bombers flying from Scotland could just reach *Tirpitz* with their Tallboys. However, the Lancs would require installation of uprated Merlin engines and the removal of some weight, including the upper gun turrets.

As the hours of daylight decreased, and with only a few days of clear weather per month, the timing of another raid on the battleship was becoming critical. Such a raid would have to be carried out no later than 26 November when daylight at Tromso would become minimal. By late October, both 617 and 9 Squadrons were again in residence at Lossiemouth, and in the early morning darkness of the 28th, 32 Lancasters rose sluggishly from the Scottish base, with their bomb and fuel overloads testing their performance in the extreme. Weather reconnaissance had predicted a clear spell over the target area, but the prediction was wrong. Heavy cloud obscured the battleship by the time the bombers arrived over it, and once again the attack was essentially a failure, though one bomb did some damage to the port propeller shaft of *Tirpitz* and caused some flooding of her aft compartments.

Air Vice-Marshal R.A. Cochrane, in command of 5 Group, decided to attack the battleship one more time, even though such a raid would now be complicated further as the Germans had moved a group of fighters to a base near Tromso to defend *Tirpitz* against any new bombing attacks. Without their mid-upper turrets, the Lancasters would be easy prey for the German fighters during a new bombing mission. But Cochrane accepted the added risk and made a new plan for approaching the battleship undetected. He intended to bring his bombers in low, at an altitude 1,500 feet, through a gap in the German radar network that RAF reconnaissance aircraft had located. After penetrating the German radar chain, the bombers would utilize the cover of a nearby mountain range before turning north and then approaching *Tirpitz* from the east. Again, Cochrane aimed to surprise the Germans.

This time it all worked as planned. The Lancasters evaded German radar and the fighters it would have alerted, arriving undetected over the target, which was in the clear. The bombers were able to deliver their massive bombs from an altitude in excess of the 10,000 feet required for the Tallboys to be effective against the heavy armour of *Tirpitz*. The ten-minute raid resulted in two Tallboy hits on the great battleship, which rolled over and capsized exposing her keel. The unorthodox ideas of Barnes Wallis had once again been proven sound, and the skill and tenacity of the aircrews of 9 and 617 RAF squadrons had finally accomplished what had previously seemed all but impossible. More than a thousand crewmen were trapped in *Tirpitz*. Of those, fewer than 100 were rescued.

The end of *Tirpitz* marked the end of the German battle fleet. *Bismarck* and *Scharnhorst* had already been lost, and *Gneisenau* severely damaged by a mine explosion during her Channel dash from Brest early in 1942 and an RAF bombing raid on Kiel in November. *Lützow and Sheer* would both be sunk in April 1945, but with the loss of *Tirpitz*, the difficulty of protecting the Russian convoys was dramatically reduced for the Allies. Only two merchant ships out of 250 were lost in convoys from the fall of 1944 to the end of the war.

This is war: / Boys flung into a breach / Like shoveled earth; And old men, / Broken, Driving rapidly before crowds of people / In a glitter of silly decorations Behind the boys And the old men, / Life weeps, And shreds her garments / To the blowing winds.
— Amy Lowell

THE OLD LADY

"War's spite, indeed, and we to do him right—
Will call the ship he fought in the 'War's-Spite.' "
– Queen Elizabeth I, in a 1605 play by Thomas Heywood

The English love their country with a love / Steady, and simple, wordless, dignified; / I think it sets their patriotism above / All others. / We Americans have pride— / We glory in our country's short romance. We boast of it and love it. Frenchmen when / The ultimate menace comes, will die for France / Logically as they lived. But Englishmen Will serve day after day, obey the law, / And do dull tasks that keep a nation strong.
Once I remember in London how I saw / Pale shabby people standing in a long / Line in the twilight and the misty rain / To pay their tax.
I then saw England plain.
– Alice Duer Miller

right: HMS *Warspite* in drydock at Rosyth for the repair of stern battle damage received at Jutland, damaging her steering control.

THERE HAVE BEEN eight ships called *Warspite* in the history of Britain's Royal Navy. The spelling of the name has evolved from the time of Elizabeth the First and has included *Warspight*, *Wastspight*, and *Warspitt*. The first *Warspite* was the vessel of the Elizabethan privateer, Sir Walter Raleigh. Armed with 36 guns, it was launched in 1596 at Deptford on the Thames and displaced 650 tons.

On 1 June of that year, a huge force of Royal Navy and Dutch warships set out from Plymouth to raid their Spanish enemy's port of Cadiz in an effort to destroy Spain's principal naval vessels and eliminate the growing Spanish threat to England. Raleigh, in *Warspite*, was leading one of the four Royal Navy squadrons. The British flagship was *Repulse*, under command of the Earl of Essex, who had displaced Raleigh in the Queen's affections. Raleigh hated him.

After three weeks at sea the fleet neared Cadiz. Raleigh's squadron was assigned to clear the approaches to the port of Spanish warships which might put up resistance. Meanwhile, the other squadrons of the fleet began putting hundreds of troops ashore for a direct assault on the city. On learning of this, Raleigh was enraged, knowing that in the chaos of such an attack the Spanish ships might well escape. Raleigh immediately set out to rescue the mission from the folly he saw developing.

At Elizabeth's order, command of the British fleet was shared between Essex and Lord Howard of Effingham. Raleigh rowed to the *Repulse* to confer with Essex, whom he soon persuaded to discontinue the assault on Cadiz. He then had a similar conversation with Effingham who concurred. Raleigh was appointed to command an attack on Cadiz harbour in which *Warspite* would take the lead.

The next morning Raleigh's force entered the harbour and encountered a savage response from

right: A handsome view of *Warspite* at anchor, believed to be lying off Portsmouth, England.

the Cadiz fortifications and the Spanish vessels. *Warspite* and many of the other British warships were badly damaged in the battle. Raleigh himself was wounded in the leg, but was utterly determined that his force would prevail and capture the Spanish treasure ships which he knew were trapped in the harbour. Essex and Effingham chose, instead, to plunder the town, ignoring Raleigh's insistence that their priority should be the treasure galleons. The Spaniards set fire to their treasure ships to prevent their three million pounds worth of goods being grabbed by the enemy. The British did, however, manage to capture more than twenty important Spanish vessels and 1,000 cannon before withdrawing to Plymouth. Thus went the maiden voyage of the very first *Warspite*.

The last Royal Navy warship to bear the name *Warspite* was a nuclear attack submarine of the 1960s. The seventh and last *surface* warship to be called *Warspite* was completed at Devonport, England in 1915. A *Queen Elizabeth* class battleship, she displaced 27,500 tons amd was 646 feet long, with a beam of 90 feet 6 inches and a draft of 29 feet 10 inches. Manned by a crew of 951, *Warspite* was armed with eight fifteen-inch guns and 16 six-inch guns. With a range of 4,500 nautical miles at ten knots, her quadruple screw turbines were capable of propelling her at a top speed of 23 knots.

The seventh *Warspite* came to be in 1912 when King George V provided names for the new *Queen Elizabeth* class of super dreadnoughts, which consisted of the lead ship and the *Barham*, *Valiant*, *Malaya* and *Warspite*. Winston Churchill, the 37-year-old First Lord of the Admiralty, was determined to establish and maintain British fleet superiority over the Germans. In an address to the House of Commons in May, one of the first occasions in which he enlisted the language of Shakespeare and sent it to war, he sought the members' support for the new class of vessels. He described the amazing armour of the ships, up to thirteen inches thick for a new

standard of protection, and the fifteen-inch main guns, together with powerful secondary six-inch guns, all vastly superior to anything the Germans had. He spoke eloquently of the oil-burning boilers which would provide the great speed, which Churchill saw as essential. It was imperative, in his view, that the new battleships be able to "curl around the head of the enemy's line and concentrate awesome firepower, shattering those vessels and throwing all the ships behind them into disarray".

Britain's naval experts confirmed that the new super dreadnoughts would have to be capable of a 25-knot speed to achieve what Churchill had described. Virtually all arguments favoured oil-fuelled power for the ships, instead of traditional coal. The speed of an oil-fired ship could changed easily and quickly by increasing or decreasing the number of ignition sprayers activated in the boilers. An oil-powered vessel was more easily kept stable because the oil could readily be pumped from tank to tank for optimum ballasting, and an oil-powered ship could be quickly refuelled at sea, eliminating the time and inconvenience of a port call at a coaling station. In his book *The World Crisis*, Churchill states: "As a coal ship used up her coal, increasingly large numbers of men had to be taken, if necessary from the guns, to shovel the coal from remote and inconvenient bunkers to bunkers nearer the furnaces themselves, thus weakening the fighting efficiency of the ship perhaps at the most critical moment in the battle." The advantages of oil over coal were obvious. Coaling a ship took longer and required more manpower. A full load of coal weighed more than one of oil. Oil saved weight and thus allowed for the use of bigger guns, more room for other facilities including additional boilers which meant greater speed, and other improvements including better crew facilities. Finally, the Navy's own evaluation established that the energy generated by a coal-burning battleship of *Warspite*'s displacement could not propel the vessel at anything approaching the 25-knot requirement set for her. Churchill was committed to the use of oil-fired boilers in the *Queen Elizabeth* class battleships, though many in Britain and the British government were vigorously opposed to the abandonment of coal in favour of oil. They saw the move as unpatriotic, an insult to the British coal miner, and a senseless rejection of an abundant British natural resource for one that came from a foreign, and thus vulnerable, source. The First Lord of the Admiralty sought the help of the former First Sea Lord, Sir John Fisher and in 1913 the Royal Commission on Oil Fuel declared in favour of oil for all new British warships and recommended the creation of fuel oil reserves sufficient for four years of fleet operation. Parliament was persuaded and the oil-burning super dreadnought programme was approved.

Churchill had to gamble on more than a switch to oil-burning for the new battleships. To achieve and maintain an advantage over the fleet of the German Kaiser, he would have to commit the new warships to being armed with new, untested 15-inch main guns. Again, from *The World Crisis*: "No such thing as a modern 15-inch gun existed. None had ever been made. The advance to the 13.5-inch had in itself been a great stride. Its power was greater; its accuracy was greater; its life was much longer. Could the British designers repeat this triumph on a still larger scale and in a still more intense form?" The gamble might have cost Churchill his career, and left Britain largely unprepared and ill-equipped in the period leading up to war with Germany, her ready and powerful naval adversary.

The keel of *Queen Elizabeth*, the lead ship of the class, was laid down at Portsmouth dockyard on 21 October 1912 and the keel-laying of *Warspite* followed ten days later at Devonport, with work beginning on *Valiant*, *Barham* and *Malaya* during 1913. *Warspite* was finished and fitted out early in 1915 and was put through her working-up exercises at Scapa Flow in April and May of that year. She joined the British Grand Fleet in June, engaging in North Sea sweeps preparatory to

entering action in the war with Germany. By early March, all five *Queen Elizabeth* class vessels had completed their work-ups and been formed into the Royal Navy's new fast battleship organization, the Fifth Battle Squadron, five ships which collectively mounted 40 massive 15-inch guns.

Late in the evening of 30 May, *Warspite* sailed from Rosyth, joining the vessels of the Grand Fleet to take part in the Battle of Jutland (see chapter four, *Jutland*). The Executive Officer of *Warspite*, Commander Humphrey T. Walwyn, recorded events of Jutland from 2.40 p.m of 31 May: "I realised that there was something serious doing. I passed the word round to everybody that we were in for the real thing and went round all the mess- decks . . . and lit all Action candles, etc. Saw all doors and everything closed, and went up on deck; they were just finishing washing down the weather decks. I sent all hands away to their stations and went up [to the bridge] to report everything ready. There was nothing in sight except our own ships, but we were steaming hard. Hoisted Battle Ensigns and Union Jack at after struts and masthead. Went to my action station, B turret . . . It was now about 4 o'clock . . . Got orders to 'load and train on Red 20˚ [i.e. 20˚ on port bow]. Could not see anything at all, hazy and a lot of smoke about . . . I made out five columns of smoke in the mist and that was all I could see— no masts or anything else."

At this point all of the principal vessels of both the German and British fleets were sailing to the southeast, and the Germans seemed to have the advantage. Their gunnery was producing results, with HMS *Indefatigable* being severely damaged, as was *Lion*, flagship of Admiral of the Fleet Sir David Beatty. *Indefatigable* soon exploded and sank.

Now the ships of the Fifth Battle Squadron came into play. Manoeuvring behind Beatty's ship and at a range of some 23,000 yards from their targets, *Warspite* and her sister ships quickly began to earn their keep. This part of the fight commenced when the giant guns of *Warspite* fired a few initial salvoes at one of the German light cruisers, which soon

You shall not hear their mirth: / You shall not come to think them well content By any jest of mine. These men are worth Your tears. You are not worth their merriment.
– from *Apologia Pro Peomate Meo*
by Wilfred Owen

HMS *Warspite* is believed to have scored the longest-range hit ever achieved on a moving target in a naval combat engagement. In July 1940, the British battleship fired on and struck the Italian battleship *Giulio Cesare* from a distance of 26,000 yards.

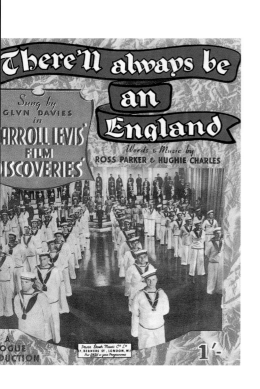

took leave. Commander Walwyn: "We were turning fast to starboard . . . and as we came round eight points [90 degrees] I saw five enemy battle cruisers on the port bow. They were steaming the same way as we were and going very hard . . . I could only see their masts and the tops of their funnels above the horizon. We opened fire on number five [the *Von der Tann*, which had just destroyed the *Indefatigable*]. . . range, I think, 23,000 yards . . . I distinctly saw one salvo hit. She turned away in a cloud of black and white smoke, and we turned our attention to number four [the *Moltke*]."

According to German Vizeadmiral Reinhard Scheer: ". . . superiority in firing and tactical advantages of position were decidedly on our side until 4.19 p.m., when a new unit of four or five ships of the *Queen Elizabeth* type, with a considerable surplus of speed, drew up from a northwesterly direction and . . . joined in the fighting. It was the English Fifth Battle Squadron. This made the situation critical for our battle cruisers. The new enemy fired with extraordinary rapidity and accuracy . . ."

Just before 5.p.m. the Fifth Battle Squadron came under heavy, intensive fire from the German battle cruisers. All were hit, but *Barham* and *Malaya* took the worst of it. The German vessels were also coming under extremely heavy fire and, although *Warspite* was taking several hits at the time, her executive officer remembered the moment: "I distinctly saw two of our salvoes hit the leading German battleship. Sheets of yellow flame went right over her mastheads, and she looked red fore and aft like a burning haystack. I know we hit her hard . . . [B turret] machinery working like a clockwork mouse, no hang-up of any sort whatever." *Warspite* herself was now receiving some very hard hits, with one round passing through the mess-decks and the side armour. [It]". . . burst in a terrific sheet of golden flame, stink and impenetrable dust. Another hit below in the side aft and began to flood the steering compartment. Yet another burst in the captain's lobby, reducing it to a state of indescribable

wreckage. Farther forward, X Turret was hit, and water was flooding through a hole in the side, and going down the engine-room [air] supply trunk. Another took away the engineer's office."

For the next hour and a half, fire and damage control parties struggled to stabilize and repair *Warspite*, to keep her in fighting condition. During this period, *Warspite* and *Malaya* again became engaged in combat with elements of the German High Seas Fleet.

As *Barham*, *Valiant*, *Warspite* and *Malaya* were manoeuvring at high speed to form up line astern of the Grand Fleet, *Warspite*'s helm suddenly jammed. Meanwhile, the British armoured cruisers *Defence*, *Warrior* and *Black Prince*, intent on finishing off the crippled German cruiser *Weisbaden*, had come under intense fire from the main body of the German battle fleet. *Defence* was quickly destroyed, while *Warrior* and *Black Prince* were badly damaged and vulnerable. With her rudder jammed, *Warspite* was soon turning in uncontrolled circles around *Warrior*, with the effect of shielding the cruiser from the worst of the enemy shelling, while drawing much of the fire onto herself. The sailors of *Warrior* would always be grateful to *Warspite* for the favour, whether or not it was intended, and *Warspite* would become legendary among the British people. In his book *H.M.S. Warspite*, S.W. Roskill quotes a *Warspite* midshipman who witnessed the situation from the after torpedo control position: "Suddenly we found ourselves hauling out of the line and rushing towards the German fleet . . . All that we knew was that we were in a hail of fire; in fact, so much so that the salvoes falling short and over made such splashes that a lot of water came into the tower, and we got quite wet . . . Once or twice we got a good view of the Germans, the range being only about 8,000 yards, and they looked enormous at this distance. We thought that our own six-inch guns were firing, but discovered later that it was the enemy's shells bursting on our armour belt. This had not been going on for long when the end of the world seemed to come. The deck below me seemed to open up, and I had the sensation of falling—falling."

Warspite was by now nearly unmanageable. Her captain was ordered to withdraw from the battle and take her back to Rosyth. Thus ended her involvement in the action of Jutland. Her adventure continued, however, when, as she neared port, she was attacked by U-boats and narrowly escaped two torpedoes which passed close by her bows.

Her Jutland damage repaired, *Warspite* joined with 220 Royal Navy ships, six American battleships and three French warships at the end of the First World War to take the surrender of the ten German battleships and five battle cruisers in the Firth of Forth. Following the war, only *Warspite* and her *Queen Elizabeth* class sister ships, together with the five Royal Sovereigns, survived a cull of the Royal Navy's main striking force. She participated in several annual cruises to the Mediterranean as part of the Atlantic Fleet and underwent her first major refit between 1924 and 1926.

With the ascent of Adolf Hitler to power in Germany during 1933, the British government authorized a major rebuilding programme for the *Queen Elizabeth* class battleships and *Warspite* remained in Portsmouth dockyard from 1934 until 1937, when she emerged thoroughly reconstructed and considerably improved.

After the start of the Second World War in September 1939, the Royal Navy's Home Fleet came under U-boat attack in Scapa Flow when Kapitän Leutnant Gunther Prien attacked and sank the battleship *Royal Oak*. *Warspite* was immediately recalled from her Mediterranean assignment to join the Home Fleet and was sent directly to Halifax, Nova Scotia with orders to escort slow Convoy HX9, 30 ships, leaving from Halifax on 18 November. In the sixth day of the crossing, she was ordered to depart the convoy and intercept the German battle cruisers *Scharnhorst* and *Gneisenau* in the Denmark Strait. But, in the terrible weather conditions, the German warships eluded her.

In April 1940 the German Army invaded Denmark and Norway, landing troops at many Norwegian ports including Narvik in the frigid Arctic. The invasion was supported by ten Kriegsmarine destroyers. *Warspite* was again redirected, this time to meet the Home Fleet off the coast of Norway. On 10 April, British destroyers engaged and sank two of the German destroyers near Narvik. Realizing that roughly a third of the Kriegsmarine destroyer force was trapped in port at Narvik (heavily battle damaged and short of fuel and ammunition), the Royal Navy decided to mount an attack on the Germans, using a hunting pack of destroyers formed around *Warspite*. The raid was to be led from *Warspite* by Vice Admiral William 'Jock' Whitworth.

In a heavy swell and freezing conditions, the British force set out for Narvik at 5.00 a.m. on 13 April. As they approached the Norwegian port, they encountered the German destroyer *Koellner* lurking in a fiord, ready to fire its shells and torpedoes at the first British warship target to present itself. The gunners of *Warspite* sent two full broadsides from eight fifteen-inch guns and four six-inch salvoes into *Koellner*. The German vessel was literally torn apart by the barrage and sank immediately.

Earlier, a Swordfish floatplane launched from *Warspite* had been patrolling the Herjangsfiord when the pilot spotted a U-boat. It was the *U-64* and the British pilot dived to attack it with the two 250-pound armour-piercing bombs he carried. As it closed on the submarine, the Swordfish was met with 37mm anti-aircraft fire from the German boat. The bi-plane's observer responded with machinegun fire and the pilot released his bombs, one of which struck and severely damaged the sub, which soon sank by the bows. She was the first German submarine to be sunk by a British naval plane in World War II.

In Narvik harbour, the German destroyer *Giese* was trying to escape when she was shelled by some of the British destroyers. Badly damaged, she became easy prey for *Warspite*. At this point all but

Former crew members of the Royal Navy battleship HMS *Warspite* met in Bremerton, Washington for a reunion several years ago. While there the group visited the battleship *New Jersey*. In late 1941, after *Warspite* had suffered major damage in the naval battle for Crete, the British warship was repaired at Bremerton. British shipyards were fully occupied at that time and, though the United States was not yet in the war, she offered to repair *Warspite* in a U.S. yard. For some at the reunion, it was a nostalgic return to Bremerton.

below: *Warspite* stamp issued by the Royal Mail as part of a D-Day anniversary block of commemorative stamps.

Camouflaged, they detach
lengths of sea and sky
When they move; offset,
speed and directions are a
lie.

Everything is grey anyway;
ships, water, snow, faces.
Flanking the convoy, we
rarely go through our
paces.

But sometimes on
tightening waves at night
they wheel
Drawing white moons on
strings from dripping keel.

Cold cases them, like ships
in glass; they are formal,
Not real, except in
adversity. Such deception
is normal.

At dusk they intensify
dusk, strung out, non-
committal: Waves spill
from our wake, crêpe
paper magnetised by gun-
metal.

They breathe silence, less
solid than ghosts,
ruminative
As the Arctic breaks up on
their sides and they sieve

Moisture into mess-decks.
Heat is cold-lined there,
Where we wait for a
torpedo and lack air.

Repetitive of each other,
imitating the sea's lift and
fall, On the wings of the
convoy they indicate
rehearsal.

Merchantmen move
sideways, with the gait of
crustaceans,
Round whom like eels
escorts take up their
stations.

three of the German warships had been destroyed
or run aground. The crews of the remaining three
Kriegsmarine vessels ran them aground as well,
abandoning them after setting scuttling charges.

After the raid, *Warspite* remained in the area as
flagship for the Royal Navy task group assigned to
bombard the port of Narvik preliminary to a British
amphibious assault. The bombardment did not
cause the Germans to surrender, as the British
hoped it might, and it was not until 28 May that
Narvik was finally captured—by elements of the
French Foreign Legion. *Warspite* returned in
triumph to Scapa following the Narvik battle. She
would soon be off to the Mediterranean as flagship
of Admiral of the Fleet Lord Andrew Cunningham.

When Italy entered the war as Germany's ally on 10
June 1940, Admiral Cunningham in *Warspite* led his
fleet in a brief sweep off Crete and the coast of Libya,
looking for the Italian navy. When France fell to the
Germans on 22 June, Britain lost her naval partner in
the western Mediterranean. Cunningham was now at
a distinct disadvantage, seriously short of
submarines, destroyers, fighter planes and
minesweepers. Many of his ships were old and slow,
but he had great confidence in the quality and
character of his sailors, believing them to be superior
to those of his Italian naval adversary. And, he had
those big guns of *Warspite* and *Malaya* at his call.

In an effort to protect the vital British convoys to
Malta and Alexandria, Cunningham apportioned
his fleet into three groups, one being *Warspite*
and five destroyers, the second consisting of the
battleships *Royal Sovereign* and *Malaya* together
with ten destroyers, and the third the aircraft
carrier HMS *Eagle* and ten destroyers. On 7 July
the three task groups departed the British base at
Alexandria. They were dependent for primary
reconnaissance on a picket line of British
submarines in the central Mediterranean, one of
which reported a very large force of Italian warships,
including two battleships, steaming 200 miles east

of Malta. Soon the British warships came under air
attack by Italian bombers. The cruiser HMS
Gloucester was hit and a bomb destroyed her
bridge, killing her captain and twelve sailors.

In the morning of 9 July Cunningham's fleet lay
southwest of Greece. The Battle of Calabria began at
3 p.m. when the carrier HMS *Eagle* launched her
aircraft in what turned out to be an ineffectual strike
against some of the Italian cruisers. By 3.30 a sea
battle was under way with an exchange of fire
between the Italian and British cruisers.
Cunningham and his fast cruisers had outrun his
slower battleships, which now lagged ten miles
behind him, making his position quite vulnerable.
Fortunately, *Warspite* was soon able to help by
sending salvoes of fifteen-inch shells into the
formation of Italian cruisers, causing them to flee.
The Italian battleships *Giulio Cesare* and *Conte di
Cavour* began shelling *Warspite,* but their fire was
inaccurate. *Warspite* returned fire with her big guns
at a range of 26,000 yards and scored one critically
important amidships hit on *Giulio Cesare,* which
won the battle for the British. Admiral Cunningham
wrote of the incident: "The *Warspite*'s shooting was
consistently good. I had been watching the great
splashes of our fifteen-inch salvoes straddling the
target when, at 4 p.m. I saw the great orange-
coloured flash of a heavy explosion at the base of
the enemy flagship's funnel. It was followed by an
upheaval of smoke, and I knew that she had been
heavily hit at the prodigious range of thirteen miles."

The crew of the Italian battleship suffered 100
casualties and some of the vessel's boilers were
destroyed, making retreat through the Straits of
Messina the only course for the Italian warships. At
the end of the afternoon, *Warspite* and *Eagle* came
under a further Italian bombing attack near the
Calabrian coast, but suffered little if any damage.
After Calabria, the Italian Fleet had no interest in
further contact with the Royal Navy.

By October 1940, Cunningham's warship fleet
had grown in strength and capability, with

Warspite, *Valiant* and the new aircraft carrier *Illustrious* being supplemented by *Malaya*, *Ramillies* and *Eagle*, and joined by another *Queen Elizabeth* class battleship, HMS *Barham*. Frustrated by the Italian fleet's refusal to come out and fight, Cunningham decided to mount a raid on the key enemy ships in the harbours at the Taranto naval base. The attack was set for the evening of 11 November. *Eagle* was to participate, but mechanical problems caused her withdrawal, with some of her Swordfish aircraft being transferred to *Illustrious* for the action. Earlier that day a reconnaissance pilot overflew the Taranto harbours and confirmed the presence of all six Italian battleships, *Littorio*, *Cesare*, *Duilio*, *Vittorio Veneto*, *Conte di Cavour* and *Doria*. The night was calm and quiet with bright moonlight as 21 Fairey Swordfish armed with bombs and torpedoes took off from *Illustrious,* beginning at 8.40 p.m. In an action that would cause considerably more damage to the Italian fleet than was done to the German warships at Jutland, the Fleet Air Arm planes hit *Littorio* with three torpedoes, sinking her at her moorings. They managed to sink *Conte di Cavour* and *Duilio*, each with a single torpedo hit, and heavily damaged a cruiser and two destroyers. *Warspite*, in support of the carrier operation, had played her part in one of the most dramatic actions of the war.

With the Germans poised to begin their assault on the Soviet Union, they did not need the hassle of having to rescue their Italian allies from a failed adventure in Greece and Yugoslavia, but they were compelled to do so in April 1941. To support this effort, they demanded that the Italian Navy send a battleship and supporting warships to cut supply lines between Egypt and Greece. The Germans offered air cover for the task force to protect them against more punishment from British torpedo planes.

On 27 March, Admiral Cunningham determined to take his battle fleet to sea that night from their port at Alexandria. Among his ships were *Warspite*, *Valiant* and *Barham*, as well as the carrier HMS *Formidable* and nine destroyers. *Warspite* was handicapped by clogged condensors and could not make more than a 20-knot top speed.

Following an initial exchange off Cape Matapan near Crete early on the 28th, between the Italians and three Royal Navy cruisers, *Gloucester*, *Ajax* and *Orion*, the cruisers located the battleship *Vittorio Veneto* sixteen miles north of their position. The battleship began firing her nine fifteen-inch guns at the cruisers and HMS *Valiant* quickly moved forward to take her on. *Warspite*'s condensor problem was resolved and she was soon able to join *Valiant* as they chased the fleeing *Vittorio Veneto*, which had just come under torpedo attack by Albacore bombers from *Formidable*. One torpedo struck the battleship below the waterline near one of her propellers, slowing her to a top speed of fifteen knots.

Just after 6 p.m., the *Vittorio Veneto* and her escorts were spotted 45 miles from *Warspite*. The British warships were gaining on the crippled Italian battleship. Later that evening, Cunningham, who had set his mind on catching and sinking *Vittorio Veneto*, ordered eight of his destroyers ahead in pursuit of the battleship. As the night wore on, Cunningham was informed that two *Zara* Class Italian heavy cruisers and a destroyer escort were nearby. The Italians were in the dark, literally, and unaware of the British fleet presence. Lacking radar, it must have been a great shock to them when they were suddenly illuminated by the searchlights of *Warspite* as she and the other British warships opened fire. Five massive shells from *Warspite*'s guns found their mark, smashing into the cruiser *Fiume* and shattering her. This was followed less than a minute later by a second salvo. At the same time, *Valiant* was busy destroying her target, the cruiser *Zara*, while *Barham* was dealing with the destroyer escort, *Alfieri*. Within the hour, the three Italian warships, and the cruiser *Pola*, had been sunk. The battleship *Vittorio Veneto* had escaped, but in every other

Landfall, Murmansk; but
starboard now a lead-
coloured Island, Jan
Mayen. Days identical,
hoisted like sails, blurred.

Counters moved on an
Admiralty map, snow like
confetti
Covers the real us. We
dream we are counterfeits
tied to our jetty.

But cannot dream long;
the sea curdles and
sprawls,
Liverishly real, horizon and
water tilting in to walls.

– *Destroyers in the Arctic*
by Alan Ross

above: Royal Navy
Admiral of the Fleet Sir
Andrew Cunningham,
First Sea Lord and Chief
of Naval Staff.

Napoleon tried. The Dutch
were on the way, / A
Norman did it—and a Dane
or two.
Some sailor-King may
follow one fine day; / But
not, I think, a low land-rat
like you.
– A.P. Herbert

"We were at sea for a much longer time than it would ordinarily take to make a beeline journey from England to France. The convoy we sailed in was one of several which comprised what is known as a "force." As we came down, the English Channel was crammed with forces going both ways, and as I write it still is.

"Minesweepers had swept wide channels for us, all the way from England to France. These were marked with buoys. Each channel was miles wide. We surely saw there before us more ships than any human had ever seen before at one glance. And going north were other vast convoys, some composed of fast liners speeding back to England for new loads of troops and equipment. As far as you could see in every direction, the ocean was infested with ships. There must have been every type of oceangoing vessel in the world. I even thought I saw a paddle-wheel steamer in the distance, but that was probably an illusion. There were battleships and all other kinds of warships clear down to patrol boats. There were great fleets of Liberty ships. There were fleets of luxury liners turned into troop transports, and fleets of big landing craft and tank carriers and tankers. And in and out through it all were nondescript ships—converted yachts, riverboats, tugs, and barges. The best way I can describe this vast armada and the frantic urgency of the traffic is to suggest that you

sense, Matapan had been a great British victory.

After Matapan, *Warspite* experienced a series of tragic episodes which would test the mettle of her crew. With the Germans preparing a seaborne invasion of Crete, to be preceded by a paratroop assault in May 1941, warships of the Royal Navy were attempting to defend the island. On 22 May, *Warspite* was sailing 100 miles west of Crete as flagship of the 1st Battle Squadron, with *Valiant*, one cruiser and ten destroyers. At 1.30 p.m. several Luftwaffe aircraft, including three Me109s, began to attack *Warspite* from low altitude. One bomb from one of the 109s rent a 100-foot tear in the forecastle deck. A six-inch gun mount disappeared and a massive fire spread rapidly from there through a ventilation shaft to a boiler room. 38 men were killed and 31 wounded. Most of the battleship's starboard anti-aircraft guns had been knocked out, leaving her highly vulnerable. But the operational weapons on the port side continued blazing away at the increasing numbers of enemy dive-bombers attacking *Warspite*. Admiral Cunningham, who had temporarily moved his headquarters ashore before this operation, signalled his ships: "Stick it out. Navy must not let Army down. No enemy forces must reach Crete by sea." The damage to *Warspite* was so severe as to be unrepairable by the dry dock facilities at Alexandria and arrangements were made for her to be repaired at the Puget Sound Naval Shipyard in Bremerton, Washington on the west coast of the United States. In a German bombing raid on Alexandria shortly before she was to leave for the U.S., *Warspite* incurred additional major damage.

In the July 1943 Allied landings in Sicily, *Warspite* carried out a bombardment of enemy shore positions and, to reach her assigned station for the shelling which was to begin at 6.30 p.m., she had to hurry. A full speed of 22.5 knots was somehow achieved and, following the shelling Admiral Cunningham signalled her captain: "Operation well carried out. There is no doubt that when the old lady lifts her skirts she can run."

Off the beaches of Salerno on 15 September 1943 *Warspite* and *Valiant* were shelling German tank, artillery and troop concentrations in the nearby hills, when *Warspite* came under attack by a new and deadly weapon of the enemy, a radio-controlled aircraft glider bomb. In the early afternoon, three of the glider bombs were launched from German bombers at high altitude. One fell on *Warspite*, slamming into her amidships near the funnel. A second glider bomb then hit in the sea near her starboard side, tearing a great gap in her hull. With only partial power, she continued her shelling of the shore targets until the task was completed. Then, as she slowly steamed from the area her old chronic steering malfunction recurred and she began running in circles into a mined area. The first glider bomb had done far more damage to the battleship than most of the crew had realized. In addition to the helm trouble, she was listing five degrees to starboard, had settled four feet deeper in the water, was heavily flooded and under threat of further bombing attacks, and there was a four-foot by twenty-foot hole in her bottom. With immediate shoring and counterflooding, the situation was somewhat eased and soon *Warspite* was taken in tow by American tugs through the Straits of Messina, shielded by a protective screen of destroyers. Through that long night the blacked-out battleship was kept afloat by the efforts of a 200-man bailing-out team. For much of the night, the crippled ship swung on her tow ropes in the strong currents, completely out of control. She crept into harbour at Malta behind her tugs on 19 September.

Wounded and showing her age, HMS *Warspite* put to sea from Greenock on 2 June 1944 in company with the battleship *Ramillies* and several other Royal Navy warships comprising the Eastern Task Force. Their immediate destination was Plymouth, England and, from there, to just off the Isle of Wight. They were part of a force of several thousand vessels assembling in the English Channel for the Normandy invasion. *Warspite* was one of the ships assigned to provide fire support for the British troops who would be landing at SWORD, one of five beaches along the French coast between Cherbourg and the Caen region. In particular, she was tasked with knocking out the German gun batteries near Le Havre. *Warspite* would have the honour of firing the opening shot of the Normandy landings at 5.30 a.m. on D-Day, 6 June. All that day the old veteran of Jutland, and so many other combat actions since 1916, continued to fire on German infantry positions and vehicle concentrations, gun emplacements and a command headquarters. Some of her gunnery was conducted with the benefit of spotting by forward observers and observation aircraft, but much of it was not. Return fire from German shore batteries frequently peppered *Warspite* with shrapnel, but she suffered no significant damage during the operation. She remained on station off shore until late in the evening when finally ordered to pull back and anchor a few miles out from SWORD. On the 7th, *Warspite* resumed firing, this time at enemy strongpoints and troop concentrations.

On 8 June, her ammunition magazines nearly empty after having fired more than 300 fifteen-inch rounds, *Warspite* returned briefly to Portsmouth to reload. On the 9th she was again lying off Normandy but now in support of troops on the American invasion beaches. She took over for the battleship USS *Arkansas* which was also running out of ammo. Late that day she put nearly 100 of her big shells onto an important German artillery site, winning high accolades from U.S. commanders in the area. On the 11th, she lay off GOLD beach where she was asked to shell an assembly of enemy tanks and troops in a nearby wood, receiving the command "Fifty rounds fifteen-inch rapid fire." The action helped to save the British 50th Division from what would have been a savage counterattack.

With her main guns nearly worn out, *Warspite* was ordered back to Rosyth on 12 June to have replacement guns fitted. She sailed through the Straits of Dover and received the attentions of several German coastal gun batteries as she passed. No real harm was done, but on the 13th, off Harwich, she came too close to a magnetic mine which exploded, damaging her steering and, once again jamming her helm. She was dead in the water and began listing to port. There were no casualties and the crew were able to correct the list through counterflooding and restart her engines within an hour. She crawled back to Rosyth at just seven knots, arriving to the cheers of other warship crewmen.

In October 1944, *Warspite* was assigned to provide gunfire support for a British commando brigade in the final major assault of the Allied campaign in northwest Europe. The targets were German gun emplacements on the island of Walcheren near the port of Antwerp. The Allies desperately needed the port to bring in the great quantities of supplies required for their advance on Germany in the final months of the European war. It was the last time her guns were fired.

On 20 April 1947, HMS *Warspite* was off Land's End, being towed by two tugs to Gareloch in the Clyde, where she was to be cut up for scrap, when she was overtaken by an incredibly violent Atlantic storm. A tow line parted and the old battleship began taking on water by the bows. A new tow line was eventually attached and she was taken to Mount's Bay, Penzance, to wait out the lengthy storm. There she broke free of her anchor and soon ran aground at Prussia Cove on the far side of the bay, ripping her bows, flooding her forward compartments and sinking down by the bows. Her small caretaker crew was rescued from the threatened vessel. She lingered there, gradually disintegrating, until the summer of 1950, when she was refloated and towed to Marazion Beach near St Michael's Mount. There her remains were blasted and cut apart into sections small enough to be transported by rail to Welsh smelters. Fragments of her boilers are still buried in the beach.

visualize New York Harbor on its busiest day of the year and then just enlarge that scene until it takes in all the ocean the human eye can reach, clear around the horizon. And over the horizon there are dozens of times that many."
– Ernie Pyle
American war correspondent describing the D-Day invasion fleet

"As our teams were called, we assembled on the landing craft and were lowered into the water, and it was tremendously rough and the spray from the sea was cold, and it came over the sides of the landing craft and nearly everybody got soaked. We were taking water from the rough sea over the bow, and we were bailing to try to keep afloat. Some of the landing craft sank before they got in because of the rough sea. In fact, we picked up some of our buddies who had floundered eight or nine miles from shore, and we had taken them on as extra cargo; and some that we should have picked up or would have liked to have picked, we left because we didn't have room. We hoped somebody else would.
"It was a terrible ride to the beach. Over to our right, the battleship *Texas* was firing into the cliffs, and every time that big fourteen inch gun went off, a tremendous tsunami swamped our boat, and the water would come over the side and just soak us and make our seasickness worse."
– Bob Slaughter
D-Day landings veteran

Countless are the mountains in Yamato, / but perfect is the heavenly hill of Kagu; / when I climb it and survey my realm, / over the wide plain the smoke-wreaths rise and rise, / over the wide lake the gulls are on the wing; / a beautiful land it is, the land of Yamato!

– from *Climbing Kaguyama and looking upon the land, Nippon Gakujutsu Shinkokai*

by Emperor Jumei, seventh century AD

The region surrounding the ancient Japanese capital of Nara was called Yamato. In time this poetic name became that of the nation.

CONSIDERED BY MANY to have been the ultimate battleships, the World War II giants, *Yamato* and her sister ship *Musashi*, were truly extraordinary. They provided the Imperial Japanese Navy with the largest guns and the heaviest armour ever employed in warships.

By the time *Yamato* was laid down in 1937, she had been the subject of 23 major proposals and revisions, each intended to refine her design to meet the exacting requirements set for her by Japanese naval planners. At 72,809 tons fully loaded, her displacement was surpassed only by

that of the Cunard liner, *Queen Mary*. Her four steam turbines developed 153,553 shaft horsepower and could move her through the water at up to 27.5 knots. Each of her nine eighteen-inch guns in triple turrets could fire two 3,240-pound shells per minute over a distance of nearly 30 miles. With a length of 863 feet and a beam of 121 feet, her basic dimensions were similar to those of the American *Iowa* class battleships, *Iowa*, *New Jersey*, *Missouri* and *Wisconsin*, though *Yamato* and *Musashi* were considerably heavier.

In the 1930s Japan was set on expansion in the Pacific. To achieve it she would have to overcome the inevitable resistance of the British, with their bases and territories in the Far East, and confront the significant naval forces of the Americans, already hostile towards Japan. The battleship limitations and prohibitions of the 1922 Washington Treaty spelled the end of Japan's on-going warship programme which called for the building of eight large battleships and eight battle cruisers. Knowing that they could not match the industrial capability of the United States, the Japanese then elected to build a small number of an entirely new class of super battleship, enormous in both size and capability. They would be vessels of such quality and superior performance that it would be virtually impossible for the Americans to reply in kind. A comparable vessel would be too large to pass through the Panama Canal, which the Japanese believed would always be a primary requirement for U.S. warships. They had estimated that the Canal could not accommodate a vessel larger than 63,000 tons with ten sixteen-inch guns and a 23-knot speed, so they instructed their planners to design a new battleship substantially larger than that. With massive armour, eighteen-inch guns and a speed of 30 knots, it would be a vessel clearly superior to anything that any potential enemy possessed or was likely to build.

The preliminary design for the new ship was ready

BATTLESHIP YAMATO

"The war comes through the air . . . dripping death." — H.G. Wells

left: Japan's *Yamato*, the world's largest battleship, at top speed outside Sakumo Bay during her full-power trials in October 1941

below: 7 April 1945, *Yamato* is targetted by conventional and torpedo bombers of U.S. carrier aircraft. At 2:23 p.m. she sank with the loss of 2,498 of her crew.

in March 1935. With a hull 964 feet long and a displacement of 70,000 tons, she was meant to be powered by turbines generating 200,000 hp and a speed of 31 knots. In the next two years many tests were carried out to determine the optimum specifications and performance factors for the ship, the armour and armament. Fifty models of the new vessel were built for basin testing; after repeated revisions of the blueprints and the reduction of the speed requirement to 27 knots in

1937, the final design was completed and construction began.

Work on the new class of Japanese battleships was to be done in utmost secrecy at the Nagasaki, Kure, Yokosuka and Sasebo shipyards. As it happened, the slipways of the Nagasaki yards were clearly visible from both the American and British consulates there. Thus, the first task for the builders was the erection of a large warehouse to obscure the view from the consulates, followed by

the erection of 75,000 square metres of hemp screening which completely surrounded the slipways. Engineering and construction then proceeded under the tightest security. The few lapses and infringements were dealt with harshly and, while the West was aware that something special was going on in the shipyards, little if any significant intelligence was gathered about the specifics of the project.

Size mattered in several important ways with the new battleships. Their immense hulls, for example, could not be manoeuvred in the water by the use of conventional tugs, so a new, purpose-built 1,600 hp tug had to be designed and constructed. To deliver the extremely heavy armament from the Kure Naval Arsenal to the Nagasaki yards, a specially constructed freighter was needed. *Yamato* was assembled in a dry dock at the Kure Kaigun Kosho yards, but the hull of her sister ship *Musashi* would have to be launched down a slipway. Japanese engineers knew from their analysis of launch data from the *Queen Mary* and other large-hull vessels that *Musashi* might gain too much momentum as she left the slipway and continue across the harbour to run aground on the opposite shore. On the day of the launch, however, they were able to control the momentum through the use of special friction chains, though the hull still caused a wave so large that it flooded some houses on the bank.

The Type 94 18.1-inch guns of the *Yamato* class battleships were ranged by a complex of three 49-foot rangefinders mounted high on the tower superstructure with the fire director. Each of the three triple turrets weighed 2,774 tons, roughly equivalent to the weight of a large destroyer. The ship carried a total of 900 projectiles for the great guns, or 100 for each gun. At an elevation of 40° a shell took 89 seconds to reach its target at a distance of 40,000 yards. The blast effects when the main armament was fired were catastrophic to anyone caught topside in an exposed position. In a test experiment, guinea pigs in cages were positioned on deck when the main guns were fired and the poor animals were disintegrated by the shock wave. The *Yamato* vessels were also mounted with a mix of 52 anti-aircraft and anti-torpedo boat guns and the latest radar, sonar arrays and electronic equipment. Each battleship carried seven Aichi E13A 'Jake' or Mitsubishi F1M2 'Pete' floatplanes. These aircraft were launched from two 63-foot catapults. They were retrieved from the water by a six-ton, 60-foot crane and were stowed in a hangar near the stern. The aircraft were used for general purpose and long-range reconnaissance.

Yamato was the heaviest armoured vessel ever built. The weight of her armour plating alone was 22,895 tons; twenty-two-inch armour protected her barbettes. All of her vital areas were covered by 16.1-inch armour, each sheet of which weighed 68 tons. It was sloped outwards to help deflect falling shells and was intended to defeat eighteen-inch enemy shells (though no such threat existed from any other naval power) when fired from a range beyond 22,000 yards. The hull armour extended down to the bottom plates with a slight extra bulge to cope with the force of torpedo explosions. With her 7.8-inch armoured deck, she was theoretically protected against even a 2,200-pound armour-piercing bomb dropped from 10,000 feet. Her great hull contained a network of more than 1,150 flood-control watertight compartments.

The designers of *Yamato* utilized 50 experimental hull models in their tests at the Tokyo Naval Technical Research Centre, which contained the largest marine test basin in the country. The purpose of the testing was to find ways to increase hull efficiency and minimize resistance in order to achieve the desired speed and performance for the massive new warship. One conclusion resulting from the experiments was that a huge and bulbous bow forefoot would have to be adopted to aid in reducing hull resistance and achieving the required 27-knot speed capability. In actual trials, *Yamato* reached a

"It is impossible to escape from other men's wrongdoings, when they are cruel and hard to remedy, or even wholly irremediable, otherwise than by victorious fighting and self-defence and by punishing most rigorously; and this no soul can achieve without noble passion."
– Plato

speed of 27.46 knots. Another important characteristic of her hull design was a rather shallow draught which would allow her to utilize most of the existing dry dock and base facilities of the Imperial Japanese Navy.

Having been laid down on 4 November 1937, the battleship *Yamato* was launched on 8 August 1940. Her main engines had been fitted in September/November 1939, with her boilers going in between May and October of that year. Between May and July of 1941, the main gun armament was fitted and on 16 December 1941, she was commissioned and became part of the First Battleship Division of the Imperial Japanese Navy and training in her commenced. The next significant event in her career came on 12 February 1942 when she became the flagship of Admiral Isoroku Yamamoto, Commander-in-Chief, Combined Fleet, IJN. The Battle of Midway (3-6 June 1942) was her first major combat engagement and as Yamamoto's flagship she became the Japanese command centre for the battle. Midway Island was an American naval airbase and refuelling station located 1,136 miles west of Hawaii. Yamamoto wanted to draw out and destroy the U.S. Navy aircraft carriers from Pearl Harbor and the confrontation would take place in the area of Midway. Japanese naval forces outnumbered the U.S. forces substantially, with eight aircraft carriers, eleven battleships, eighteen cruisers and 65 destroyers against America's three carriers, no battleships, eight cruisers and fifteen destroyers. In the event these superior numbers did not help the Japanese: Midway was an air battle between Japanese and U.S. carrier-based aircraft and a major defeat for the IJN. They suffered the loss of four aircraft carriers, *Kaga*, *Akagi*, *Hiryu* and *Soryu*, in their first naval defeat since 1592. The U.S. Navy lost the carrier *Yorktown*. From the Battle of Midway on, Japanese aircraft carriers were no longer a significant threat to American forces and after the battle the capability of both the Japanese and U.S. fleets was roughly comparable, enabling the U.S. to

right: Bridge and superstructure details of the Japanese battleship *Nagato* which is being inspected by U.S. Navy personnel in August 1945.

right: The listing, heavily damaged Japanese battleship *Ise* in August 1945, with the details and camouflage of her bridge superstructure clearly defined. Following their loss of four aircraft carriers at Midway in June 1942, the Japanese began converting *Ise* and her sistership *Hyuga* to hybrid battleship-carriers. Both vessels took part in the Battle of Leyte Gulf. They ended the war out of fuel and stranded near Kure, where they were attacked by Allied planes and sunk in the shallows.

begin an offensive role in the Pacific war. In this major air fight, the big guns of *Yamato* did not come into play and after the battle, she returned to Japan's Inland Sea. By this point the Japanese admirals had begun to accept the spreading belief that the aircraft carrier had supplanted the battleship as the key naval weapon. They ordered the immediate conversion of *Shinano*, the third *Yamato*-class battleship, then under construction, to a heavy aircraft carrier.

In August 1942, *Yamato* was sent to Truk in the Solomon Islands to participate, with *Musashi*, in a campaign to recapture Guadalcanal from the Americans. The recently completed *Musashi* arrived in the area on 22 January 1943 and became the new flagship of Admiral Yamamoto on 11 February. Now the Japanese were rapidly losing ground in the Solomons and were forced to abandon Guadalcanal. On 18 April, over the island of Bougainville, P-38 fighters of the Fifth U.S. Army Air Force intercepted and shot down a Japanese bomber carrying Admiral Yamamoto. The admiral died in the crash and his ashes were returned to Tokyo aboard *Musashi*. After a refit, both *Yamato* and *Musashi* returned to Truk where, on 25 December, *Yamato* was struck by a torpedo fired from the U.S. submarine *Skate*, causing flooding in her upper powder magazine near the number 3 main turret and necessitating another return to Japan for repairs.

By mid-May 1944, the main Japanese fleet had become an aircraft carrier strike force with a supporting battleship group which included *Musashi* and *Yamato*. On 9 July the battleships went to Lingga anchorage to train in preparation for the coming defence of the Philippines. On 22 October both *Yamato* and *Musashi* moved swiftly through the Philippines to launch an attack on the U.S. fleet in Leyte Gulf. The next day the Japanese heavy cruisers *Atago* and *Maya* were the victims of American submarines off Palawan Island and Admiral Kurita transferred his flag from *Atago* to *Yamato*.

The two giant battleships came under heavy air attack on 24 October, with *Musashi* receiving twenty torpedoes and many bombs in the four-hour raid. *Yamato* took just three bomb hits, none of which caused serious damage, but her sister ship had been mortally wounded and went down with the loss of 1,039 crew. On the following day, *Yamato* engaged in what would be her only battle with enemy vessels, firing 104 salvoes of her massive shells and sinking one American escort carrier, the USS *Gambier Bay,* and a destroyer in the Battle of Samar Gulf. The IJN lost the battle and with it the Philippines. *Yamato* left the area for Brunei Bay in Borneo and from there returned to Japan.

The last important stop in the Allied island-hopping campaign of World War II was Okinawa, an island group of the central Ryukus, in the East China Sea about 50 miles southwest of the southernmost Japanese island, Kyushu. Okinawa was serving as a base for the last-ditch Kamikaze attacks which were attempting to halt the Allied drive on Japan. U.S. naval forces assaulted the main island in Operation Iceberg, the most complex Allied invasion landing of the Pacific war, on Easter Sunday, 1945. Fleet Admiral Chester W. Nimitz was in overall command of 1,500 ships and 250,000 men.

Yamato was now called on to perform one of two final assignments. She was ordered to Okinawa to destroy the enemy invasion fleet with her big guns or, failing that, she was to be run aground there and use her great firepower in support of the Japanese defenders. The plan had originated with Admiral Soemu Toyoda, the new Commander-in-Chief of the Combined Fleet. While the Japanese believed *Yamato* to be virtually unsinkable, the assignment was, on any realistic assessment, suicidal. She was to attempt it against the opposition of many Allied aircraft and warships and with little or no Japanese air cover.

Yamato sailed at 3 p.m. on 6 April 1945 from Tokuyama Bay on Japan's Inland Sea. She was part

"Only technology has permitted us to put a city to the sword without quite realizing what we are doing."
— Joseph Wood Krutch

"A weapon is an enemy even to its owner."
— Turkish proverb

In blossom today, then
scattered: / Life is so like a
delicate flower. / How can
one expect the fragrance
To last forever?
— *Blossoms in the Wind*
by Vice-Admiral Ohnishi

of a task force commanded by Vice-Admiral Seiichi
Ito, and was only fuelled for a one-way trip to
Okinawa, but carried a full load of ordnance for
her armament. At 10 a.m. the next day, her radar
showed enemy aircraft in the area and her crew
was put on a high state of readiness for attack. Just
after noon two large groups of American carrier
aircraft were sighted approaching the task force
and the battleship was ordered to a speed of 24
knots. Shortly before 12.30 p.m. she was struck by
three torpedoes on the port side and by three
bombs near the number 3 turret. Substantial
damage was done to the flying deck and to many
of the smaller guns. Additional bombs hit her in
the next five minutes and a large fire was started.

There was a lull in the attacks lasting about 40
minutes. At approximately 1.00 p.m. *Yamato* was
struck by three more torpedoes on the port side
and by one on the starboard side. She began a
severe list to port, which was largely corrected by
counter-flooding of many compartments. Two of
her boiler rooms, one engine room and one
hydraulic machinery room were flooded and her
speed now fell to 18 knots.

Ensign Mitsuru Yoshida was Assistant Radar Officer
serving in *Yamato*. In his book, *Requiem For
Battleship Yamato*, translated by Richard H. Minear,
Yoshida recalls life aboard the great ship, and her
last days: "I was an average O.C.S. officer, a run-of-
the-mill military man. Among the countless young
men sent into battle at the end of the Pacific war, I
was entirely unremarkable. It is only that the
experience I was confronted with was unique,
nothing more.

"29 March, early morning: over the ship's P.A.—
'Preparations for getting underway commence at
0815 hours; getting underway is scheduled for
1500 hours.' There has never been so sudden a
sailing. Is this it? From the communications
people, reports that wireless and signal traffic is
heavy. This is it—the sortie we've been waiting for.

Being anchored 'in preparation for entering the
dock' was in fact a cover for our imminent
departure.

"When I first came on board, a novice, an officer
drafted out of college, I found a four-hour watch
very demanding. Without a moment's letup, one
must maintain close watch over everything around
the ship and keep an eye on the movement of
other ships at anchor; in addition, one must plan,
implement, and inspect the daily schedule on
board. The junior officer of the deck must always
function on the double; walking will not do.

"About 0100 hours: a single B-29 passes directly
over *Yamato*. 'Continue refueling, but man anti-
aircraft batteries.' The plane is much too high, so
we do not fire. The tenacity with which this ship is
being reconnoitered is enough to make us gnash
our teeth. Day after day the American
reconnaissance planes have come in a diligent
effort to capture *Yamato*'s movements. And they
have not missed the golden opportunity offered
by this refueling for the mission.

"Once more we check that hatches, doors, and
covers have been sealed. The work of getting ready
is almost completed. In the midst of growing
tension on board, all remains calm. Time hangs
heavy.

"The ship's P.A.: 'The deadline for mail is 1000
hours.' Even though we are in no mood for it, we
all encourage each other and try to write home.
How difficult to write a letter to be read after one's
death! But I must requite those kind enough to
hope for even a single word written by me. What
to do about mother's grief? Is there any way that I,
unfilial in dying ahead of her, can now console her?

"My place of duty is in the middle of the bridge,
the heart and brains of the ship; my duty is to
supervise the lookouts stationed at sixteen places
on board and to evaluate their reports, deciding
which to pass on to the staff officers, from the
captain on down. When we are steaming on alert,
it is a most important duty.

"*Yamato* advances inexorably, throwing up a bow wave to either side. Thanks to the incomparable seaworthiness of the ship's construction, there is no pitch or roll; even on the bridge, we have the illusion of standing on firm ground.

"The broad outlines of the operation are as follows. First, all ships will charge ahead, attract the American naval and air forces, and open the way for the success of the special attack planes. Any ship still afloat will simply press forward into the very midst of the enemy until she runs aground; all hands will fight with might and main until all ammunition is expended. Then any men still alive with one bound will become footsoldiers and join the fray. Hence machine guns and pistols have been distributed to each division.

"Never in the annals of naval warfare has there been such a special attack, nor will there ever be another.

"Breakfast. Probably the last meal we can enjoy in a normal atmosphere. I cannot bear to eat it inside this gloomy compartment. I scramble up the ladder outside the radar compartment, come out atop the platform of the antenna used in sending out transmissions, a flat area a little more than two meters square. I take a big bite out of my ball of rice. An ideal spot, surrounded by sky. When the sea wind blows up and threatens to knock me off, I hold on by wrapping my legs around the support.

"1200 hours. We have just reached the halfway point. The entire task force advances serenely. The commander in chief looks to each side of him and smiles a broad smile: 'We got through the morning all right, didn't we?'

"These are his first words since the mission began, when he took his seat in the commander in chief's chair, in front and to the right on the bridge. The sequence of alerts, the choice of zigzag, the speed, the changes of course—he has left everything to the captain of *Yamato*; and he has merely nodded silently in response to the reports of his chief of staff.

"From now on, until the ship capsizes, he will sit, arms folded, like a rock amid the smoke of the guns and the rain of bullets. All those around him will be killed or wounded, but he will move not at all.

"Was he too proud to assert control over this operation forced through over his opposition, opposition so strong he risked losing his command? Or was this his silent protest against the fate of being remembered as the highest-ranking officer of an operation that will live in naval annals for its recklessness and stupidity? A man of refreshing directness, the tall and graceful Admiral Ito."

At 1.45 p.m. yet another series of attacks began and this time the giant battleship took at least two torpedoes to port and one to starboard. Now she was listing up to 18° to port and the list was increasing rapidly. Additional counter-flooding was ordered but the degree of list continued to grow. The ship was now moving through the water at barely ten knots, steaming in a giant circle. By 2 p.m. all power failed in *Yamato* and the captain ordered that the crew make ready to abandon ship. The great vessel began to capsize and shortly thereafter, an immense explosion of the stern ammunition magazines was followed immediately by a secondary blast which ripped the ship apart. The huge smoke cloud was visible 110 miles away on Kagoshima Island. In the campaign for Okinawa, which was finally secured by U.S. forces on 22 June, more than 12,000 Americans were killed. Japanese dead amounted to just over 110,000 (including 24,000 civilians). The Japanese lost sixteen ships sunk, with four damaged, while the Americans lost 36 ships, with 368 damaged. The Americans lost several hundred aircraft and the Japanese several thousand.

The end came for *Yamato* at 2.23 p.m., 7 April, when she sank taking 2,498 of her crew with her. Only 280 survived. The Japanese Navy of World War II was no more. It marked the end of the ultimate battleship and nothing like her was ever attempted again.

Out of a fired ship, which, by no way / But drowning, could be rescued from the flame, / Some men leap'd forth, and ever as they came / Near the foe's ships, did by their shot decay; / So all were lost, which in the ship were found, / They in the sea being burnt, they in the burnt ship drowned.
— *A Burnt Ship*
by John Donne

BY 1946, when HMS *Vanguard* was commissioned, the battleship era had nearly finished. The Second World War had clearly demonstrated that the aircraft carrier would now be the new capital ship of the world's navies.

Seven years earlier, however, there had been much talk in Royal Navy circles of building a new, "one-off" battleship which would utilize the fifteen-inch guns that had been removed from the old light battlecruisers *Glorious* and *Courageous* in the 1920s, when they were converted into aircraft carriers. These guns and their turrets had been held in reserve for the *Queen Elizabeth* and *Revenge* class battleships. In March 1939, Sir Stanley Goodall, Director of Naval Construction, wrote a proposal suggesting that the guns be the basis for a new battleship. He argued that the precious time spent in designing, constructing and testing main-battery guns and turrets for the new vessel could be saved. All the significant European navies appeared to be using fifteen-inch guns in their newest battleships. Actually, the fifteen-inch main guns mounted in Germany's *Bismarck*, Italy's *Vittorio Veneto* and France's *Richelieu* were all capable of shooting to a substantially greater range than those intended for the new British battleship. Goodall believed that the new warship should be based on a hull utilizing the armour standards of the *King George V* class, with a *Lion* class propulsion system. As well as the eight fifteen-inch guns, in four turrets, the new battleship, *Vanguard*, would carry sixteen 5.25-inch guns in eight mounts, 48 two-pounder pom-poms and two spotting aircraft. She was to be capable of between 27 and 31.5 knots. Her vertical armour protection was intended to resist fifteen-inch 1,938-pound shells fired at a range of 14,000 yards. Horizontal protection was meant to resist 1,000-pound armour-piercing projectiles dropping from 14,000 feet. Her hull would be designed to resist the explosion of a 1,000-pound charge of TNT. Her fully-loaded displacement would be 51,400 tons.

It was believed that *Vanguard* would be needed to help counter the growing Japanese naval capability in the Far East, where, it had been estimated, Japan would be operating at least four more capital ships than the Royal Navy by 1944. *Vanguard* would be assigned to help protect British trade routes in Australasian and Indian waters, and to serve as a stop-gap show of force until a Royal Navy battle fleet could arrive.

In May 1940 the design of *Vanguard* was approved and her keel was laid at the John Brown & Company yard on the Clyde on 2 October 1941. However, with highest construction priority going to Britain's newest aircraft carriers, the *Illustrious*, *Implacable*, *Majestic* and *Colossus* class vessels, it was not until early 1944 that *Vanguard* gained a top priority status. She was launched on 30 November 1944 and was sponsored by HRH Princess Elizabeth, the eighteen-year-old future Queen, in one of her first important public appearances. "I am very proud to come here to launch this truly magnificent addition to the Royal Navy. You may be sure I shall always follow the movements of this fine ship and of all who serve in her with the greatest possible interest. When I first saw her I found it hard to realise that this vast structure, now safely afloat, is the work of men's hands. The men and women of this shipyard may indeed feel proud of this evidence of their patience, their skill, and their hard work through many months. They must surely have put something into her which is part of the staunchness of our race."

Deriving from the French "avant-garde", the word vanguard refers to "the foremost position in an army or a fleet advancing into battle", and the motto of HMS *Vanguard* was "We Lead". Similar in appearance to the battleships of the earlier *King George V* class, *Vanguard* was fully fitted out and left the John Brown yard on 2 May 1946, the ninth Royal Navy warship to be called *Vanguard*. The tenth *Vanguard* was to be a nuclear-powered ballistic missile submarine which was laid down in

AFTER WORLD WAR II

"And so the great democracies triumphed. And so were able to resume the follies that had nearly cost them their lives."
– Winston Churchill, on the rapid disarmament, defence budget-cutting and return to complacency by the Western powers following World War II.

HMS *Vanguard* was Britain's most powerful battleship, and her last. Her predecessors, the battleships of the King George V class, were known as "wet boats" because of the absence of shear forward in their hull design, which caused them to take a lot of water over the deck in heavy weather. *Vanguard* had considerable forward shear, making her one of the best sea boats in the world. When sailing in company with the USS *Iowa* in heavy seas during a storm, she was noted to be rolling just 13 degrees, while *Iowa* was rolling 26 degrees.

left: A warm welcome back at war's end.
overleaf: HMS *Vanguard* in Gibraltar's No. 1 drydock for an annual overhaul visit.

September 1986 and launched in March 1992. The 15,000-ton sub was armed with sixteen Trident D5 intercontinental ballistic missiles and was also fitted with four torpedo tubes. Together with her sister ships, *Vigilant*, *Vengeance* and *Victorious*, this last *Vanguard* leads Britain's nuclear deterrent capability.

Vanguard was the last battleship of the Royal Navy. She did not, in the end, utilize the eight fifteen-inch guns originally fitted to HMS *Glorious* and HMS *Courageous*. What she did incorporate were the four main turrets from these old ships, giving her thick turret armour. In these turrets were mounted fifteen-inch Mk 1 guns which fired a 1,938-pound shell with a 2,458fps muzzle velocity, but her crews never fired her guns in anger.

In March 2002, the world of seafarers was shocked and outraged by news that the London-based daily shipping newspaper, *Lloyd's List*, had elected to stop referring to vessels as "she" and to henceforth refer to them as "it". The paper's editor stated that ships were nothing more than mercantile real estate, and that calling an elegant cruise liner "she" was all very well, but it could be offensive to apply the feminine pronoun to some rusting old hulk.

Merchant sailors and Britain's Royal Navy were defiant in their opposition to the move. The Ministry of Defence said: "*Lloyd's List* can do what they want. The Royal Navy will continue to call its ships 'she' as we have always done. It is historic and traditional."

below: HMS *Vanguard* under way ca. 1953.

TYPICAL DAILY SEA ROUTINE IN HMS VANGUARD
03.55 Morning Watch men to muster.
05.30 Call the hands.
06.00 Hands fall in. Scrub decks.
07.05 Starboard Watch to breakfast.
07.25 Port Watch to breakfast.
07.55 Forenoon Watch men to muster. Both Watches of hands fall in. Prayers. Detailed for work.
09.00 Training classes to instruction.
11.55 Grog issue.
12.00 Starboard Watch to dinner.
12.25 Afternoon Watch men to muster.
12.30 Port Watch to dinner.
13.15 Both Watches of hands fall in. Detail for work. Training classes to instruction.
15.55 First Dog Watch men to muster.
16.00 Port Watch to tea.
16.20 Starboard Watch to tea.
16.30 Cinema show for

To some extent, the design of *Vanguard* was influenced by lessons learned with the loss of the Royal Navy battleship, *Prince of Wales*, which sank on 10 December 1941 in the South China Sea following an attack by Japanese land-based aircraft. Specifically, major improvements were made in such areas as pumping facilities, internal watertight subdivisions, additional diesel generators and escape routes from the lower compartments.

Finally completed and commissioned in late 1946, *Vanguard* was the last British dreadnought battleship and the only one never to go to war. In a three-month tour of South Africa by King George VI, she operated as the royal yacht and in 1949 was assigned to the Mediterranean Fleet. She served as a training vessel from summer 1949 until summer 1952 and later served as flagship of the Home Fleet. In 1955 a proposal was floated to convert *Vanguard* into a guided-missile warship, but the plan was shelved as unaffordable. The battleship entered the Reserve Fleet in 1956 and, in August 1960, she

was sent to Shipbuilding Industries, Faslane, for scrapping.

On 12 May 1951, the newly recommissioned USS *New Jersey* (BB-62) arrived in Yokosuka, Japan, recalled to active duty for the Korean War. North Korean communist troops had invaded South Korea in June 1950 and *New Jersey* was being reactivated to join her sister ship *Missouri* in bombarding the North Korean enemy. When the North Koreans had moved south, *Missouri* had been pulled from her midshipman training assignment and dispatched to Korea. Within two months, she was re-equipped and on station there.

The United Nations had agreed to oppose the

North Korean invasion of its southern neighbour, but was unsure of North Korea's military capability. The only certainty was that there would be jet fighters on both sides capable of flying at much higher flying speeds than their World War II fighter counterparts. A major concern of the U.S. Navy was that the Soviet Union and China would provide enough front line aircraft to the North Koreans to create an air defence nightmare for the Navy. As it happened, that concern was not justified. At the time, however, it was believed that the American carriers would require protective cover from the remaining *Iowa* class fast battleships.

Missouri and *New Jersey* went to war in Korea looking essentially the same as they had in World War II. The only major equipment changes were the addition of new, advanced radar and electronics for greater efficiency in detecting and identifying air and surface targets, as well as assisting in the direction of air strikes. The single major change to the armament of the reactivated Iowa class ships was the programme to add automatic 3-inch/50 calibre medium range anti-aircraft guns, to replace many of the quadruple 40mm mounts.

The first job given *New Jersey* was to provide anti-aircraft cover for the *Essex* class carriers of Task Force 77 off the Korean east coast. While on this mission, the battleship was detached from

Red Watch of Engine Room Department. Fo'c'sle and Torpedo Divisions muster on Quarter-deck for Deck Hockey.
16.45 Tombola in main Dining Hall. Miniature Rifle Range open on the Fo'c'sle for shooting practice.
17.55 Last Dog Watch men to muster.
18.25 Hands to supper.
19.30 Cinema show for Starboard Watch of Royal Marines.
19.55 First Watch men to muster.
20.00 Port Watch fall in. Clear up Mess Decks and Flats. Gramophone Concert in the After Schoolroom.
20.30 Rounds.
21.30 Pipe down.
21.45 Chief and Petty Officers pipe down.
23.55 Middle Watch men to muster.

On a post-war Western Pacific deployment of the battleship USS *New Jersey*:
34,500 nautical miles were steamed.
174 sixteen-inch bullets were fired.
481 five-inch rounds were fired.
7,855,466 gallons of fuel oil were burned.
1,248,333 gallons of fuel oil were transferred.
6,218,108 gallons of water were desalinated.
2,800 gallons of paint were used.
40 replenishments underway were conducted.
310 helicopter landings were accomplished.
93.1 remote-piloted vehicle flight hours were logged.
6,275 messages were received.
$696,834. worth of provisions were consumed.
420,627 meals were served.
28,188 gallons of milk were consumed.
580,320 eggs were consumed.
412,000 pounds of laundry was washed.
$3,250,000 of wages were paid.
500,000 pounds of mail was received.
20,000 VIPs were given tours.
4,185 medical outpatients received care.
2,192 dental patients received treatment.

HMS *Vanguard* is the only British battleship never to have fired her guns in anger.

the task force to bombard North Korean shore installations and enemy supply movements. She gradually proceeded northward to Wonsan harbour, where her main guns were fired at the enemy transportation centre there through the night of 20-21 May. The next morning began with North Korean artillery shelling the battleship. Some relatively minor damage was caused when an enemy round hit turret one, destroying a periscope there. The ship's crew was ordered to battle stations. The shelling continued and, on the battleship's port side, Seaman Robert Osterwind was mortally wounded when shrapnel fragments from an exploding round struck him in the chest. Osterwind became the only man ever to be killed in action on the *New Jersey*.

When the Army of the Republic of Vietnam (ARVN) was unable to cope with the North Vietnamese communist insurgents in 1965, the United States sent a large ground force into South Vietnam in an attempt to stabilize the situation. Once again, the U.S. Navy was called on to provide fire support and air cover in that region. Internal squabbling in the Navy between proponents of battleship reactivation and the naval aviation community, including the Chief of Naval Operations at the time, caused a nearly two-year delay in the next recommissioning of the USS *New Jersey*. Then, on 31 July 1967, the CNO retired and the very next day the Navy announced that *New Jersey* would be reactivated for deployment to Vietnam. *New Jersey* got the nod over her *Iowa* sisters because she was the nearest to combat-ready of the four vessels.

Despite the decision to bring *New Jersey* back for service in Southeast Asia, there remained a feud within the Navy. The air community felt threatened by the presence of the battleship and resented the funding it was drawing. The Marine Corps, though, mindful of the support it needed from the old warship, lent its considerable support to the

involvement of *New Jersey* in the Vietnam conflict. The Department of Defense, moreover, took the view that the battleship offered the capability of hitting many of the targets normally assigned to aircraft, without suffering the losses normally incurred in pilots and aircraft on those assignments.

New Jersey is credited with having achieved an outstanding level of performance in Vietnam. Operating all along the coast there, with virtual impunity, the battleship was considered extremely effective in the destruction of important targets within range of her big guns. Her intimidating presence caused the Vietcong forces to move well inland, easing pressure on South Vietnamese troops near the coast. Yet, by 1969, this same power to intimidate by her very presence was seen as a problem by the new Nixon administration in Washington. Though she was scheduled for a second deployment to Vietnam in September, the White House ordered that she be deactivated instead, along with 100 other Navy ships. Washington, it seems, was concerned that the threatening shape of *New Jersey* off the Vietnamese coast would impede peace negotiations and prolong the war. As it happened, both the peace talks and the war went on and on, and in 1972 the North Vietnamese launched a major spring offensive and stalled the peace negotiations, causing the U.S. president to resume significant offensive operations against the North. It seems probable that, had the battleship not been mothballed at the end of her first deployment to Vietnam, she could have contributed importantly to the action against Haiphong harbour and other vital targets in the North.

All four *Iowa* class battleships participated in action during World War II and the Korean War, but *New Jersey* was the only battleship to participate in the Vietnam War. She also saw action when ordered to the Mediterranean to fire on Syrian anti-aircraft batteries in Lebanon from December 1983 through February 1984. By this time she had been re-equipped to carry 32 Tomahawk cruise missiles, 16 Harpoon anti-surface missiles, four Vulcan-Phalanx close-in "Gatling guns" for air defence; a cruiser-style communications system; a modern electronic countermeasures system; aviation facilities and operating stations for SH-60B helicopters; updated air and surface radars; and conversion of the fuel plant to burn Navy distillate fuel.

In December 1989 a battle group led by the USS *New Jersey* steamed into the Persian Gulf region, replacing the single aircraft carrier battle group headed by the USS *Midway* that had been stationed there. *Midway* had been patrolling the Indian Ocean just outside the Persian Gulf, guarding the strategic oil waterway where more than 500 commercial vessels had been destroyed or damaged during the eight-year Iran-Iraq war. For the first time since 1986, the region was without the air-strike capability of a U.S. carrier. Iran called the arrival of the *New Jersey* provocative and an act of aggression. Saudi Arabia showed her displeasure at the presence of the battleship by refusing to allow a port call. Instead, *New Jersey* was given a warm (if low-key) welcome by the island state of Bahrain where she anchored two miles off the coast and much of the 1,800-man crew went ashore for a brief liberty visit. Most of the Gulf Arab states were balancing a quiet support for an American military presence with their overt neutrality and opposition to such a foreign presence in the region.

New Jersey was the largest warship ever to enter the Gulf and sail the Strait of Hormuz.

The crew of the USS *Missouri* (BB-63) reacted with stunned silence as their captain informed them unofficially on the internal television system that their ship was soon to be decommissioned and retired. It was 1990, and before decommissioning could take place, it was cancelled as the United States suddenly began preparations for war. In November, the *Missouri* was ordered to join her sister ship, the USS *Wisconsin* (BB-64), in the

Persian Gulf. Having had major refits, the two *Iowa* class battleships were armed with Tomahawk cruise missiles capable of striking strategic inland targets, in addition to their massive sixteen-inch main guns for shore bombardment.

In the mid-morning of 16 January 1991, Captain Albert Lee Kaiss, who would be the last captain of the *Missouri*, and the last battleship captain in the world, received orders to prepare a cruise missile strike. Fourteen hours later, just after midnight, Kaiss ordered reveille to be sounded and told his crew to go to the head because everyone would be ordered to general quarters in about ten minutes and "we are going to general quarters for real. We are currently in receipt of a strike order, and we are making preparations to launch Tomahawks in the next hour".

On 2 August, Iraqi President Saddam Hussein had sent three Iraqi army divisions into neighbouring Kuwait, taking over the tiny nation and threatening Saudi Arabia to the south. With U.S. Navy warships under way to the Gulf, President George Bush ordered Operation Desert Shield, a mobilization for action in that region. An Allied Coalition began forming, American congressional debates were held, economic sanctions and United Nations resolutions were sought in preparation for conflict with Iraq.

By October *Missouri* was in San Diego where some of her crew underwent specialist training at Navy schools. Training continued aboard the battleship as she headed to the Persian Gulf. On the morning of 16 January 1991, *Missouri* was at anchor in Bahrain when Desert Shield became Desert Storm, the Gulf War proper.

At 1.40 a.m. the first Tomahawk missile blasted from an armoured box launcher in *Missouri*'s superstructure, creating a bright white halo and a tail of orange flame as it skidded and lifted into the blackness. The battleship fired six Tomahawks into Iraq that night. By 20 January, the *Missouri* Tomahawk team had launched a total of 28 of the

The Mark 7 sixteen-inch/fifty-calibre guns of the American *Iowa* class battleships fired two basic types of round: a 1,900-pound High Capacity (HC) shore bombardment projectile, and a 2,700-pound armour-piercing projectile. Four additional projectile types were developed for the big guns during the 1980s: the Mk 143 High Explosive (HE) using an M732 Controlled Variable Time proximity fuze; the Mk 144 Improved Conventional Munitions projectile, with an electronically timed M724 fuze, a round which dispensed 400 small wedge grenades; the Mk 145 High Explosive, with the M724 ETF; and the Mk 146, also using a M724 ETF, and dispensing 666 shaped-charge bomblets.

A further projectile development of the 1980s was the Sub-Calibre Extended Range round. It was designed to achieved the longer distance and greater accuracy required to hit the mobile defences of a modern enemy. It was spin-stablized; a thirteen-inch body with a sabot outer shell adapting it to a sixteen-inch bore. The sabot discarded when the projectile left the gun muzzle. In flight, the projectile had a muzzle velocity of more than 3,600 feet per second and could reach targets 70,000 yards distant. The new shell contains submunitions, a large number of fragmentation grenades which disperse over an area equivalent to about six football fields. New radars and computers were required for the gunfire control systems of the *Iowa* class to cope with the extended range of the new shells.

precision guided missiles at Iraqi targets.

Off Khafji on 3 February, *Missouri* was called on to fire her sixteen-inch main guns in anger for the first time since March 1953 off Korea. Her task was to target concrete command and control bunkers and the terrain required the battleship to manoeuvre much closer into shoal water than safety considerations normally allowed, where there was as little as three feet of water under her keel.

This bunker targetting assignment involved the first combat use of the remotely piloted reconnaissance and scouting vehicle (RPV) system from *Missouri*. The small, pilotless aircraft was "flown" by a controller on the 0-3 level of the battleship via a television monitor and a remote control box similar to that used by flyers of powered model airplanes. The little RPV was fitted with a black-and-white television camera and an infra-red sensing system for sending a high-resolution video image at night. It was recovered aboard the ship with the aid of a net strung between poles on the fantail.

For three nights the main guns of *Missouri* fired into the Khafji area, delivering a total of 112 of the huge rounds. The ship was relieved by *Wisconsin,* for one week, and then returned to Khafji to shoot an additional 60 rounds of the big stuff in nine fire-support assignments. The targets included infantry battalions, a command bunker, a mechanized unit and an artillery battery, all with the considerable assistance of the RPV whose television pictures were shown on hundreds of monitors throughout the battleship.

In those and subsequent bombardment assignments, *Missouri*'s World War II-era plotting room computers worked well, helping her gun crews to achieve great accuracy.

The ground war began on 24 February. *Missouri* was tasked with firing into Iraqi-held territory in support of the operation to re-take Kuwait. She was part of an effort to fool the Iraqis into

believing that a Coalition amphibious landing in Kuwait was imminent. She pretended to be two battleships, frequently moving along the shore and laying down a massive bombardment to make the enemy think that they were exposed to twice the firepower. She fired 133 rounds in two hours on the night of 25 February. During the firing, the officer of the deck spotted an orange fireball that was glowing as it grew larger and nearer to the ship. Captain Kaiss recognized it as an incoming missile and the OOD ordered everyone to hit the deck. For nearly two minutes from the officer's warning, the entire crew of *Missouri* waited for the impact and many of them watched as other ships in the area fired several chaff rockets intended to decoy the radar seeker of the enemy missile. It was a Chinese-built Iraqi Silkworm anti-ship missile and it approached the stern of the battleship, crossing from starboard to port and then seeming to head down the port side. At that instant, two white streaks, Sea Dart missiles fired from the British destroyer HMS *Gloucester* at a range of four miles intercepted the Silkworm; one of them detonated it, probably saving *Missouri* from damage and possibly worse. After the Silkworm attack, an RPV was launched from *Missouri* to locate the site of the enemy missile battery. That accomplished, the battleship began firing its heavy projectiles at the enemy site, quickly destroying it.

Missouri shot 759 sixteen-inch projectiles during her Gulf War assignment, 611 of them during one sixty-hour period ending on 27 February. Her crew performed superbly in that period of about four days, spending most of it at general quarters and, for many of them, with little or no sleep.

Wisconsin became the Tomahawk missile Strike-warfare Centre during Operation Desert Storm and the last naval gunfire of that conflict came from her sixteen-inch main weapons. The Tomahawk and gunfire strikes, naval gunfire support in Kuwait, and

"Last year I successfully led the fight to preserve these ships as a key part of the U.S. force projection capability. This enabled them to be used in Operation Desert Storm. I agree that we should not rush to eliminate them, in spite of the cuts in defense spending. I have consistently advocated reductions in our strategic and nuclear forces in order to preserve the battleship element of our force projections capability."
– U.S. Senator John McCain

left: A sixteen-inch salvo fired from the USS *Missouri* at Chong Jin, Korea, in an effort to cut North Korean communications on 21 October 1950, overleaf: The *Missouri* under way to her recommissioning at San Francisco,1986.

The USS *Missouri* (BB-63) was armed with nine sixteen-inch/fifty-calibre guns in three triple turrets. She also carried twenty five-inch/thirty-eight-calibre guns in ten twin mounts (in her 1984-86 modernization, this was reduced to twelve guns in six twin mounts). Originally, the ship carried 49 20mm guns in single mounts (reduced to 22 by 1947). By the Korean War period, these had been the remotely piloted vehicle operations were all coordinated through *Wisconsin*. She acted as the Persian Gulf Force "over-the-horizon targetting coordinator", both at sea and in port. In February 1991 *Wisconsin* destroyed or inflicted severe damage on Iraqi communications facilities, special forces boats, artillery batteries, command posts, infantry bunkers, mechanized units, troop housing and surface-to-air missile sites. On 1 March, at Faylaka Island, the television camera of a *Wisconsin* RPV recorded the first instance of Iraqi troops waving white flags in an attempt to surrender to an unmanned aircraft. In her six months of service in the Gulf War, *Wisconsin* fired 324 sixteen-inch rounds, 881 five-inch rounds, 5,200 20mm rounds and launched 24 land-attack cruise missiles. She operated there without incurring a serious fire, flood or collision casualty or personnel injury.

replaced with 32 in dual mounts. All such guns were removed by the ship's 1955 decommissioning. During her 1984-86 modernization, four Vulcan/Phalanx Gatling guns were added, as well as four Harpoon anti-ship missile canisters containing a total of sixteen missiles. She also received eight quadruple Tomahawk cruise missile launchers containing a total of 32 missiles.

Alone, quite alone now; / Only the slap of the hump-backed wave / Can reach him here, / Washing away his manhood, far away.

Awake, all agape his face, / Stabbing surprise at the sea-stretched sky / That saw him fall. / And O his mouth but a cut for the tide.

His was no newspaper death. / No high-explosive slogan-burst / Heightened his heart, nor did the singing lead / Write headlines in the prophet-sky for him.

Merely the heart of the world / Turned cold; and he was erased; his head / Is a seed that never took root, / A stub that is crushed before it's alight.

Do not watch, do not watch; / This is the issue, the pay-book, the number, / This is not him; / Too casually he slips and ebbs with the running tide.

O, do not look for an answer. / The birds of the drowned as they mew, / Do not know. / And under all the sea lies, vast and menacing.
– *Missing—Believed Drowned* by Michael Greening

"I WAS IN THE after control with half a dozen men, the Sub. and the clerk. We crouched down behind the tenth of an inch plating and ate bully beef, but it didn't seem to go down very easily. It seemed rather a waste of time to eat beef, for surely in the next ten minutes one of those 11-inch shells would get us; they couldn't go on falling short and just over indefinitely, and well, if one did hit us—light cruisers were not designed to digest 11-inch high explosives in their stomachs."
– An officer in HMS *Southampton* at Jutland

" 'Remember Pearl Harbor' became an American shibboleth and the title of the country's most popular war song, but it was the loss of that great ship which seared the minds of navy men. Six

left: The USS *Wisconsin*, BB-64, currently berthed at the Hampton Roads Naval Museum, Norfolk, Virginia.

215

below: The USS *Iowa*, BB-4, is seen entering drydock in 1898.

We had many challenges with the restoration of USS *New Jersey*. You have to take into account that the *Iowa* Class battleships weren't designed for bombardment duty, and that is what the ship was being brought back to do. The Iowa class was built to fight enemy battleships and to be totally self-sustaining if they were damaged. So they had an extensive compartmentation design for sealing off the ship, and huge machine shops that could rebuild almost anything, so the ship could repair itself. But none of this was needed for bombardment assignments.

Of course, you couldn't remove anything, so you had to improvise around the obstacles. Galley changes were going to be needed because of the new technology for preparing and storing foods that were far different from what we used in WW2 and in the Korean War. And during earlier times, many U.S. Navy ships used deep fat fryers. These fryers gave Captain Snyder fits because he had shipboard experience with their dangerous side and saw them as potential fires just waiting to happen. To fight [such fires] we needed to install Halogen fire systems, and the space to install

months later, when naval Lieutenant Wilmer E. Gallaher turned the nose of his Dauntless dive-bomber down toward the *Akagi* off Midway, the memory of that volcanic eruption in Pearl Harbor, which he had witnessed, flashed across his mind. As the *Akagi* blew up, he exulted: '*Arizona, I remember you!*' "
– from *Goodbye, Darkness*
by William Manchester

A week after the Japanese attack on Pearl Harbor, Don Reid and bandleader Sammy Kaye released the song *Remember Pearl Harbor*. It became an immediate hit as Americans were mobilizing for war with Japan.

"Yesterday, December 7, 1941— a date which will live in infamy—the United States of America was suddenly and deliberately attacked by naval and air forces of the Empire of Japan.

"The United States was at peace with that nation and, at the solicitation of Japan, was still in conversation with its Government and its Emperor looking toward the maintenance of peace in the Pacific. Indeed, one hour after Japanese air squadrons had commenced bombing Oahu, the Japanese Ambassador to the United States and his colleague delivered to the Secretary of State a formal reply to a recent American message. While this reply stated that it seemed useless to continue the existing diplomatic negotiations, it contained no threat or hint of war or armed attack.

"It will be recorded that the distance of Hawaii from Japan makes it obvious that the attack was deliberately planned many days or even weeks ago. During the intervening time, the Japanese Government has deliberately sought to decieve the United States by false statements and expressions of hope for continued peace.

"The attack yesterday on the Hawaiian Islands has caused severe damage to American naval and military forces. Very many American lives have been

lost. In addition, American ships have been reported torpedoed on the high seas between San Francisco and Honolulu [these reports were incorrect].

"Yesterday the Japanese Government also launched an attack against Malay.

"Last night Japanese forces attacked Hong Kong.

"Last night Japanese forces attacked Guam.

"Last night Japanese forces attacked the Philippine Islands.

"Last night the Japanese attacked Wake Island.

"This morning the Japanese attacked Midway Island.

"Japan has therefore undertaken a surprise offensive extending throughout the Pacific area. The facts of yesterday speak for themselves. The people of the United States have already formed their opinions and well understand the implications to the very life and safety of our nation.

"As Commander in Chief of the Army and Navy I have directed that all measures be taken for our defense.

"Always will we remember the character of the onslaught against us.

"No matter how long it may take us to overcome this premeditated invasion, the American people in their righteous might will win through to absolute victory.

"I believe I interpret the will of the Congress and of the people when I assert that we will not only defend ourselves to the uttermost but will make very certain that this form of treachery shall never endanger us again.

"Hostilities exist. There is no blinking at the fact that our people, our territory, and our interests are in grave danger.

"With confidence in our armed forces—with the unbounded determination of our people—we will gain the inevitable triumph, so help us, God.

"I ask that the Congress declare that, since the unprovoked and dastardly attack by Japan on Sunday, December 7, a state of war has existed between the United States and the Japanese Empire."
— President Franklin Delano Roosevelt, 8 December 1941

"As soon as I heard, last night, that Japan had attacked the United States, I felt it necessary that Parliament should be immediately summoned. It is indispensible to our system of government that Parliament should play its full part in all the important acts of State and at all the crucial moments of the war; and I am glad to see that so many Members have been able to be in their places, despite the shortness of the notice. With the full approval of the nation, and of the Empire, I pledged the word of Great Britain, about a month ago, that should the United States be involved in war with Japan, a British declaration of war would follow within the hour. I therefore spoke to President Roosevelt on the Atlantic telephone last night, with a view to arranging the timing of our respective declarations. The President told me that he would this morning send a message to Congress, which, of course, as is well known, can alone make a declaration of war on behalf of the United States, and I then assured him that we would follow immediately."
— Prime Minister Winston Churchill, from a speech to the House of Commons, 8 December 1941

Following the December 1941 Japanese attack on American battleships in Pearl Harbor, the wreck of the USS *Arizona*, BB-39, lay at her mooring, her hull resting on the shallow harbour bottom and her deck awash. The remains of her superstructure still projected skyward, if not precisely erect. For weeks after the attack, U.S. Navy personnel worked tirelessly to locate and recover the bodies of *Arizona*'s crew, and her ship's records. When, at last, it was judged that no more bodies could be retrieved, it was determined that at least 900 of her men remained entombed in her.

them. Also, in years past, we used freezers designed for storing whole sides of beef on hooks, and now we needed shelves to handle the way food was being frozen and packaged today. We also had to retrofit for a much colder freezer to meet the modern requirements. There were so many problems, and they just kept coming.
— Charles T. Thomas, Assistant Program Manager for Battleships, Philadelphia Naval Shipyard, 1967-1968

Out of the chill and the shadow,
Into the thrill and the shrine;
Out of the dearth and the famine,
Into the fulness divine.
— *Going Home*
by Margaret E. Sangster

Through 1942, salvage efforts concentrated on the removal of the main masts and superstructure of the 31,400 ton *Pennsylvania* class battleship. Her after turrets were given a new use as shore batteries in Hawaii. On 1 December 1942, Arizona was formally stricken from the registry of U.S. Navy vessels.

For the next eight years, there was little interest in the wreck of *Arizona*. There was, after all, a world war to be fought and won, and after that most people wanted, more than anything, to put the war, and its dreadful memories, behind them. But in 1950, the Navy began the practice of raising and lowering the American flag over the wreck each day. Interest in the idea of creating a memorial for the ship and the men who died in her began to grow. Finally, in 1958, the Congress passed legislation authorizing construction and fund-raising for the present *Arizona* memorial which straddles the hull of the battleship. The new monument was dedicated on America's Memorial Day in 1962. Now managed by the National Park Service, the white rectangular structure serves as a fitting reminder of 1,177 men who died on *Arizona* in the hours before America's entry into World War II. Only a few hundred yards from the memorial, the USS *Missouri*, BB-63, is berthed. As the host vessel for the signing ceremony of the Japanese surrender on 2 September 1945, *Missouri* represents the final day of that conflict.

"I beg to move: That an humble Address be presented to His Majesty to convey to His Majesty the deep sorrow with which the House has learned of the death of the President of the United States of America, and to pray His Majesty that in communicating his own sentiments of grief to the United States Government, he will also be generously pleased to express on the part of this House their sense of the loss which the British Commonwealth and Empire and the cause of the Allied nations have sustained, and their profound sympathy with Mrs Roosevelt and the late

left and bottom: Views of the USS *Arizona* Memorial in Pearl Harbor, Hawaii. below: The Memorial site as it appeared in the 1950s.

219

BATTLESHIPS STRUCK BY
KAMIKAZE AIRCRAFT IN
WORLD WAR II
6 January 1945 USS *New
Mexico* (BB-40) at Lingayen
Gulf, 117 casualties.
9 January 1945 USS
Mississippi (BB-41) at
Lingayen Gulf, 86
casualties.
12 April 1945 USS
Tennessee
(BB-43) at Okinawa, 129
casualties.
6 January 1945 USS
California
(BB-44) at Lingayen Gulf,
199 casualties.
27 November 1944 USS
Colorado (BB-45) at Leyte
Gulf, heavy casualties.
29 November 1944 USS
Maryland (BB-46) at Leyte
Gulf, 70 casualties.
7 April 1945 USS Maryland
(BB-46) at Okinawa, 53
casualties.
1 April 1945 USS *West
Virginia* (BB-48) at
Okinawa, 30 casualties.
11 April 1945 USS *Missouri*
(BB-63) at Okinawa, no
listed casualties.

President's family, and with the Government and people of the United States of America.'

"My friendship with the great man to whose work and fame we pay tribute today began and ripened during this war. I had met him, but only for a few minutes, after the close of the last war, and as soon as I went to the Admiralty in September 1939, he telegraphed inviting me to correspond with him direct on naval or other matters if at any time I felt inclined. Having obtained the permission of the Prime Minister, I did so. Knowing President Roosevelt's keen interest in sea warfare, I furnished him with a stream of information about our naval affairs, and about the various actions, including especially the action of the River Plate, which lighted the first gloomy winter of the war.

". . . He has left a successor who comes forward with firm step and sure conviction to carry on the task to its appointed end. For us, it remains only to say that in Franklin Roosevelt there died the greatest American friend we have ever known, and the greatest champion of freedom who has ever brought help and comfort from the new world to the old.

— Prime Minister Winston Churchill, from a speech to the House of Commons, 17 April 1945

Sponsored by the USS Missouri Association, a new surrender plaque was installed in the deck of the battleship *Missouri* and a dedication ceremony was held aboard the ship on 21 August 1989. The new plaque is an exact duplicate of the original plaque, which had become extremely worn after four decades of polishing. After the Japanese signed the instrument of surrender ending the Second World War, Admiral Chester W. Nimitz, Commander in Chief of the U.S. Pacific Fleet, decided that a bronze plaque would be placed on the exact spot on *Missouri*'s Veranda Deck where the surrender document had been signed. Since that day, *Missouri*'s 'Surrender Deck' has been the

equivalent of a national shrine, with millions of visitors from around the world making the pilgrimage to view the historic spot. Following her decommissioning in 1955, *Missouri* was opened to the public as a National Historic Site at the Puget Sound Navy Yard, Bremerton, Washington. "At the dedication ceremony, the *Missouri*'s teakwood decks gleamed to perfection," said Marcel Damiens of the USS Missouri Association. A recording of Supreme Allied Commander General Douglas MacArthur's concluding remarks at the surrender on 2 September 1945 was played: "From this solemn occasion a better world shall emerge out of the blood and carnage of the past, a world dedicated to the dignity of man and the fulfillment of his most cherished wish for freedom, tolerance and justice." The original plaque has been retired to the Navy Museum in Washington, DC.

As of 2003, disposition of the four *Iowa* battleships was as follows: the USS *Iowa* (BB-61) is currently berthed in Suisan Bay, California. She was reinstated on the Naval Registry of the United States in Class B Mobilization status on 4 January 1999. Her future is considered uncertain; the USS *New Jersey* (BB-62) is currently docked at Camden, New Jersey, having been removed from the Naval Registry on 4 January 1999. She is undergoing refurbishment for her new role as a floating museum; the USS *Missouri* (BB-63) is now berthed at Ford Island, Pearl Harbor, Oahu, Hawaii and is open to the public as a floating museum; the USS *Wisconsin* (BB-64) was reinstated on the Naval Registry on 12 February 1998 (Inactive Status) and is now a floating museum located at the Hampton Roads Naval Museum, Norfolk, Virginia.

The USS *Alabama* (BB-60) is preserved as a memorial at Mobile, Alabama. The USS *Massachusetts* (BB-59)is preserved as a memorial at Fall River, Mass. The USS *North Carolina* (BB-55) is preserved as a memorial at Wilmington, North Carolina. The USS *Texas* (BB-35) is preserved as a memorial at San Jacinto, Texas. In Britain, HMS *Victory* and HMS

Allotted a battleship tonnage of 70,000 by the 1922 Washington Naval Treaty, the French elected in 1932 to build the *Dunkerque* class, two vessels of 26,500 tons each. With eight thirteen-inch guns and a 30-knot speed, they had a significant advantage over the German pocket battleships of the early '30s. Built to specs well within the treaty limits, the *Dunkerque* and *Strasbourg* battleships quickly inspired the Germans to design and construct the two *Scharnhorst* class vessels laid down in 1935. Also influenced by the *Dunkerques*, the Italians laid down the first of their *Vittorio Veneto* class battleships in 1934.

Unique to the *Dunkerques* was their superfiring main armament arrangement with four big guns in each of two turrets. The arrangement saved some 1,700 tons of weight.

With the appearance of the *Scharnhorst* and *Gneisenau* to threaten the Allied convoys in the north Atlantic, both the *Dunkerque* and *Strasbourg* were sent after them. They were then transferred to the Mediterranean. Both were based at Oran in July 1940 when a British attack on the port severely damaged *Dunkerque*. In November 1942, both vessels were at Toulon when the French fleet was destroyed to prevent its seizure by the Germans. Both *Strasbourg* and *Dunkerque* were eventually salvaged but

Warrior are preserved in the Naval Dockyard at Portsmouth, England, as are the remains of the *Mary Rose*.

"Battleships are not the dinosaurs of the Navy, but examples of American ingenuity, design, flexibility and resolve. We in *Wisconsin* do not consider it an end. It is a temporary lay-up until America has a need to recall our firepower once again."
– Captain Conrad van der Schroeff, last commander of the USS *Wisconsin*, speaking at the decommissioning of the battleship in 1991.

"I had the honor to be the last battleship captain in the world, and that was while in command of the USS *Missouri*. I was CO when she was re-commissioned on 10 May 1986 and when she was de-commissioned on 31 March 1993. She served the United States in three wars and always did her job in the highest possible professional manner. If you were to ask me what made her great, there is only one answer in my opinion . . . and that is HER CREW. From 1944 to 1992 they were always equal to the task and true professionals. I always believed they stood six inches taller than any other sailors in the fleet. That is the story of the 'Mighty Mo', the last of the great ships."
– Albert Lee Kaiss, Captain USN Ret.

When Margaret Truman, the daughter of Missouri's native son, Harry S. Truman, christened the battleship *Missouri* with a ceremonial bottle of champagne on 29 January 1944, the spray from the breaking bottle spattered her fur coat. 42 years later, as an honoured guest at the recommissioning of the *Missouri*, she recalled: "I never did get the smell of champagne out of that muskrat."

"[When the *Missouri* took the Kamikaze hit] . . . it was more of a glancing blow. The plane and pilot were already being turned into a colander by the massive AA fire of 20mm, 40mm and 5"/30 VT frag.

It came up along the starboard side and the left wing tip hit the shell plating just below the main deck. The plane then spun around and slammed the nose spinner into the shell. Its bomb went off outboard of the ship. The upper half of the pilot's body landed on the main deck aft of a 40mm gun tub. One of the Jap machine guns penetrated the flash hider of another 40mm gun and stuck there. There was some fuel fire on the deck and scattered bits of the airplane lying around. The dents in the shell plating are still there."
– Richard Landgraff, Long Beach Naval Shipyard

Radioman Ted Mason's first duty station was the USS *California* at Pearl Harbor in December 1941. His boot camp training took placeat San Diego. "Downtown San Diego was dirty and sleazy. For a dozen blocks east from the Broadway and Navy piers, the merchants devoted themselves to the welfare of sailors and marines. There were many bars like Bradley's 5 & 10, and a number of cabarets—the Paris Inn, the Rainbow Gardens, and The Hofbrau—all guarded by husky bouncers who checked IDs closely and barred all who were not twenty-one. Approaching these in number were glass-fronted coffee shops like the Silver Dollar, serving thin greasy hamburgers and fat greasy French fries in the hot glare of fluorescent lamps. The most famous of these places was the Right Spot, which specialized in ham and eggs grilled in the front window. There a crowd usually gathered, marveling at an ambidextrous cook who manipulated three smoking skillets, flipping ham, eggs, and hash-brown potatoes with controlled abandon and flair. One had to wait for a stool or booth at the Right Spot.

"Nourishment for the outer man was not neglected. On nearly every block could be found a 'locker club' equipped with rows of green metal lockers and minimum, usually dirty, toilet facilities. Here enlisted men could shed their uniforms and change into the 'civvies' that enabled them to temporarily escape the onus of being sailors in a navy town.

"Lockers rented for about $1.50 a month, and it was customary for two or three sailors to split the expense. For the several thousand men in the "tin-can" squadrons at the destroyer base at the foot of Thirty-Second Street, it was a sensible investment. Not so for the recruits, who chanced losing their civvies when they were shipped out. An even better reason for foregoing locker clubs was given many years later by my friend Tom Hall, a former aviation radioman and fellow member of the Pearl Harbor Survivors Association. 'Who the hell did we think we were fooling with our GI haircuts?' he laughed.

At the zoo in Balboa Park, the only merchants were purveyors of popcorn, cotton candy, Orange Crush, and Delaware Punch. But the animals made me homesick for my dogs and my gun. And the giggling high-school girls in their pleated skirts, colorful blouses, tan-and-white saddle shoes, and bobby-socks reminded me achingly of the girl I had lost and could never have again. I watched the bolder of my fellow recruits approach them and invariably be rejected, and saw no reason to believe I would fare any better."

In a speech he gave at the Minnesota State Fair of 1901, U.S. President Theodore Roosevelt said: "Speak softly and carry a big stick." With the U.S. victory in the Spanish-American War, came a new popularity for the Navy. As former Secretary for the Navy, Roosevelt had ridden the tide of this popular sentiment and planned construction of a huge new battle fleet intended to project the nation's power to the world. Half a century earlier, heavily armed American ships under the command of Commodore Matthew Perry had shown the Japanese an example of "Gunboat Diplomacy" when, in 1854 and again in 1855, they sailed into Tokyo Bay. On the second occasion Perry delivered a letter from the U.S. president

neither would see action again. They were both scrapped in the 1950s.

The *Richelieu* class followed the Dunkerques. This time the French were seeking a far more powerful battleship, which they armed with eight fifteen-inch main guns. Capable of a 32-knot speed, the ships of the class, *Richelieu* and *Jean Bart* had a displacement of 47,500 tons fully loaded. *Jean Bart* and *Richelieu* were active early in World War II, fighting against the Allies. But *Richelieu* was heavily damaged by a torpedo from an HMS *Hermes* aircraft in September 1940 and came into possession of the Free French who had her repaired in the New York Navy Yard. She later became part of the British Pacific Fleet.

left: The battleship *Richelieu,* pride of the French navy, in New York harbour during November 1943.

'requesting' that the Shoguns open Japan's ports for trade with the West. The representative of the feudal Shogun relunctantly yielded to the demand.

The backbone of Teddy Roosevelt's "Big Stick" policy was the American battleship. During his first term in office, eleven new battleships joined the fleet under previous naval acts passed by Congress between 1895 and 1899. While he served as president, a series of congressional acts provided for the build-up of the Navy, including sixteen additional battleships. They were sent around the world by the president from 16 December 1907 to 22 February 1909 in an impressive parade of American sea power. Painted entirely white, except for gilded scrollwork on their bows, the warships became known as "the Great White Fleet". Crewed by more than 14,000 sailors, the ships made twenty port calls on six continents in their 43,000-mile odyssey. Accompanying the battleships were six destroyers and several auxiliary vessels. The flagship of the fleet was the USS *Connecticut*, under the command of Rear Admiral Robley D. Evans, but his poor health necessitated command being assumed by Rear Admiral Charles S. Sperry when the ships arrived at San Francisco on 6 May 1908. Following port calls at Honolulu, Auckland, Sydney, Melbourne, Manila, Yokohama and Columbo, the fleet reached Suez, Egypt where the commander was informed of a major earthquake which had just occurred in Sicily. In a display of friendship, he immediately dispatched the *Connecticut*, *Illinois*, *Culgoa* and *Yankton* to Italy to offer aid. In Sicily, the *Illinois* recovered the bodies of the American consul and his wife who had been buried in the ruins.

"We were up at Scapa and 24 hours before we sailed for what ultimately turned out to be the action with the *Scharnhorst*, Guy Russell, who had been the captain of *Nelson*, came over and took command of *Duke of York*. He was a very fine man.

He would sit, slouched in his chair when we were at sea and he would administer approbation or approval by reference to London streets. So, if you as the Officer of the Watch, were doing that well-known manoeuvre, turning in the wake of your next ahead, and you got it right, he would nod and say, 'Ah, Bond Street.' But if you made a Horlicks of it, he would growl and say, 'Um, that was a bit White Chapel.' And there were gradations in between. It was a marvellous way of letting you know exactly what he thought of what you'd just done."
— Admiral of the Fleet Sir Henry Leach, HMS *Duke of York*

The USS *New Jersey* fought 26 major engagements. With sixteen battle stars and thirteen other ribbons and citations, she is the most highly decorated battleship in American naval history. Career Navy men considered assignment to her a plum, and the Bureau of Navy Personnel said it was perpetually backlogged with four times as many requests for transfer to the *New Jersey* as the ship could accommodate.

About the USS *New Jersey*, former World War II Seabee, George Reider said: "We used to see her going from island to island, and every time you saw her going ahead, you knew the enemy was going to catch it. It made you feel good."

Entrance and exit wounds are silvered clean, / The track aches only when the rain reminds. / The one-legged man forgets his leg of wood, / The one-armed man his jointed wooden arm. / The blinded man sees with his ears and hands / As much or more than once with both his eyes. / Their war was fought these twenty years ago / And now assumes the nature-look of time, / As when the morning traveller turns and views / His wild night-stumbling carved into a hill.
— from *Recalling War* by Robert Graves

"Over the next three days I would learn something about the ever-changing moods of the ocean misnamed the Pacific. From great rising masses of cumulonimbus the ship was bombarded by intermittent rain squalls. Almost hour by hour the ocean changed personalities, from smiling to sullen to grim to angry. Whitecaps formed; spray blew along the wing; the seas heaped up and began to break in a fury of white water. Unlike a surf marching in to shore, there was no disciplined movement. Waves that seemed as tall as oak trees, moving with the speed of freight trains, collided with each other in rolling shock and flung spindrift. The ocean resembled an expanse of the Dakota Bad Lands heaving in continuous earthquake.

"At first the *California* breasted the seas with a long, easy roll. When assailed from all quarters, she shrugged the waters aside like a grizzly bear shaking off a pack of hounds. As the sea redoubled its attack she gave a little ground, dipping her mighty prow into the troughs, letting the green water roll up her forecastle to break in vain against the solid steel of turret. Then her bows rose triumphantly, tons of ocean fell away, she showed her black boot topping in disdain, and smashed into the next trough in a hiss and roar of defiance.

"I grew to love the *California* in those three days when she was tested and washed clean, as if purified by storm. Then I began to understand the feeling a sailor can have for his ship. The *California* was honest and she was virtuous and she was valiant. What more can a man ask of his mistress?"
— Ted Mason, USS *California*

"I joined the Navy in December of 1942. I had never been more than eighteen miles from my home in Melrose Park, Illinois. Then I joined the Navy and suddenly I found myself in Great Lakes Naval Training Station. It was January, the dead of winter, and I was at Camp Green Bay in boot camp. Then I was on a train to Philadelphia, and then on the *New Jersey* and her shakedown cruise. I'd never seen the ocean and I couldn't believe the colour of it, that it could be so blue. That shows you how green I was."
— Tony Iacono, USS *New Jersey*

"If, as the protesters claim, there is danger of a nuclear accident with these ships, why do so many protesters take their children along? They either don't care for their children's safety or they don't believe their own propaganda. Which is it?"
— from a letter to the Sydney, Australia *Sun-Herald*, in response to a demonstration by protesters to a visit of the USS *New Jersey*.

Lieutenant William S. Bennet served aboard the USS *New Jersey* as executive officer of the Marine Detachment. The 26-year-old Bennet had always been fascinated by battleships. "I knew about the recommissioning [of *New Jersey*], but had no idea that service aboard her would be available. I never put in for sea duty. But one day there was a call from a Marine Corps assignment officer in Washington. I thought he might ask me to become part of the Marine Detachment on the *New Jersey*, but couldn't believe it. He did and I said yes on the spot."

"After my first few weeks on board the *California*, it was apparent that, while I was in the battleship navy, I was not yet of it. I would have to prove myself before I truly belonged. Meeting that challenge would mean more than I could have imagined then. It would mean comradeship of a high order. It would mean membership for life in what I later described as a harsh and mystic brotherhood of arms. It would mean a quiet, secret pride and a deep, inner satisfaction I would never quite lose, no matter what happened."
— Ted Mason, USS *California*

RAF Group Captain Montagu Dawson died on 7

1948
BB-39 *Arizona* 1916-1941
BB-40 *New Mexico* 1918-1947
BB-41 *Mississippi* 1917-1956
BB-42 *Idaho* 1919-1947
BB-43 *Tennessee* 1920-1959
BB-44 *California* 1921-1959
BB-45 *Colorado* 1923-1959
BB-46 *Maryland* 1921-1959
BB-47 *Washington* cancelled
BB-48 *West Virginia* 1923-1959
BB-49 *South Dakota* cancelled
BB-50 *Indiana* cancelled
BB-51 *Montana* cancelled
BB-52 *North Carolina* cancelled
BB-53 *Iowa* cancelled
BB-54 *Massachusetts* cancelled
BB-55 *North Carolina* 1941-1961
BB-56 *Washington* 1941-1961
BB-57 *South Dakota* 1942-1962
BB-58 *Indiana* 1942-1963
BB-59 *Massachusetts* 1942-1965
BB-60 *Alabama* 1942-1964
BB-61 *Iowa* 1943-
BB-62 *New Jersey* 1943-1999
BB-63 *Missouri* 1944-1998
BB-64 *Wisconsin* 1944-
BB-65 *Illinois* cancelled
BB-66 *Kentucky* not completed
BB-67 *Montana* cancelled
BB-68 *Ohio* cancelled
BB-69 *Maine* cancelled
BB-70 *New Hampshire* cancelled
BB-71 *Louisiana* cancelled

The only battleships in the world currently under Mobilization Reserve Status are the USS *Iowa*, BB61 and the USS *Wisconsin*, BB64.

January 2003. He had been a navigator in one of fifteen unescorted Halifax heavy bombers which attacked the German battle cruiser *Scharnhorst* on 24 July 1941. Though normally berthed in Brest, *Scharnhorst* was temporarily in port at La Pallice on the Brittany coast of France that bright summer morning when the Halifaxes approached. From their bases in England, the bombers crossed the Channel at 100 feet, finally climbing to their bombing altitude of 15,000 feet as they neared La Pallice. They were suddenly attacked by Me 109 fighters. Near the target, they received intense anti-aircraft fire from German shore batteries and from the *Scharnhorst*. Five of the Halifaxes were downed in the attack. Dawson's plane banked sharply away from the target after dropping its bombs, and just then a cannon shell from a 109 exploded in the rear turret of the Halifax, severely injuring the rear gunner. Dawson struggled back to the turret and pulled the wounded man into the fuselage where he administered a pain-killer. In the air battle, the remaining British bombers came under attack by 21 German fighters. The gunners in Dawson's plane managed to shoot down two of the enemy craft before the Halifax was nearly brought down. Cannon and machine-gun fire smashed the windscreen and instrument panel, and ruined the port inner engine. The crew brought their bomber back to England on three engines and then lost power on the port outer engine as they approached their base. The Halifax landed with just her two starboard engines functioning and was a total write-off. In the effort, just five bombs from the RAF force struck the German warship and of these, two failed to explode. But *Scharnhorst* had been seriously damaged and had to be removed to Brest for major repairs. For his part in the raid, Group Captain Dawson was awarded the Distinguished Flying Medal.

"With most areas of interest both above decks and below barred to us, Fisher and I often found

226

ourselves at the ship's gedunk stand, despite the quality of ice cream served there. A thin, gooey concoction that tasted of dried milk solids and strong vanilla extract, slapped into a conical paper cup, passed for ice cream. Since it was unfit for human consumption without disguise, we added a nickel to the ten-cent price and ordered it dripping with chocolate or strawberry syrup topping. Never having heard of the dietary hazards of sugar and being unconcerned about weight—it was impossible for me, in those halcyon days, to gain an ounce no matter what I ingested—we ate great quantities of these horrendous sundaes until, faced with the cruel economics of sixty dollars a month, we switched to soft drinks at a third the cost. Our cokes were disguised, too, with cherry or lime flavoring: a squirt of syrup into the already sugary drink.

"The old-timers derided these effete practices of the new navy. 'Goddam gedunk sailors!' they sneered, turning to their joe pots. But the gedunk stand, to us younger ones, brought back memories of the neighborhood soda fountains that were teenage social centers in our home towns, and there were always fifteen or twenty of us in the service line."
– Ted Mason, USS *California*

On 4 August 1960, the last battleship of the Royal Navy, HMS *Vanguard*, began her final voyage, to the breaker's yard. When leaving Portsmouth Harbour, she ran aground off Customs Watch House, Old Portsmouth, and had to be pulled free by two tugs. Many locals, along with the patrons of the nearby Still & West public house, gathered outside the pub to witness the event.

By 9 August *Vanguard* was being manoeuvred by tugs through the Clyde approaches to the Faslane yard of Shipbreaking Industries. Large crowds of onlookers and photographers turned out to view her arrival. The breakers had paid £560,000 for her and she would ultimately yield nearly 40,000 tons of saleable metals and materials. By 4 September, some of her 100-ton fifteen-inch guns had been removed. It would not be until 2 April 1962 that her denuded hull would be towed from its deepwater berth at Faslane, to a beaching ground. By June, there was nothing left of her.

"When we shipchecked *Missouri* in 1982 for reactivation, we found all tools and spare parts for each part of each turret laid out in grade 2 preservative on wax paper on the decks of the compartments they belonged to. Outside the door was a check-off list of every item including the smallest screwdriver."
– Richard Landgraff, Long Beach Naval Shipyard

"They came to the Navy as strangers; served as shipmates and friends; and left the Navy as brothers in eternity . . . In the finest Navy tradition, they served a great battleship."
– President George Bush, speaking of the USS *Iowa* gun turret explosion victims, 1989.

Four decades after the D-Day landings on the Normandy coast of France, the U.S. battleship *Iowa* returned to the English Channel. Commenting on her September 1985 visit was Desmond Wettern, Naval Correspondent for the London *Daily Telegraph*: "A blinding orange flash, a searing blast of heat and a shock wave that stunned the senses marked the firing of a broadside of 16in. guns in the Channel yesterday.

"Not since the Normandy landings 41 years ago has the region experienced such a fearsome display of military firepower.

"The occasion was a demonstration by the *Iowa*, the 52,000-ton American battleship.

"Earlier, the *Iowa* had fired her Vulcan-Phalanx Gatling guns whose 3,000 rounds a minute are intended to down sea-skimming missiles. This was followed by the firing of her 5" guns whose sharp crack some gunnery officers would claim is more

above left: One of the last photos taken of the German battleship *Bismarck*, left: A still from the film *Sink The Bismarck!*, above: The Plymouth, England war memorial ca. 1925.

disturbing to the nervous system than the roar of the "Sixteens."

"But it was nine of those massive guns the *Iowa* carries which stole yesterday's show.

"After the flash it was possible to see the sea agitated by shock waves. As the cloud of cordite smoke cleared, the whine, like a distant underground train, could be heard of the one-ton shells travelling at about three times the speed of sound.

"Then, after about three seconds, there was a series of dull underwater booms as the practice shells broke up on hitting the water, sending up plumes of spray as high as a three-storey house.

"On this occasion the range was limited to 10,000 yards, and the shells lacked the high explosive of armour-piercing warheads that could penetrate 30ft of reinforced concrete at 25 miles."

"I think we need one or two battleships in commission at all times because there's still a lot of unrest in the world. I'm not alone; there are a lot of people who feel that way."
– Harold Porter, USS *Maryland*

"It's impossible to get more bang for the buck than by maintaining ships like the *New Jersey*. Replacement cost for a vessel with our firepower exceeds $2 billion. And the U.S. doesn't even have the capacity to roll steel to build a ship like this anymore. Moreover, the *New Jersey* is not the same ship she was during World War II. We still project the image of a floating platform for gargantuan cannons, but our arsenal of missiles is actually far more devastating."
– Captain W. Lewis Glenn Jr., former commander of the USS *New Jersey*

"I would defy any person to come to this ship and tell me it's a relic. We have the most sophisticated cruise missiles and the most powerful guns. It is the most powerful surface ship afloat and the most survivable."
– Captain John J. Chernesky, Commanding Officer, USS *Missouri*, 1989

The USS *Missouri* (BB-63) was armed with nine sixteen-inch/fifty-calibre guns in three triple turrets. She also carried twenty five-inch/thirty-eight-calibre guns in ten twin mounts (in her 1984-86 modernization, this was reduced to twelve guns in six twin mounts). Originally, the ship carried 49 20mm guns in single mounts (reduced to 22 by 1947). By the Korean War period, these had been replaced with 32 in dual mounts. All such guns were removed by the ship's 1955 decommissioning. During her 1984-86 modernization, four Vulcan/Phalanx Gatling guns were added, as well as four Harpoon anti-ship missile canisters containing a total of sixteen missiles. She also received eight quadruple Tomahawk cruise missile launchers containing a total of 32 missiles.

left: An *Iowa*-class battleship in a Pacific sunset.

231

While the practice of containing powder charges in metallic cartridges for use in smaller calibre naval guns was relatively common, prior to World War I such a practice had only been used by the German and Austro-Hungarian navies in their large naval guns. There were certain advantages to the use of the metallic powder cartridges, including an improved sealing of the breech opening, reduced possibility of burning remnants of a previous powder charge causing a dangerous flareback, less liklihood of damage to the stored cartridge powder charges in a magazine than with powder bags stored in lightweight canisters, and a higher rate of firing for the big guns. The downside of using cartridge powder charges for main guns includes is that they are awkward, more difficult to handle, thus they require special handling equipment. Powder bags, being easier to handle, require lighter and less complex handling equipment.

GLOSSARY

Abaft: behind; toward the stern.

Abeam: at right angles to the keel.

Amidships: the middle portion of a vessel.

Armour: steel plating designed to defeat shells, bombs, torpedoes or underwater explosions.

Armour belt: a band of armour extending along the sides of a ship above and below the waterline.

Athwart: across; from side to side; transversely.

Barbette: vertical armoured surround for guns which could be fired over it; evolved into an armoured protective cylinder around a revolving gun turret on a warship.

Battleship: Any one of a class of warships of the largest size, having the greatest number of weapons and protected with the heaviest armour.

Beam: the extreme width of a ship.

Bearing: angular direction measured from one position to another, using geographical or celestial reference lines.

Bilge: the curved part of a ship's hull where the sides and the flat bottom meet.

Blister: a bulge built into a ship's side as a protection against torpedoes.

Blockade: to prevent an enemy fleet from leaving port by the threat of military action.

Boom: a free-swinging spar used to secure boats or to handle cargo, boats or aircraft.

Break: the point at which upper decks are discontinued.

Bridge: a raised forward platform from which a ship is conned and navigated.

Broadside: the simultaneous discharge of all the heavy guns of a warship having centreline armament.

Bulkhead: transverse of longitudinal partitions subdividing the interior of a ship.

Bulwarks: a light plating or wooden extension of a ship's sides above upper deck.

Calibre: the diameter of a cannon ball, bullet or other missile.

Cannon: a large, mounted gun that fires heavy projectiles.

Casemate: an armoured gun mount built into the sides or superstructure of a ship.

Class: vessels of the same type built to a common basic design.

Cofferdam: narrow space between watertight compartments of a vessel.

Combined Operations: joint operations conducted by non-homogeneous forces or forces of different services and/or nationalities.

Companionway: a hatchway providing access from one deck to another.

Compartmentation: the subdivision of ship's hull by means of transverse and/or longitudinal bulkheads.

Conning tower: an armoured ship control station. In submarines, the main deck structure.

Cowl: a smoke baffle located on top of a funnel; the opening of a ventilator.

Damage Control: comprehensive term for all means of mitigating or offsetting the effects of damage aboard a ship.

Deflection: an adjustment to the aim of a gun from a straight line to the target to compensate for wind or the movement of the target while the projectile is in flight.

Depth charge: an explosive device projected or dropped from air or surface craft; detonated at predetermined depths by a hydrostatic mechanism.

Displacement: the weight of water displaced by the hull of a ship.

Doubling: firing on an enemy ship from both sides.

Fantail: the after section of a ship's main deck.

Fore: that part of a ship between the bow and the midship section.

Forecastle: a forward upper deck extending to the bow.

Freeboard: the height of a ship's sides from the waterline to a weather deck.

Flying bridge: a light, self-supporting structure extending from the side of a ship's bridge.

Fuse/fuze: device timed to explode a shell at a specific time after firing, on contact with a target, or after contact with the target.

Gedunk: snack bar or ice cream stand on a U.S. Navy ship, where sailors could purchase snacks, etc.

Gun house: a lightly protected, rotating mount for guns of lesser calibre.

Gun shield: any protection for gun crews which

does not completely enclose a gun mount.

Gunwale: the upper edge of a vessel or boat's side.

Halyards: light lines used in hoisting signal flags.

Hatch: an opening in a ship's deck.

Hawse pipes: tubes leading anchor chains from deck down and forward through bow plating.

Helm: the mechanism for operating a ship's rudder.

Holy-stoning: a method of smoothing and cleaning the teakwood deck utilizing stones with an abrasive surface.

Hull: the main body of a vessel exclusive of elements of superstructure.

Island: a free-standing section of a ship's superstructure. The superstructure of an aircraft carrier.

Keel: the centreline strength member running fore and aft along the bottom of a ship.

Knot: a unit of nautical distance; a unit of speed, equalling one nautical mile per hour.

Laying: adjusting the elevation of a gun.

Leeward: opposite to windward.

List: a transverse inclination of a vessel.

Main battery: the heaviest calibre gun armament carried by a naval vessel.

Main deck: a ship's highest continuous deck.

Mine: a device containing a high explosive charge, free-floating or anchored at a fixed depth, or resting on the seabed; detonated by contact, or by electrical or magnetic impulse.

Multiple mast: an exposed mast having one or more supporting elements.

Ordnance: military material, such as weapons, ammunition, combat vehicles, and equipment.

Port: the left-hand side of a vessel when looking towards the bow; an opening; a harbour.

Quarter: that portion of a vessel's side near the stern.

Quarter deck: part of the upper deck reserved for officers; also the deck near the stern.

Radio direction finder: a device for determining the direction of a source of radio impulses.

Rake: fore and aft inclination from the vertical.

Rangefinder: an optical instrument for determining the distance to a target or other object.

Reciprocating engine: a steam-actuated piston engine as distinguished from a turbine.

Rigging: a collective term for ropes and chains employed to support the masts, yards, and booms of a vessel.

Salvo: one gun from each turret firing simultaneously.

Secondary battery: the gun armament next in calibre to the main battery.

Sheer: the longitudinal upward or downward curvature of the deck or gunwale of a ship.

Sheer line: a line formed by the intersection of the deck and sides of a ship.

Splinter screen: a light armour shield for the protection of the crew.

Stack: the exposed uptake from a ship's boilers; a funnel.

Starboard: the righthand side of a vessel when looking towards the bow.

Stem: the extreme forward line of a ship's bow.

Stern post: the main vertical post in the stern frame of a ship, upon which the rudder is hung.

Superstructure: any structure built above a ship's hull.

Task force: a naval force organized to carry out a specific mission.

Trajectory: the flight path of a projectile.

Turret: a rotating mount enclosed by armour for guns of large calibre.

Twin turret: a turret housing two guns.

Type: all vessels built or converted for the same purpose.

Weather deck: any deck exposed to the weather.

Well: a lateral opening in a ship's hull or superstructure.

Windage: difference between the bore of a cannon and the calibre of its missile.

Windward: side from which the wind is blowing.

Even in the 1930s, prior to the introduction of radar in gunfire control systems on battleships, such vessels were capable of accurately firing their big gun projectiles at unseen, manoeuvring targets to ranges of fifteen miles and more. The introduction of mechanical analog fire-control computer systems, along with radar, to battleships in the 1940s enabled major increases in the effective ranges of their big guns. The new equipment also gave the gun teams the ability to accurately shoot at targets hidden in fog, smoke or darkness.

PICTURE CREDITS

Photographs by Philip Kaplan are credited: PK. Photographs from the author's collections are credited: AC. Photographs from the United States National Archives are credited: NARA. Photographs from the United States Navy are credited: USN. Photographs from the Tailhook Association are credited: TH. Jacket front: TH. Jacket back: Michael Fisk. Jacket back flap: Margaret Kaplan. Front endsheet: Courtesy Henry Leach. Back endsheet: PP2-3: TH, P5: TH, P7: AC, P8: NARA, P9: AC, PP10-11: Courtesy Charles Addis, P11: PK, P12: U.S. Library of Congress, P13: NARA, P15: AC, PP16-17: National Maritime Museum, PP18-19: National Maritime Museum, PP22-23: AC, P23: AC, P25: Naval Historical Center, P26 top: AC, P26 bottom: NARA, P27 all: AC, P29: Naval Historical Center, PP30-31: AC, P34: AC, P35: AC, PP36-37: NARA, P38: AC, P39: AC, PP40-41: NARA , P41: AC, P42 top left: AC, P42 bottom left: AC, PP42-43 centre: NARA, P43 both: NARA, PP44-45: NARA, PP46-47: NARA, P48: AC, PP48-49: NARA, P50: Courtesy Warner Brothers, P51: AC, P52: NARA, P53: Coourtesy The Rank Organisation, P55: Courtesy Brian McMaster, PP56-57: NARA, P57: AC, P59: PK, P60 both: Courtesy Richard 'Mac' McCutcheon, PP62-63: NARA, P64 both: Courtesy Richard 'Mac' McCutcheon, P65 top left and right: Courtesy Richard 'Mac' McCutcheon, P65 bottom: NARA, P66 top and bottom: Courtesy Richard 'Mac' McCutcheon, PP66-67: TH, P68: NARA, P69 all: NARA, P70 top: NARA, P70 bottom: Courtesy Buena Vista, P71 top left and right: TH, P71 bottom: Courtesy Buena Vista, PP72-73: NARA, PP74-75 all: NARA, P76: both: NARA, P77: NARA, P78 top: NARA, P78 bottom left: PK, P78 bottom right: AC, P79: NARA, P80: NARA, PP82-83: NARA, P83 all: AC, P85: NARA, PP86-87: U.S. Navy, PP88-89: NARA, PP90-91: NARA, PP92-93: NARA, P94: NARA, P95: AC, P96: AC, PP96-97: NARA, P98: NARA, P 99: NARA, P99 bottom: AC, P101: NARA, P102: Courtesy Tony Iacono, P103: NARA, P105: NARA, P106 all: AC, P107: AC, P109: NARA, P110 both: AC, P111 left: AC, P111 right: Courtesy Robert Sambataro, P112: AC, P113 top: Courtesy Universal, P113 bottom: Courtesy Paramount, P114 all: Courtesy David Mellor, P115: NARA, P116: NARA, P117: NARA, P119 top: Courtesy Maynard Loy, P119 bottom left: Courtesy Richard 'Mac' McCutcheon, P119 bottom right: AC, PP120-121: Imperial War Museum, P122: NARA, P123 top left: AC, P123 top centre: NARA, P123 top right: AC, P123 bottom: NARA, P124 both: Naval Historical Center, P125 both: NARA, PP126-127: NARA, P128: NARA, P131: NARA, P132: TH, PP134-135: NARA, PP136-137: Naval Historical Center, P138: NARA, PP140-141: Courtesy Henry Leach, P142: TH, P143: PK, PP144-145: Courtesy Henry Leach, PP148-149: NARA, PP150-151: TH, P152: NARA, P153: NARA, PP154-155 all: PK, P156 both: NARA, P158 top: PK, P158 bottom left: Courtesy Tony Iacono, P158 bottom right: PK, P159: Courtesy Maynard Loy, P161: NARA, PP162-163 all: PK, P164: TH, P166 both: PK, P167 top left and right: PK, P167 bottom: TH, P169: NARA, P170 top left: NARA, P170 top right: AC, P170 bottom: NARA, P171 top: Courtesy Tony Alessandro, P171 centre and bottom: NARA, PP172-173: NARA, PP174-175: Courtesy Robert Bailey, P176: NARA, P178: NARA, P180: Imperial War Museum, P182: AC, PP184-185: AC, P186: AC, P187: AC, P189: AC, PP192-193: NARA, P194: NARA, PP196-197: NARA, P198: NARA, P199: AC, P202: NARA, PP204-205: HMS Drake Photo Section, PP206-207: HMS Drake Photo Section, P210: NARA, PP212-213: TH, PP214-215: TH, P216: NARA, P218: TH, P219 top: Courtesy Maynard Loy, P219 bottom: TH, P220: NARA, P221: U.S. Navy, P223: TH, PP226-227: TH, P229 top: Naval Historical Center, P229 bottom: Courtesy 20th Century-Fox, PP230-231: TH, PP234-235: TH,

left: The sixteen-inch forward gun turrets of the USS *Missouri, BB-63,* at Ford Island, Pearl Harbor, Hawaii.

235

"I looked aft, to see how the other battleships were faring. I couldn't see any. The fuel oil that had poured from the *Arizona* and *West Virginia* by the hundreds of thousands of gallons had formed a viscous sludge on top of the water. It had caught fire. Orange flames rose into great ebony clouds. The prevailing wind was pushing the fire toward us. Passing inshore from the *Oklahoma*, it had already engulfed the *Tennessee* and *Maryland*. Unless the wind shifted, it would very soon be at our stern.

" 'Abandon ship! Repeat: Abandon ship!' Carefully, I unplugged my headset and stowed it away with the unused message pad and pencil. I felt very calm as I joined the exodus from the maintop. Halfway down, the seaman behind me on the ladder began pushing at me impatiently.

" 'Christ, let's hurry it up!' he said in a thin, fearful voice. As I turned, I could see that his eyes were wide and unfocused.

" 'Take it easy, mate,' I said soothingly. 'We've got plenty of time. No problem.' That put an end to his brief loss of control. I learned then that hysteria must be dealt with immediately, and cooly, before it spreads and becomes general.

" 'Everyone put a life jacket on!' was the shouted command. On the starboard quarterdeck, life preservers had been pulled from their storage space inside the mainmast and piled up in a heap. I slipped into one of the bulky jackets, pulled

ACKNOWLEDGMENTS
The author is grateful to the following people for their generous help in the development of this book:
Charles Addis, Tony Alessandro, Robert Bailey, Malcolm Bates, Quentin Bland, Tony Briscomb, Charles Brown, Phoebe Clapham, Jack Delaney, Keith De Mello, Roger Ebert, Herb Fahr, Gary Fisher, Michael Fisk,Ella Freire, Kate Freire, Oz Freire, Joseph Gilbey, The HMS Drake-Photo Section, Mike Holloman, Eric Holloway, Ellen Iacono, Tony Iacono, Jan Jacobs, Albert Lee Kaiss, Hargi Kaplan, Neal Kaplan, John Keegan, Richard Landgraff, Henry Leach, Maynard Loy, Eric Marsden, Ted Mason, Judy McCutcheon, Rick McCutcheon, Rita McCutcheon, Richard McCutcheon, Tilly McMaster, James McMaster, David Mellor, Richard H. Minear, Robert Oelrich, Ted Pederson, Harold Porter, Robert Sambataro, John E. Shelton, Christy Sheaff, Doug Siegfried, Mike Sizeland, Robert V. Shultz, Ian Smith, Mark Stanhope, Mark Thistlethwaite, Andrew Toppan.
Grateful acknowledgment is made to the following for the use of their previously published material:
Coward, Cdr B.R., RN, for extracts from his book *Battleship At War*, Ian Allan, 1987.
Ebert, Roger, for an extract from his column on *The Battleship Potemkin*
Gilbey, Joseph, for extracts from his book *Langsdorff of the Graf Spee, Prince of Honour*, Joseph Gilbey, 1999.
HMS *Victory* website, for extracts, 2003.
Kipling, Rudyard, for extracts from his book *Sea Warfare*, Macmillan and Co., 1916.
Manchester, William, for an extract from his book *Goodbye Darkness*, Little Brown, 1980.
Mason, Ted, for extracts from his book *Battleship Sailor*, Naval Institute Press, 1982.
Mitsuru,Yoshida, for extracts from his book *Requiem for Battleship Yamato*, University of Washington Press, 1999.
Wouk, Herman, for an extract from his book *The 'Caine' Mutiny*, Jonathan Cape Ltd., 1951.
Royal Navy, for extracts from the booklet *Your Ship. Notes and Advice to an Officer On Assuming His First Command*.

BIBLIOGRAPHY

Adams, Simon, *World War I*, Dorling Kindersley, 2001.
Arroyo, Ernest, *Pearl Harbor*, MetroBooks, 2001.
Baldwin, Hanson W., *Battles Lost & Won*, Smithmark, 1966.
Ballantyne, Iain, *Warspite*, Leo Cooper, 2001.
Beeler, John, *Birth of the Battleship*, Naval Institute Press, 2001.
Berecuson, David J. & Herwig, Holger H., *Bismarck*, Hutchinson, 2001.
Bonney, George, *The Battle of Jutland 1916*, Sutton Publishing, 2002.
Bradford, Ernie, *The Mighty Hood*, Hodder & Stoughton Ltd., 1959.
Breyer, Siegfried, *Battleships of the World 1905-1970*, Conway Maritime Press, 1980.
Brown, G.I., *The Big Bang*, Sutton Publishing, 1998.
Browne, G.Lathom, *Nelson*, Trident Press International, 1999.
Buxton, Ian, & Warlow, Ben, *To Sail No More, Parts One and Four*, Maritime Books.
Campbell, John, *The Experience of World War II*, Oxford University Press, 1989.
Canby, Courtland, *A History of Ships and Seafaring*, Hawthorn Books, 1963.
Congdon, Don, *Combat WWII, Pacific Theater of Operations*, Arbor House, 1958.
Costello, John, *Love, Sex & War*, William Collins Sons & Co Ltd., 1985.
Cowburn, Philip, *The Warship in History*, Macmillan, 1965.
Crawford, Steve, *Battleships and Carriers*, Dempsey-Parr, 1999.
Cutler, Thomas J., *The Battle of Leyte Gulf*, Harper Collins, 1994.
Davies, J.B., *Great Campaigns of World War II*, Little, Brown, 2000.
Edwards, Bernard, *Salvo!*, Brockhampton Press, 1999.
Ethell, Jeff, *The Victory Era in Color!*, Reiman Publications, 1994.
Faulkner, Keith, *Jane's Warship Recognition Guide*, Harper Collins, 1999.
Fawcett, H.W. & Hooper, G.W.W., *The Fighting At Jutland*, Chatham Publishing, 2001.
Flower, Desmond, & Reeves, James, *The Taste of Courage, The War, 1939-1945*, Harper & Row, 1960.
Fowler, Will, *Modern Weapons and Warfare*, Hermes House, 2000.
Frankland, Noble & Dowling, Christopher, *Decisive Battles of the Twentieth Century*, Sidgewick & Jackson Ltd., 1976.
Gardiner, Juliet, *D-Day, Those Who Were There*, Collins & Brown, 1994.
Gilbey, Joseph, *Langsdorff of the Graf Spee, Prince of Honour*, Joseph Gilbey, 1999.
Goldstein, Donald M., Dillon, Katherine V., Wenger, J. Michael, *Pearl Harbor, The Way It Was*, Brassey's, 1991.
Haines, Gregory, & Coward, Cdr B.R., RN *Battleship, Cruiser, Destroyer*, Ian Allen, 1995.
Hamer, David, *Bombers Versus Battleships*, Conway Maritime Press, 1998.
Holmes, Richard, *Battlefields of the Second World War*, BBC Worldwide Limited, 2001.
Holt, Toni and Valmai, *The Visitor's Guide to Normandy Landing Beaches*, Moorland Publishing, 1989.
Hough, Richard, *The Great War At Sea 1914-1918*, Birlinn Ltd, 2000.
Hough, Richard, *The Longest Battle*, Cassell, 1986.
Ireland, Bernard, *Jane's Battleships of the 20th Century*, Harper Collins, 1996.
Ireland, Bernard, *War At Sea 1914-45*, Cassell, 2002.
Ireland, Bernard & Grove, Eric, *Jane's War At Sea 1897-1997*, Harper Collins, 1997.
Jackson, Robert, *History of the Royal Navy*, Paragon, 1999.
Jackson, Robert, *The World's Great Battleships*, Greenwich Editions, 2000.
Johnston, Ian, and McAuley, Rob, *The Battleships*, Channel 4 Books, 2000.
Keegan, John, *Battle At Sea*, Pimlico, 1988.
Kennedy, Ludovic, *Pursuit*, Cassell, 1974.
Kipling, Rudyard, *Sea Warfare*, Macmillan and Company, Ltd., 1916.
La Forte, Robert S., & Marcello, Ronald E., *Remembering Pearl Harbor*, Ballantine Books, 1991.
Linder, Bruce, *San Diego's Navy*, Naval Institute Press.
Macintyre, Captain Donald, *Jutland*, Evans Brothers Limited, 1957.

Man, John & Newark, Tim, *Battlefields Then & Now*, Quarto Inc, 1997.
Mason, Theodore C., *Battleship Sailor*, Airlife, 1982.
McCart, Neil, *HMS Vanguard 1944-1960*, Maritime Books, 2001.
Mearns, David, & White, Rob, *Hood and Bismarck*, Channel 4 Books, 2001.
Mehl, Hans, *Naval Guns*, Chatham Publishing, 2001.
Messenger, Charles, *World War II in the Atlantic*, Brampton Books, 1990.
Middlebrook, Martin and Mahoney, Patrick, *Battleship*, Allen Lane, 1977.
Miller, James, *Scapa*, Birlinn Limited, 2000.
Mitsuru, Yoshida, *Requiem For Battleship Yamato*, Constable, 1999.
Moore, John, *Jane's Fighting Ships of World War 1*, Random House, 2001.
Names, Larry, *Ironclads Man-of-War*, Avon Books, 1995.
Newhart, Max R., *American Battleships*, Pictorial Histories, 1995.
Newman, Bill, *"Sparks", R.N.*, Bill Newman, 1993.
Padfield, Peter, *Battleship*, Birlinn Limited, 2000.
Plevy, Harry, *Battleship Sailors*, Chatham Publishing, 2001.
Pope, Dudley, *The Battle of the River Plate*, William Kimber, 1956.
Preston, Antony, *Battleships 1856-1977*, Chartwell Books, 1977.
Rasmussen, Henry, *D-Day Plus Fifty Years*, Top Ten Publishing, 1994.
Rawls, Walton, *Disney Dons Dogtags*, Abbeville, 1992.
Reynolds, Clark G., *The Carrier War*, Time-Life Books, 1982.
Rhys-Jones, Graham, *The Loss of the Bismarck*, Cassell, 1999.
Roskill, S.W., *H.M.S. Warspite*, William Collins & Sons Ltd., 1957
Rule, Margaret, *The Mary Rose*, Conway Maritime Press, 1982.
Skulski, Janusz, *The Battleship Yamato*, Conway Maritime Press, 1988.
Smith, Myron J., *Mountaineer Battlewagon USS West Virginia (BB-48)*, Pictorial Histories, 1982.
Smith, Myron J., *The Sophisticated Lady: The Battleship Indiana in World War 2*, Fort Wayne Public Library, 1973.
Snyder, Louis L., *The War A Concise History 1939-1945*, Dell, 1960.
Steinberg, Rafael, *Island Fighting*, Time-Life Books, 1978.
Stern, Robert C., *U.S. Battleships in Action Part 1*, Squadron/Signal Publications, 1980.
Stern, Rob, *U.S. Battleships in Action Part 2*, Squadron.Signal Publications, 1984.
Steven, Martin, *Sea Battles in Close-Up, World War 2*, Ian Allen, 1988.
Stillwell, Paul, *Battleships*, MetroBooks, 2001.
Stillwell, Paul, *Battleship Missouri*, Naval Institute Press, 1996.
Stillwell, Paul, *Battleship New Jersey*, Naval Institute Press, 1996.
Stone, Cdr Scott C. S. USNR Ret., *The Last Battleship*, The Donning Company, 1999.
Sturton, Ian, *All The World's Battleships*, Conway Maritime Press, 1987.
Sulzbergerm C.L., *The American Heritage Picture History of World War II*, American Heritage, 1966.
Sumrall, Robert, *Iowa Class Battleships*, Naval Institute Press, 1988.
Sumrall, Robert, *Warship's Data 3, USS Iowa (BB-61)*, Pictorial Histories, 1986.
Sumrall, Robert, *Warship's Data 2, USS Missouri (BB-63)*, Pictorial Histories, 1999.
Sweetman, John, *Tirpitz, Hunting the Beast*, Sutton Publishing, 2001.
Terrant, V.E., *King George V Class Battleships*, Arms and Armour, 1991.
Thompson, Julian, *The Imperial War Museum Book of the War At Sea*, Pan Books, 2003.
Thompson, R.W., *Spearhead of Invasion D-Day*, Ballantine Books, 1968.
Van der Vat, Dan, *The Pacific Campaign*, Birlinn Limited, 2001.
Viney, Nigel, *Images of Wartime*, David & Charles, 1991.
Wels, Susan, *Pearl Harbor, America's Darkest Day*, Tehabi Books, 2001.
Whitley, M.J., *Battleships of World War Two*, Arms and Armour, 1998.
Whitley, M.J., *German Capital Ships of World War Two*, Arms and Armour, 1989.
Willmott, H.P., *Battleship*, Cassell, 2002.
Willmott, H.P., *Pearl Harbor*, Cassell, 2001.
Wouk, Herman, *The 'Caine' Mutiny*, Jonathan Cape Ltd., 1951.
Young, Stephen Bower, *Trapped At Pearl Harbor*, Airlife Publishing Ltd., 1991.
Zich, Arthur, *The Rising Sun*, Time-Life Books, 1977.

the tapes snug, and tied them off, as I had long ago been instructed.

"My mates of the maintop had scattered. I would never see any of them again. I was alone at the abandon-ship station—and that is to be very much alone. *Abandon ship*—those two words turn a disciplined crew into a mass of individualists, held together by the tenuous bonds of common loyalty, tradition, and courage. Without these, the mass becomes a mob. All around me, men were donning life jackets in a hurried but orderly way and heading for the edge of the quarterdeck.

"Most of the crew were abandoning over the forecastle, jumping into the water or sliding down the mooring lines to the forward quay. Some were using the rope ladders suspended from the boat booms. Just to my right, the wounded were being carried down the officer's accommodation ladder to waiting boats.

"As I stood by the lifeline, I could see that the oily water was beginning to burn around the starboard fantail. Through the smoke appeared the dim outline of a small vessel, a yard tug. Passing close astern, the tug backed down toward Ford Island. This action by an unsung hero put open water between the swimming men and the flames."
— Ted Mason, USS *California*

left: The USS *Missouri* open bridge, New York Navy Yard, July 23, 1944.